Overcoming
Violence
in Asia

Published in association with
Bethany Theological Seminary
Richmond, Indiana

Overcoming Violence in Asia *is the third in a set of books based on con-ferences called to work on conceptualizing and implementing the World Council of Churches' Decade to Overcome Violence. The prior two books are—*

- Fernando Enns, Scott Holland, Ann K. Riggs, eds., *Seeking Cultures of Peace: A Peace Church Conversation* (Telford, Pa.: Cascadia Publishing House, 2004; copublished with Geneva: World Council of Churches Publications; and Scottdale, Pa.: Herald Press, 2004).

- Donald Eugene Miller, Scott Holland, Lon Fendall, and Dean Johnson, eds. *Seeking Peace in Africa: Stories from African Peacemakers* (Telford, Pa.: Cascadia Publishing House; copublished with Geneva: World Council of Churches Publications; and Scottdale, Pa.: Herald Press, 2007)

Overcoming Violence

Violence

in Asia

The Role of the Church in Seeking Cultures of Peace

Edited by

Donald Eugene Miller,
Gerard Guiton, and Paulus S. Widjaja

Foreword
by Konrad Raiser

Cascadia

Publishing House
Telford, Pennsylvania

copublished with

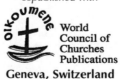

World
Council of
Churches
Publications

Geneva, Switzerland

Cascadia Publishing House orders, information, reprint permissions:
contact@CascadiaPublishingHouse.com
1-215-723-9125
126 Klingerman Road, Telford PA 18969
www.CascadiaPublishingHouse.com

The paper used in this publication is recycled and meets the
minimum requirements of American National Standard for Information
Sciences—Permanence of Paper for Printed Library Materials, ANSI Z39.48-1984.

Bible quotations are used by permission, all rights reserved, and unless otherwise
noted are from *The New Revised Standard Version of the Bible*, copyright 1989, by the Division of Christian Education of the National Council of the Churches of Christ in the
USA

Library of Congress Cataloguing-in-Publication Data
Overcoming violence in Asia : the role of the church in seeking cultures of peace
/ edited by Donald Eugene Miller, Gerard Guiton, and Paulus S. Widjaja
    p. cm.
"The chapters in this book are based upon a conference of representative members of the Historic Peace Churches in Asia that took place in Solo, Indonesia, December 2-7, 2007"--Introd.
  Includes bibliographical references and index.
  ISBN-13: 978-1-931038-89-8 (trade pbk. : alk. paper)
  ISBN-10: 1-931038-89-9 (trade pbk. : alk. paper)
  1. Violence--Religious aspects--Christianity--Congresses. 2. Peace-building--Religious aspects--Christianity--Congresses. 3. Violence--Asia--Congresses. 4.
Peace-building--Asia--Congresses. 5. Christianity and culture--Asia--Congresses. I. Miller, Donald E. (Donald Eugene), 1929- II. Guiton, Gerard. III. Widjaja, Paulus. IV. Title.

BT736.15.V493 2011
261.8'3--dc22

2011015030

18 17 16 15 14 13 12 11   10 9 8 7 6 5 4 3 2 1

Dedicated to those who gathered at
the Historical Peace Churches International Conference,
Solo, Indonesia,
December 2-7, 2007

Contents

Part IV: RELIGIOUS RADICALISM

Part V: POVERTY

Part VI: PRINCIPALITIES AND POWERS

Part VII: OVERCOMING VIOLENCE

Foreword

THE HISTORIC PEACE CHURCHES, i.e. the Society of Friends (Quakers), the various Mennonite denominations, and the Church of the Brethren, have provided decisive impulses for the ecumenical "Decade to Overcome Violence: Churches Seeking Reconciliation and Peace 2001-2010" which was proclaimed by the World Council of Churches 1999 and will be concluded with an International Ecumenical Peace Convocation at Kingston/Jamaica in May 2011. This present book, which is the result of the Third International Historic Peace Church Consultation at Solo/Indonesia in December 2007, brings an important Christian witness from Asia into the worldwide ecumenical discussion about overcoming violence and building cultures of peace.

Christianity is a minority religious community in most of the Asian countries and the Historic Peace Churches represent an even smaller minority within Asian Christianity. The conference included peace church representatives from India, Indonesia, Japan, Korea, Philippines, Australia, and New Zealand. While their contributions to the conference and their exchange of experiences cannot claim to be representative for Asian struggles with the culture of violence, the three principle themes discussed at the conference—religious pluralism, injustice, and poverty—do touch the context of daily living for most people in Asia, whether Christian or followers of other religious traditions.

What makes this publication particularly valuable for the continuing ecumenical discussion is the fact that the major presentations focussing on one of the principle themes are followed by a record of lively discussion between participants from different Asian countries with the presenters. Too often ecumenical reflections on overcoming violence and building cultures of peace remain focused on global issues and are relatively far removed from experiences in local commu-

9

nities. The Decade to Overcome Violence was intended to stimulate the exchange between Christian communities about their witness for reconciliation and peace in their local context. This book makes a very rich contribution in serving this purpose of the Decade.

Among the issues addressed in the presentations and exchanges emerging from the conference are these: responding to the harassment of Asian Christian communities by religious extremists; transforming conflicts through restorative justice; rethinking mission as reconciliation; unmasking the culture of empire through a culture of earth community; seeking cultures of peace; and throughout—the role of peace churches in overcoming violence.

This volume is another example of the very creative contributions the Historic Peace Churches are continuing to make to the ecumenical search for reconciliation and peace. For teachers and students engaged in developing a new approach to an ecumenical ethics of peace and for those committed to overcoming violence in their local context, the book provides valuable insights and welcome encouragement.

—*Konrad Raiser, Berlin, Germany*
World Council of Churches General Secretary, 1992–2003

An Introduction to *Overcoming Violence in Asia:* The Role of the Church in Overcoming Violence

Donald Eugene Miller

THE PURPOSE OF THIS VOLUME is to discover what churches in Asia and around the world are able contribute to a culture of peace. Our particular concern is the role of religion in promoting and/or overcoming violence. The question of the relationship between religion and violence has become increasingly urgent, and the present volume addresses the question directly. John C. Danforth, former ambassador to the United Nations, has lamented the absence of religious comment on the widespread violence of our time. He asks where are the religious voices in the world are? The silence has seemed deafening.[1] The present volume is a response to that invitation. Our goal is to speak to the silence.

A second and closely related purpose of this volume is to explore the uniqueness of Asian peace theology. In the twenty-first century every region of the world needs a careful consideration of what contributes to peace and overcoming violence. Not only do traditional

11

conflicts continue, but they have become intertwined with global threats of world terrorism, increase of number of nations possessing atomic weapons, global environmental changes, separation of the rich and the poor, violations of human rights, and clash of religious traditions. What is the unique contribution of the Asian churches to the discussion of the relationship between religion and violence? Here the reader will be a part of a conversation between eighty Asians searching to answer to the question of the contribution of the church to overcoming violence. Theirs is a uniquely Asian discussion.

These questions lead to a series of related questions. How important is the role of the Asian churches in overcoming violence? What can the churches contribute to a culture of peace in Asia? What is the relationship between peacemaking and evangelism in the churches' debate about mission? How can the churches respond effectively to religious radicalism in an era of global violence? How do political, economic, regional, and global realities affect efforts to achieve peace in Asia? What theological, institutional, and practice issues are related to violence and overcoming violence in Asia? How does Asian peace theology related to peace theology in other parts of the world? Ultimately, what does an Asian peace theology say about the role of the church in overcoming violence in any part of the world? These are the questions that guide the articles and discussions in this volume.

THE IMMEDIATE CONTEXT

The World Council of Churches has recognized the importance of these issues by authorizing the Decade to Overcome Violence, 2000-2010, and inviting the Historic Peace Churches to share their experiences and insights with the ecumenical church as a part of the Decade to Overcome Violence. The chapters in this book are based upon a conference of representative members of the Historic Peace Churches in Asia that took place in Solo, Indonesia, December 2-7, 2007. The Historic Peace Churches include those denominations that throughout their histories have claimed the peace witness of the New Testament and the apostolic church to be an essential part of the Christian gospel.

The members of the Historic Peace Churches, namely Quakers, Mennonites, and Church of the Brethren, are an extremely tiny minority of the population of Asia. Quakers are found in the Philippines, Australia, New Zealand, India, and Indonesia. Mennonites are active in the same five countries plus Korea and Japan. All of the Brethren are located in India. Of the total eighty-two participants in the Solo conference, eleven came from outside Asia, namely from the USA and Europe.[2] So only a few of the many countries in Asia are represented in this discussion, simply because the Peace Churches are to be found in those few countries. Furthermore, of the seven Asian countries represented here, most persons came from Australia, India, and Indonesia, with Indonesia having the heaviest voice.

So we cannot say that these articles represent the peace theology of all of Asia. Voices from many Asian countries are not to be found here at all, especially China, but also many others. It might be more accurate to say that these articles represent the views of a few members of the Peace Churches within several Asian countries. Furthermore, these views may not be representative of all of the members of the Peace Churches in those several countries. For example conference planners hoped for an equal number of women and men, but the voices here are primarily male. They hoped for a distribution of both young and old, but not many youth voices are here. Nevertheless these articles are from select Asian members of the Historic Peace Churches speaking from within their Asian context. That in itself makes them worth listening to, and in that sense we can listen for a uniquely Asian peace theology.

Several of the articles are from writers outside of Asia. Hansulrich Gerber is a staff member for the World Council of Churches Decade to Overcome Violence (DOV), and his article interpreting the DOV is necessary to the volume. The editors have made every effort to keep the articles in the words of the Asians who wrote the articles, although admittedly editorial selection, arrangement, and correction can affect the message being conveyed. The editors' intention is to be scrupulously faithful to the perspective and message of the Asian authors and commentators while presenting the material in an orderly manner and readable style while looking for relationships to the wider discussion of peace theology.

A key factor in looking for a uniquely Asian peace theology is the radical diversity within the continent. Asia is by far the earth's largest land mass; it has the largest population of all continents, and its countries are more diverse than those of any other continent. The cultural diversity is striking, something that can be seen from the variety of religions to be found there. The world's five religions with the greatest number of adherents are Hinduism, Buddhism, Confucianism, Christianity, and Islam. All five originated in Asia and continue their powerful influence there. The continent is a quilt work of radically different cultural traditions. Asia Minor, India, China, and Southeast Asia all were the home of ancient civilizations. The variety is greater than

can be found on any other continent. This makes it exceedingly difficult to find a voice that represents the uniqueness of Asia, unless that
uniqueness is the very diversity we have been describing.

Furthermore, Western civilization has had a great impact upon
Asia, although that too varies. India was under British control for
more than a century, and many Indian institutions, including education, are of British origin. Australia was populated as a British colony,
so that Australian ties to the U.K. and the West is especially strong.
Finding a unique peace theology in Australia that is not influenced by
the West are unlikely. Indeed Australia and New Zealand actually are
not a part of Asia, but their nearness to the Asian countries, especially
Indonesia, led us to include them. Admittedly, this makes it more difficult to find a common voice for a peace theology of Asia. Japan was
conquered by the United States during World War II, so the American
influence in Japan is considerable. The Chinese Cultural Revolution
was intended to throw off the influence of the West. Any of the mission programs of the Peace Churches in China have either been cast
out or muted. Hence there is no voice from China in these articles.
Korea has had strong ties to the U.S. since the Korean War, and one
voice from Korea is represented in the articles in this book.

Those who planned the conference in Solo, Indonesia, from
which these articles have been gleaned, intended to hear genuinely
Asian voices, with those from the West present primarily as listeners.
However the West has heavily influenced those voices from Asia,
something that the reader will quickly perceive. It is difficult to distinguish between the Peace Church voices in Australia/New Zealand
and those in the West. True, they may vary somewhat from the West,
but they are clearly closely related to the West. The uniqueness may
be found in this variation rather than in dramatic difference. The circumstances in India are not the same as Australia, because India has a
considerably different history and culture. Still the influence of the
West is very evident in India. Indonesia has not been under past Western colonial control in the same way as Australia and India. Yet Indonesia was under Dutch colonial control, and more recently under
Japanese control during World War II. However the influence of the
West is seen directly in the Western training of Indonesian Peace
Church leaders. Indonesian peace church leaders are in close touch
with educators in the United States and Europe.

So can we find a uniquely Asian Peace Church theology from a
small group of Peace Church leaders from several of the many Asian
countries? If one looks for something that is not influenced by the
West, the answer is no. But if one looks for something that is shaped

by the varieties of historical circumstances and conditions already mentioned, even though clearly influenced by dialogue with the West, then the answer may be yes. The uniqueness is more subtle than we had anticipated.

A further consideration should be raised, namely the global influence upon Asia. The Asian continent has more poverty than any other continent in the world. Millions of people live with minimal food or less. The world economy is decisive in determining the standard of living for these people.

International trade affects the price of market products that are grown by farmers in Asia. International corporations help to determine what kind of employment is or is not available. Such corporations often are related to businesses that use child labor knowingly or unknowingly. Asian sex slavery is affected by the international tourist business. In many ways the global economy affects everyday life in Asia, often raising questions about poverty, human rights, and social justice.

Global international politics also affects violence and the response to violence in Asia. What happens in the global war against terror, including the wars in Iraq and Afghanistan, can have dramatic local effects in Asia. A radical Islamic group gave the war in Iraq as the reason for attacking restaurants in Java that are frequented by Western and Australian tourists. The international tension between Christianity and Islam provokes local conflicts in Asia. International pressure by the United States to locate troops in Asia or to build atomic energy plants also affects Asian politics. Asians vary dramatically in their attitudes toward such political pressure, which can lead to violence that provokes discussion of peace theology. International concerns about global warming are of extreme interest to Asia, particularly global areas that are experiencing flooding and tsunamis. The conflicts and agreements between individual Asian nations and other nations are a part of the political scene in Asia.

Can one find a unique Asian peace theology among the Historic Peace Churches in Asia? A. A. Yewangoe has declared that more than two-thirds of the world's poor live in Asia, and poverty is closely related to religiosity in Asia.[3] Therefore an Asian theology of peace will consider both poverty and religious pluralism. But it must also include a discussion of justice and human rights. While justice and human rights may seem more Western than Asian in origin, this is a place where Asian peace theology will show the Western influence that is so widely present in Asia. So the discussion of an Asian peace theology in this book is organized around the topics of religious pluralism, poverty, and justice, and it will attempt to discuss the radical diversities and variations that constitute the Asian experience. Having said this, we reiterate that a primary purpose of this book is to let Peace Church voices from Asia make their own assertions about these issues without straining them through a Western sieve.

The effort to give voice to a peace theology for Asia came about because of an invitation from the World Council of Churches to the Historic Peace Churches to give council and advice regarding the World Council's Decade to Overcome Violence (2001-2010). The Peace Churches had been active in World Council discussions of peace issues since its original meeting in 1948 in Amsterdam. The intention of both the Peace Churches and the World Council is to broaden and deepen the discussion of the churches' role regarding violence and its resolution. Scholars of religion often point out that religion historically has held a central role in defining the occasions for exercising or overcoming violence. The articles assembled here are a contribution to that discussion.

A discussion of peace and overcoming violence requires some description of the violence to be overcome and of the peace to be sought. Hansulrich Gerber, Mennonite and staff member of the World Council of Churches, offers a list of eight types of violence to be overcome and therefore types of peace to be sought.

(1) The first is a theology of violence and of peace. Religions have often been in the position of advocating violence as God's will, as in the instance of the Christian support of crusades and just wars. Similarly Islam has at time advocated *Jihad*, which may refer to either holy warfare or to inward spiritual struggle. At other times religions have advocated peace and forgiveness. The Historic Peace Churches are defined by their understanding that peace and reconciliation are at the heart of the relationship between God and humanity, and therefore they are not an optional consideration for believers. Many theologies assert that both peace and justice are necessary considerations regarding situations of violence. So the relationship between peace and justice becomes central to a theology of peace.

(2) Peace at heart refers to deep tranquility in one's innermost being, and therefore includes the overcoming of self-destructive passions. Peace at heart also refers to the overcoming of despair, accepting one's being, as well as faith, hope, and contentment. Questions of mental health, suicide, and self-sacrifice for a larger cause are a part of peace at heart.

(3) Peace at home refers to caring, affirming, and supportive relationships with those who are one's closest acquaintances. This in-

cludes children, parents, husbands, wives, housemates, closest friends, and family. Violence in the home may be between husbands and wives, parents and children, and the closest of acquaintances. Many murders are committed by persons who are close acquaintances of the victims. Cultural roles of family members, machismo, dowry, control, dissension, communication, exploitation, injury, and forgiveness become important questions for peace at home.

(4) Peace in the virtual world has to do with mass media, entertainment, and news sources. The mass media is full of violent entertainment, and the news media promotes violent crimes and tragedy. They tend to make violence seem normal and acceptable. Virtual violence includes degradation due to pornography. Media violence can become a primary source of influence for children and youth.

(5) Peace in the streets refers to urban violence, which includes street crimes, robbery, random shootings, gang warfare, drug violence, road rage, bombing, and arson. Of course such violence is not restricted to the city. Peace theology seeks to identify and remove the causes of such violence and to bring healing to those who are the victims of such violence.

(6) Peace with the earth addresses all of those human activities that make the earth inhabitable. It includes the depletion of nowable resources, deforestation, loss of arable land, problems with the use of atomic energy, food and water shortages, pollution of land and air, and global warming.

(7) Peace in the marketplace touches upon economic violence, in which billions of people struggle to avoid abject poverty, while a small minority of people controls a lion's share of the world's resources. The many of people who die from malnutrition, who lack adequate health care, and who are dying of illnesses such as AIDS are a part of the violence of the market place. That the earth's food supply is capable of sustaining the whole world's population while millions die for lack of food is a part of violence in the market place.

(8) Peace and warfare has to do with civil and international conflicts. Conflict has moved away from uniformed national armies seeking to destroy one another. Conflict has moved to asymmetrical warfare in which one side has enormous wealth and sophisticated, high-powered weapons, while the other side may have little wealth, uses homemade weapons, and is hidden in the population. The fact that several countries now have an enormous arsenal of atomic weapons, while others do not, has moved warfare in an asymmetrical direction. The invention of internet communication permits asymmetrical warfare to be conducted at a global level.

An Asian theology of peace may deal with any of the above dimensions of peace in terms of the Asian situation and the unique Asian perspective. The chapters in this book do touch more or less upon all eight dimensions, admittedly least on peace in the virtual media world. The chapters can be divided between the more conceptual and theological chapters, and the practical and situational chapters. We have already identified three sub-themes to a unique theology of peace in Asia: namely pluralism, injustice, and poverty. First, we shall consider the sub-themes in themselves, and then we shall consider the practices that are related to them. Finally we shall review the contribution of the Historic Peace Churches to a uniquely Asian theology of pace.

CHRISTIAN PLURALISM

Asia is a patchwork quilt of the world's five religions with the greatest number of adherents. Each of these religions was born in Asia and is thousands of years old. They are Hinduism, Buddhism, Confucianism, Christianity,and Islam. Although Islam is a few centuries less than two thousand years old, the point still remains. In terms of worldwide influence, one must include Judaism, which is also thousands of years old and also was born in Asia. Actually Judaism, Christianity, and Islam were born in Asia Minor, but that region is a part of Asia, and what happens in Asia Minor has a strong influence on the rest of Asia. Confucianism is largely contained in China and does not directly affect the remainder of Asia, as do the other religions named above.

The voices represented in this book are from India, Indonesia, Australia, New Zealand, Philippines, Japan, and Korea. In India, Indonesia, Japan, Philippines, and other Asian countries the conflict between Hinduism, Buddhism, Christianity, and Islam in some combination is always under the surface, often intense, and at times openly violent. Aristarchus Sukarto, a Mennonite Church leader in Java, Indonesia, makes a case for religious pluralism as a worldview to be a basis for peace for Asia. He points out that as long as the major religions hold to an absolute claim to truth, they will be on the edge of open conflict. He maintains that while Indonesia's national policy is unity among diversity, the conflict among the major religions is always ready to erupt.

Sukarto calls upon the Christians, and implicitly all religious adherents, to give up their claim to absolute truth. Absolute truth is in God's hands, and what each person has is one's own view of that truth as it has come through one's own experience. Therefore every believer should be willing to listen to others and learn from them. Sukarto is confident that his own Christian faith will be deepened by a humble posture of dialogue with those of other religious beliefs. He claims that such a view avoids both absolutism and relativism. Furthermore it opens the way to genuine mutual understanding and therefore to genuine peace beyond constant conflict. In addition, it is consistent with the biblical testimony.

Sukarto's doctrine of God is that God is indeed absolute truth, but that human apprehension of God's truth is culturally defined. His Christology is that Jesus is God with us as we are changing and growing in relation to all others. Thereby Jesus as the Christ truly relates to and expresses God's love to all other persons. The Holy Spirit is the divine source and vitality of love of one's neighbor, without making absolute claims, and while constantly seeking to know the absolute. The purpose of Christian mission is to share love. The eucharist is a multidimensional symbol to which everyone is invited. Although Sukarto was trained in Chicago, his perspective is tempered by his setting in Indonesia and is a genuinely Asian approach to peace theology. In an Asian community where any effort to evangelize may provoke a violent response, Sukarto calls for expressions of love without making absolute claims.

RESTORATIVE JUSTICE

An Asian theology of peace must address the question of justice. In the early 1950s, following World War II, the Historic Peace Churches declared "Peace is the Will of God," to which Reinhold Niebuhr famously replied, "Peace and Justice are the Will of God." One cannot have a theology of peace without considering justice. Atsuhiro Katano, a Mennonite professor from Sapporo, Japan, has contributed an article for this book on the meaning of injustice in the Asian context.

Katano's thesis is that the understanding of justice among the Peace Churches, particularly the Mennonites, is shifting from retribution to restoration. Retribution understands justice to be a situation in which an injury to a victim is balanced by an equal injury to the perpetrator. In biblical language retributive justice is "an eye for an eye and a tooth for a tooth." Retributive justice can also have the positive meaning that the benefit to anyone should equal the value of his/her contribution. For example, honor should be given to whom honor is due. The problem with retributive justice is that it seldom if ever heals the injury to the victim. The focus is upon injuring the perpetrator in a way that equals the injury to the victim, not upon healing the relationship.

In contrast to retribution, restorative justice seeks to restore or re-establish a relationship. The Truth and Reconciliation Commission that carried out its hearings in post-apartheid South Africa did not seek to indict or punish anyone but rather to heal the communities in which the atrocities had occurred. Bishop Tutu of South Africa considered restorative justice to be the goal of traditional African practices according to the term *Ubunto*. In the New Testament Sermon on the Mount, Jesus asks his followers to have a righteousness that exceeds that of the Scribes and Pharisee. Rather than an eye for an eye, Jesus' followers are not to resist evil, but to love their neighbors, including their enemies. Katano suggests that in Jesus' teaching restorative justice replaces retributive justice.

It is worth noting that Reinhold Niebuhr considered the kingdom of God to be an impossible ideal, even though we should constantly keep it in mind as we act. He called God's kingdom an "impossible possibility." This view leads to a life of tragic compromises, or perhaps tragic necessities. He fails to note that the balance called for in retributive justice in also an "impossible possibility." At best retributive justice is an effort of approximation, and at worst it is a miscarriage of justice. The concept of restorative justice moves beyond retributive justice in a significant way that is genuinely possible. Not that full restoration is possible—but rather that some degree of restoration goes beyond an equality of injury.

The uniqueness of Katano's argument becomes evident when he considers the situation of Japan after World War II. He asks whether injury to Japan during and following WWII ever can equal the injury done to countries like Korea and the Philippines before WWII. He says that discussion of this question never comes to an end. He subtly suggests that victims may want it never to come to an end because they deeply feel that the injury to the perpetrator will never equal the injury that they suffered. Should not the question rather be about how the relationship can be restored, or at least how some degree of restoration can be achieved? This changes the whole context of the discussion.

In a global community the question may not be about who is causing the most injury and therefore is the one who deserves retributive injury. The question may rather be how to move toward a restorative relationship that seeks to heal all injuries to some degree. For example, the question of whether Israel or the Palestinians are causing more injury might be replaced by the question of how to restore the relationship between the Palestinians and the Jews so that some healing comes to both injured parties. Many in the West see the war on terror as the injury of an unprovoked attack upon innocent victims. For some in the East it is seen as retributive injury for injustice received in the past and continuing in the present. Is it possible to work at a restorative relationship that touches both injuries? These questions come from the Asian context, and in that sense they signal a uniquely Asian peace theology.

POVERTY

Asian Peace theology must address poverty, a primary reality of the Asian context. Ashok Solanky, a Church of the Brethren pastor from Gujarat, India, writes the lead article about poverty. The poverty of India is dependent upon the economic conditions in that country, and therefore poverty in other Asian countries may not be exactly the same. Nevertheless India is the home of a significant part of the population of Asia, and so it may serve to represent poverty in Asia. Solanky points out that India is predominantly an agricultural land and that much of the poverty is among rural farmers and their families. Many factors contribute to the poverty of those living in rural areas, including illiteracy, population growth, customary practices, traditional beliefs, separation from institutional assistance, competition with local financial interests, and oppression by international corporations.

Rural families are often illiterate, and without education they have little hope of escaping poverty. They have no money for education, and so they are caught in the poverty trap. Rich agriculturalists exploit poor farmers by grabbing land whenever possible. Financial institutions cannot reach the rural areas that need them most. Poor farmers and laborers are not aware of governmental and other resources to help them. Traditional customs and beliefs make it difficult for poor families to lift themselves from poverty. The growing population means that many young people in rural areas are looking for a way to move into better circumstances. Employment is sometimes not available without bribing government officials. When youth are not able to find employment opportunities, they become restless and sometimes violent.

Multinational corporations maximize profits by policies that keep people in poverty. For example international corporations control the seeds that farmers need to plant their crops. The costs of growing these crops often exceed the loans available from the bank, and frequently the income from selling their produce exceeds the cost of producing it, especially in poor growing seasons. This puts farmers into a cycle of debt, and as the debt increases, some farmers commit suicide.

Women are especially subject to these problems. When women carry the responsibility for farming, they can be caught in the conditions named above, and they also are at times driven to suicide. The dowry is an additional burden for women in some areas of India. Traditionally the family of a bride gave a significant financial contribution as dowry to the family of the groom. If the dowry was not given, the bride could be harassed by the groom's family, even to the point of her being burned to death. National laws have been enacted to stop such harassment, but the dowry continues to be a problem for women, especially women from poor families.

Solanky observes that wherever one finds Christian churches, there one also finds schools and hospitals. One church has provided a center for orphans and for the blind. Church educational programs lifts youth out of poverty and provide them with hope that comes from the gospel. Wealthier congregations relate to poorer congregations. Churches provide food and financial help for the poor, particularly for widows. Christian love is the motive for providing care for the poor. When the church initiates such care, it will often be picked up by other community agencies. The church can help people become aware of governmental and other programs that assist the poor. The church can provide contact with financial institutions, and can help provide financial training. The church can help persons with small businesses to access micro-loans. The church can also affect customary practices and traditional beliefs that handicap the poor.

A uniquely Asian peace theology includes love for the poor based upon the last judgment scene in Matthew 25 where Jesus says in effect, "Whoever cares for the poor cares also for me." This leads to a theology of community service to address the factors that imprison persons and families in poverty. While not uniquely Asian in referring to Matthew 25, this theology is uniquely Asian in applying that passage to the circumstances in Asia that lead to poverty. The church is uniquely Asian in embodying practices that can address such poverty. Matthew 25 is powerful in showing that religious efforts can become community efforts. The "whoever" of Matthew 25 refers not only to those who say "Lord, Lord," but also to any and all in the community who love the poor. A uniquely Asian peace theology includes such a love of the poor.

PEACE CHURCH RESPONSES

Having considered an Asian theology of peace that includes the themes of religious pluralism, restorative justice, and love of the poor, we now ask about an Asian practical theology of peace. What are the unique responses of the Historic Peace Churches to violence in Asia? Again the uniqueness may be more in the historical and cultural setting rather than dramatic differences from the West in basic principles. The Western influences in Asia have already been noted.

Several common strategies seem to be present in the responses by the Historic Peace Churches to violence, the threat of violence, and injustice in Asian countries. They include prayer, fasting, nonviolent engagement, dialogue with community members, appeal to authority, service to the community, and persistence. Below we give examples of responses to harassment of Christians in Indonesia and India, and to discriminatory employment practices in the Philippines.

Harassment in Indonesia

A Mennonite pastor in Indonesia describes the harassment that Christians receive while living in a predominantly Muslim community. He says that the Christians and Muslims are often together in the streets, the markets, at social occasions, and at meals. Christians try to express the love of Christ without calling attention to it. Yet often Christians are harassed for no apparent reason at all.

One of those occasions was after an Easter service at the church. The Christians came to their church after Easter to find it closed so that they could not enter. Some of the church members wanted to fight, declaring that they had the same rights as their Muslim neighbors. The pastor entreated them not to fight, but to pray and to fast. He would try to find out from the police, the army, and other government offices why the church was closed. But the governmental officer said that there was no way he could help. The people continued to pray, and to dialogue with community leaders, but the church remained closed.

After eight months one of the Muslim leaders came to the Christian pastor to apologize for what had happened. He explained that some in the Muslim community considered the Christians to be enemies. Yet everyone realized that, for eight full months without interruption, the Christians had continued to pump water from the well on their church property to the whole community. The Christian pastor said that the church could not withhold the water, because God freely gives water to all. The Muslim leader announced that the

Christian congregation could again continue worshiping in their own church building. The pastor noted that prayer, fasting, persistent dialogue with community leaders, and continual provision of service to the community had changed the attitude of their Muslim neighbors. We might add that the church's belief that God cares and provides for the whole human family was basic to the church's response to the Muslim harassment.

Harassment in India

Several examples of violence and harassment come from India. In 2007 Hindus near Bangalore in Southern India chased away Christian worshipers as they were on their way to a worship service. The Hindus then stripped the pastor and several church members of their clothes and paraded them in the street. However the police arrested the Hindus for "forcibly converting Christians." The same year near New Delhi in north India, radicals broke down the walls of a church that Christians were building. Local people threatened to continue breaking down the walls if the Christians rebuilt them.

A faithful and openly Christian man who lived in an Indian village was harassed to the point that someone struck him in the face with a large stone, resulting in injury to his face and eye, as well as a broken jaw. The persecuted Christian transferred to a position in another village, but there he was killed in a questionable accident when hit by a truck. Nevertheless his wife and family continue to hold to their Christian faith.

Hindus in a community in north India threatened to burn Bibles at a Christian church. The Christians appealed to the District Magistrate, who stopped them. Hindus in another community pelted a Christian church with cow dung and garbage. They also accused the pastor and several church members of making sexual advances to women and young girls in the community. The accused Christians were arrested by the police but upon investigation were acknowledged to be innocent. Still another Christian church was attacked by a mob of 300, who tried to force the pastor to chant to the Hindu god Ram. When he refused, they threatened to kill him. He adamantly refused, but was not injured.

When a Christian group in India proposed building a church in their community, they were told that they must have the permission of twelve departments within the government. After six years of seeking those permissions, all departments had agreed except the police department. In continuing conversations, the Christian group obtained the ear of a local city assembly member who was a Hindu. The assembly member persuaded the police chief to give his permission. However permission was also needed from the district magistrate. When the magistrate held a meeting of the people in the community, they gave their support to the Christians, and the church was built.

The child of a Christian family in India excelled in her elementary school work in the fifth grade. On one occasion her teacher, whom she adored, asked for a drink from the girl's water bottle. Another person quickly said that the teacher ought not drink from the bottle because the girl was a Christian. The teacher immediately turned elsewhere to get a drink. The girl from the Christian family was so distraught by this incident that she no longer had any enthusiasm for her school-work.

Christians in one community of India found it difficult to obtain blood for blood transfusions because Hindus would not give blood to Christians. So the Christians organized a series of youth gatherings to collect blood to donate to the hospital. This blood was for any member of the community, Hindu or Christian. The donations from Christians became a major source of blood for the hospital, and the hospital make it available to anyone who needed it, regardless of religious belief.

In these stories of Christian response to religious harassment, we find several common threads. In one case the pastor resisted the anger of those church members who wanted to fight, and he counseled prayer and dialogue In several instances the Christians found a way of resisting nonviolently, as for example the pastor who would not chant to the Hindu god Ram. In almost every instance conversation and dialogue with community members was crucial. Nearly always there was an appeal to authority. Both India and Indonesia are countries whose laws support religious liberty, so that appeal to authority has a legal basis. The turning point for several of these instances was generous service to the community, particularly providing water to the community and donating blood for transfusions to anyone in need.

Christians sought to love their neighbors as Christ loved them, even while those neighbors were harassing them for being Christian. Notable is the element of persistence over months and years, with continual prayer, conversation, and appeal to the authorities. In summary the common elements include prayer, fasting, nonviolent engagement, dialogue with community members, appeal to authority, service to the community, and persistence in the face of continuing harassment. The uniqueness of these responses is in the wedding of nonviolence and community service.

Responses to Poverty

We have already noted that poverty is closely related to some of the most serious violence, such as suicide, rebellion, malnutrition, and starvation. The Peace Churches in Asia have addressed poverty by empowerment through linking to resources: education, assisting the poor to reach the government and private programs for the poor, linking richer churches to poorer ones, formation of coops among women, microcredit, and challenging customary beliefs.

One of the greatest resources is education. The Church of the Brethren in India has created and continues to support a vocational school to teach youth the skills they need to escape poverty. It is especially important that girls be included in the education. Such education is not limited to the Historic Peace Churches but is carried by many churches. Closely related to education is helping the poor to find and use governmental and other resources. India has many programs to help the poor, but it is difficult for the government to reach the many poor. On the other hand, the poor often are unaware of the governmental resources. Therefore the church can have a helpful role in helping the poor to be related to available resources. One of the ways this is being done is by linking wealthier churches to poorer ones.

The education and empowerment of women is critical in addressing poverty. Dr. Solanky points out that women are often the most effective persons to overcome poverty. With governmental help, the women of India have developed the Amul dairy association that includes thousands of local cooperatives, and that is now known world-wide[4].

The Grameen Bank was developed in Bangladesh in 1976 to provide microcredit to the poor without their needing to provide collateral. This movement has spread throughout Asia, and the organization and its founder, Professor Muhammad Yunus, jointly received the Nobel Prize in 2006. The majority of those who have received loans are women. Often women take the initiative to begin a small business with a micro-loan. The church can help women to be in contact with such agencies as the Grameen Bank, which has been extraordinarily successful in providing low-cost assistance to the poor.

An approach to poverty that is unique to the church is to challenge traditional beliefs and practices that hold families in poverty or that violate them in other ways. The church can do this by resisting traditional caste and class distinctions. Caste distinctions are no longer legal, but the traditional beliefs continue. A traditional practice that is often oppressive to women is the dowry. As was mentioned above, one member of the Church of the Brethren resisted the dowry by gathering the groom's family together and getting their commitment not to ask for a dowry.

All of the above approaches to poverty empower people by forging links with resources that would not otherwise be available to the poor. These approaches are unique to the circumstances and traditions of India and of Asia. They feature education and reaching out to secular resources like government and inancial institutions. They are expressions of Christ's love to the neighbor without featuring doctrinal consent, but they presume the outreach of a worshiping community devoted to overcoming poverty.

Relating to Radicalism

The Asian peace churches have their own way of relating to radicalism. Radicals include those individuals or group that are willing to use violence to achieve their purpose, whether political or otherwise. Such radicals may be hidden among the people, or they may be very visible. In an age of a global war against terrorism, radicals may be known as terrorists, but this is in part a result of asymmetrical warfare between powerful nations and loosely organized networks of radicals. Paulus Widjaja cites studies showing that radicals may be bound together as much by the need for an accepting community as by a life or death commitment to a political agenda. This suggests developing friendships as a way of relating to radicals.

Paulus Hartono, a Mennonite pastor in Indonesia, speaks of his experience of joining a Hezbollah group that was known to have killed many Christians. He approached them asking whether he could join their group. The leader said that he could join if he understood that he was *Kafir*, an unbeliever, and that he could be killed at any time. Hartono was not deterred. He visited regularly, and over a period of several years he became a close friend with the leader. Eventually the leader said that he had learned a new meaning for *Kafir*, namely "friend." When Hartono and some members of his Christian youth group joined with members of the Hezbollah group to help those who had suffered terrible damage from the 2006 earthquake, the Hezbollah leader turned to Hartono and asked, "Why are you doing this?" Hartono's answer was, "Because Jesus Christ teaches us to love one another." The leader responded, "Then I am completely wrong about Christianity. Never before have I met a Christian like you."

Hartono says that he could not have had this relationship with the Hezbollah leader without belonging to several partnership groups. Critical was the partnership group between Muslims and Christians called Interfaith Forum. It was a platform for interreligious dialogue, an occasion for sharing stories with one another, and an opportunity for joint planning. Hartono belonged to a second interfaith institution called The Indonesian Forum for Humanity and Humanhood, which was created to respond to national disasters that take place in Indonesia. Hartono also belonged to Mennonite Diaconal Services, which gave him the resources of his Mennonite colleagues. Hartono needed the resources of these several networks to do what he did. His comment is that both friendship and international networking is essential to peacemaking.

Aceh is a conservative Muslim region at the northern tip of the Island of Sumatra in Indonesia. It is considered to be the place where Islam was initiated in the region. It has been fiercely Muslim and very resistant to outside control. The Indonesian Mennonite church regularly has a volunteer group of youth offering community service in Aceh. Neither their clothing nor their conversation in any way indicates that they are Christian. They contribute to the community by teaching computer skills, planting crops, teaching English, and teaching peacemaking the schools.

East Timor is another region in which the Mennonites have several peace projects. The island of Timor was a Portuguese colony from the sixteenth century until 1975, when it was decolonized by Portugal. East Timor soon declared its independence but was invaded by Indonesia the next year. A decades-war of independence followed until Indonesia withdrew in 1999. In 2002 East Timor was recognized as an independent nation. The war left much devastation and many families permanently separated.

One of the Mennonite peace projects is in cooperation with a Christian organization from South Korea called Frontier. Together they sponsor annual international work camps in East Timor with some 50 participants coming from many parts of the world. Participants come from different religious traditions including atheist, Muslim, Buddhist, and Hindu. Another project is a *messenger* program, in which a volunteer youth makes a video tape of family members in Indonesia and then shows the video to separated members of the same family in East Timor. If the family is willing, the volunteer arranges for a family reunion at an undisclosed place where they can briefly celebrate the experiences of being reunited. Because of the continuing political tension, such a program is dangerous to carry out.

Aldo Siahaan, an Indonesian Christian pastor who now lives in Philadelphia, notes that 5000 Indonesians have moved to Philadelphia. Most are Christian, but perhaps 10% are Muslim. He invited the Muslims to use his church to celebrate breaking the fast of Ramadan. He received no response, but the next year they came and celebrated the conclusion of the fast together. However Siahaan received complaints from other Christian pastors who objected to his allowing Muslims to celebrate in his church.

A Christian from north India reports that his church has invited Hindus to celebrate Christmas together, and for three years they have been doing so. A Mennonite pastor from Hyderabad invited sixty Muslims to celebrate Christmas with his congregation. One hundred and twenty came to shout and disturb the service. The pastor managed to get their attention and asked why they should fight one another since they have the same father, Abraham. The Muslim leader replied that the Christians had remained silent when Hindu fanatics destroyed the Muslim mosque. The pastor promised the Muslim leader that he and his church would work together with them. Since then they have continued to celebrate the Christmas season together.

These stories portray the unique way that the Asian peace churches relate to radicalism. Their approach includes efforts to depolarize difference by means of friendship, interreligious dialogue, partnership groups, global networking, community service, international work camps, reconnecting separated families, and inviting shared celebration. These approaches are incognito when otherwise they would be flatly rejected, but in other instances they are openly Christian. In every instance they express the peace theology of responding to the neighbor in the love of Christ, and they move away from conceiving of anyone or any group as the enemy.

Relating to Injustice

Atsuhiro Katano makes a strong case for restorative justice to be the heart of a theology of peace that moves beyond retributive justice. Its Asian uniqueness may depend more on the context than the content. Jarrod McKenna, with the Anabaptist Association of Australia and New Zealand and an adopted Quaker from Australia, calls for jubilee acts that challenge the downward spiral of twenty-first century living. Jo Vallentine, also from Australia, calls for action to address the destructive effects of the use of atomic energy. Together the Peace Churches call for action to address global warming.

Jarrod McKenna belongs to the Vine and Fig Tree, a community that seeks to engage in Jubilee acts of restorative justice. The Jubilee refers to the year of community renewal found in the laws of Leviticus 25 and Deuteronomy 15, and also found in Jesus' inaugural declaration in Nazareth, Luke 4:16-21. The Vine and Fig Tree is a permaculture community, a concept originating in Australia. Permaculture communities seek to live an independently self-sustaining agricultural and cultural life style. The Vine and Fig Tree is dedicated to the civil disobedience of planting trees at military camps as a witness to the need to renew the earth. The community extends hospitality to refugees escaping from the violence in their own countries. Because one such refugee had been held for more than four years at the Baxter Detention Center in Australia, the community organized a protest march of 700 persons. McKenna describes how, upon arrival at the Baxter Center, police surrounded them, threatening them with raised batons. Jarrod fell to his knees and began to pray and to sing hymns. The whole group of protesters joined with him and the puzzled police stopped threatening them.

Jo Vallentine, Quaker from Australia, tells of a similar march of several thousand protesters to the NATO headquarters in Brussels. They were protesting the NATO bombings in Yugoslavia. When they arrived at the NATO headquarters, many armed police on horseback, barbed wire, and water canons surrounded them; whereupon Vallentine led the group in a spiritual dance. They danced for hours, and here again the police were perplexed. Finally the protesters submitted to arrest but without the violence that seemed inevitable.

A respondent to Professor Katano's discussion of creative justice tells of Japanese victims from the Hiroshima atomic bombing making an annual visit to the Korean Anabaptist Center where Filipino "comfort women" from World War II now reside. These women were forced to become sex slaves to the Japanese army during the war. The Mennonites and Quakers have arranged for victims of the American atomic bomb and victims of the Japanese comfort women policies to visit one another. They share in the universality of human suffering.

Restorative justice can include organizing community opinion. A Mennonite pastor in Indonesia is working with persons of all faiths to encourage them to oppose the acceptance of atomic energy in Indonesia. Restorative justice can include the appeal to public authority, as the same Mennonite pastor did when Muslim neighbors and officials closed his church. It can include training persons to use community resources, as being done by the Church of the Brethren in India. It can include use of micro-loans from an investment organization like the Grameen Bank. And it can include appealing to international authority such as the World Trade Organization.

What is uniquely Asian in these acts of restorative justice? The Asian Peace Churches challenge injustice with Jubilee acts of care for the planet. They respond to injustice with hospitality to refugees, public prayer, public dance, planting trees at army bases, public protest, willingness to be arrested, refusal to obey unjust authority, permaculture communities, efforts to influence public opinion, appeal to public authority, and appeal to international authority. Although they are influenced by peace theology around the world, especially by the theology of the Historic Peace Churches in the West, they are uniquely adapted to the Asian context. Jubilee acts of care for the planet are a unique and creative way to address the global warming and energy resources. Public dance and public prayer are a unique way to address police violence. The women's Amul Dairy Cooperatives and Grameen micro-finance loans are a unique way to address the overwhelming poverty in Asia. They were created in Asia and are uniquely Asian.

Principalities and Powers

Many scholars consider the New Testament statements about principalities and powers be to what contemporary social scientists identify as social, economic, political, moral, moral, and cultural dimensions of society. Dale Hess of Australia adopts this stance to indicate that the sources of violence can be located in the contemporary principalities and powers. Further he argues that the peace church witness, particularly the Quaker witness, can uniquely challenge the principalities and powers, moving them from support of cultures of violence to support of cultures of peace.

Christina Gibb, Quaker from Aotearoa / New Zeeland, considers the value of accompanying victims of oppression. Her comments are related to her experience as a volunteer member of Christian Peace Teams in Hebron, on the West Bank of Israel. She speaks of the nonviolent power of presence to mitigate the oppression of innocent victims. Elizabeth Duke, also Quaker from New Aotearoa/New Zealand, considers the ethics of the risk involved in volunteering for a ministry of accompaniment in a situation fraught with conflict.

The Asian Character

We have said that religious pluralism and poverty strongly shape what is uniquely the Asian identity and character. And we have said that Western Peace Theology is shaped by the Asian context. But we need to go beyond this affirmation to identify several fundamental Asian beliefs that give shape to the Asian context. One such belief is the Indonesian ideal of unity in diversity. Repeatedly Indonesians point to this ideal as basic to the Indonesian character. The concept of

Christian pluralism points directly to this belief, and in fact Professor Sukarto develops Christian pluralism as a way of deepening the traditional ideal of unity in diversity.

The ideal of harmony is another such belief. The island of Java in Indonesia is the locus of an ancient pre-Christian culture. The Javanese people have a tradition of harmony has parallels with Christianity. Consider the following Javanese traditional beliefs.

> All truth comes from God.
> Think and ask for God's mercy before acting.
> Find balance between inner form and outer life.
> Always act from love and self-respect. Do not hurt,
>   insult, or provoke people.
> We need balance and unity more than riches or beauty.

Such traditional Javanese beliefs are remarkably close to New Testament teaching. As one simple example, consider Jesus' saying that what defiles a person is not what goes into the body, but what comes from the heart. Notice the parallelism with finding balance between inner form and outer life.

The Buddhist pre-Christian concept of peace is widely influential in Asia. In this conception, peace comes from within, and we are finally at peace when we no longer are pulled or pushed by our inner desires. The walking stick is the Buddhist symbol of enlightenment. The enlightened monk walks in the life-giving nurture of the earth environment with a simple awareness of being, unfettered by desire. The Buddhist concept of peace parallels the Christian concept of the peace that comes from the grace of God without our striving for it. God's grace simply lets us be rather than requiring us to work for acceptance. The apostle Paul said that he had learned to accept whatever state in which he found himself, and all things work together for good for those who receive/accept God's love. So the Buddhist influence resonates with the Christian's awareness of God's peace, the peace beyond all understanding.

We should also remember that Mahatma Gandhi taught the Indian concept of Satyagraha. Hinduism was a primary influence for the concept, but Christianity was also influential. Gandhi's teaching has in turn deeply influenced Western peace theology. All of these traditionally Asian beliefs are the setting for a uniquely Asian peace theology.

Embodying restorative justice is in many ways uniquely Asian. Profession Katano develops the concept from reflecting about the

Japanese experience of being both military aggressors and victims of the atomic bomb. Professor Sukarto's conception of Christian pluralism is an embodiment of the unity of mission and service in the phrase "mission as love." Because Christian pluralism is so uniquely Asian, it draws restorative love into itself. It also draws into itself uniting the poor with healing resources.

Finally, relating to radicals is uniquely Asian. A person whom the West would call a terrorist leader became a friend with a Christian pastor, and the threat of violence was changed by the relationship. But the relationship was possible only because of the networks available to the Christian pastor. This strategy of friendship and networks has deeply impressed the Historic Peace Churches in Asia. They adjourned their discussions in Solo, Indonesia, pledging to carry this strategy with them because it has so much promise. The strategy of not resisting evil, but overcoming evil with good, announced in the New Testament, is not uniquely Asian, but this version of it is definitely and uniquely Asian.

AN ASIAN THEOLOGY OF PEACE

The final selections in this book elucidate the Peace Churches' vision and hope for an Asian theology of peace. Those who participated in the Solo, Indonesia, meeting had strong responses to the articles in this book. Possibly the strongest response was a commitment to pursue friendships and build networks of communication with other Christians and non-Christians in their home communities. They were more hopeful that by working and witnessing in this way they could address the injustices in their home communities, even when some of those injustices have global tentacles. They were hopeful about ways to address the nuclear arms race, terrorism, political and religious oppression, absolutist religious and political beliefs, deepening poverty, oppression of women, exploitation of children, theft of land and resources, bloody warfare, and ominous climate change. They recognized the essential importance of addressing the poverty in Asia, which is more extensive than anywhere else on earth, but they also recognized that economic gains do not guarantee the overcoming of violence

They had mixed feelings about the far-flung pluralism of Asia. Almost all voiced surprise that the struggles with pluralism of in other Asian countries matched their own struggles in their own countries. All thought that their own country's pluralism was unmatched elsewhere, but they learned that they were "all in the same boat."

Some poignantly asked whether affirming pluralism could go so far that it destroys heartfelt convictions. Can Christians participate in Hindu, Muslim, and Buddhist ceremonies without losing integrity? Yet they affirmed the possibilities of a non-relativistic, open pluralism in which the variations enrich the whole. They rejoiced that in some communities Hindus, Muslims, and Buddhists were willing to participate in Christmas ceremonies. This struggle with pluralism is certainly part of the Asian peace theology. They were willing to join with all human beings, Christian and non-Christian, who love humankind and our planet earth.

They recognized that the peace churches are a tiny minority of the Asian population. But they also were surprised to learn how many people in Asia and elsewhere are working for peace. They realized that peacemaking is an arduous task and that peacemaking is best done before violence begins. It takes a long time to build a culture of peace, but a short time to destroy it. Furthermore, money or munitions cannot finally erase injustice, but healing comes only by addressing the human problems that cause injustice.

Conference participants understood that peacemakers must address the unique problems where they live, and they must address them imaginatively and persistently. They learned how important it is to work through their own congregations to reach out to their other groups in their own communities. They were convinced that many persons from other religions are ready to join together in peacemaking activities, even though many are not. They are planning an Asian Peace Academy that would reach many countries in Southeast Asia. They were enthusiastic about the possibility of an Asian-wide, possibly worldwide, network of communication to share stories of their work and learn of new possibilities. They left the conference believing that building cultures of peace is an essential part of the gospel, a biblical mandate, deeply within the divine call to humankind.

BUILDING CULTURES OF PEACE

What do these reflections upon a uniquely Asian peace theology have to do with the countries outside of Asia? What does Asian peace theology have in common with peace theology elsewhere? For that matter what does it have to do with theology that doesn't highlight peace, or with the search for peace that is not based in theology?

The reader has likely discovered that Asian peace theology is closely related to all discussions of peace theology. The uniqueness of Asian peace theology is very much located in seeking cultures of peace in the context of Asian cultures. Implicitly cultures of peace in other parts of the world must fit their own cultural context. Questions of pluralism, justice, and poverty are to be found everywhere, but they have their own stories in other cultures. The pluralism in Africa like that in Asia involves Christianity's encounter with Islam, but not with Hinduism or Buddhism. Problems of poverty are highly important in Africa and South America as well as Asia. The relationship to governmental authority and to global conflicts is as important in other parts of the world as in Asia. One listens to Asian peace theology to discover what it might mean for other cultures in other places. The unjust treatment of women under the custom of dowry may not apply outside of Asia, but the unjust treatment of women under local customs and traditions applies everywhere. Religious pluralism may take a much different form outside of Asia, but religious difference as a source of conflict is found in many different cultures.

Peace requires the development of ongoing cultural practices that support reconciliation and alternatives to violence. The Peace Churches in Asia are seeking ways to discover and establish those practices. In doing so they are part of the wider church movement that seeks cultures of peace in every community on every continent. The articles in this book tell the stories of joining with others in their communities who want to overcome violence. This means that peace theology can be a leaven that encourages people of different traditions and convictions to cooperate with one another. The World Council's Decade to Overcome Violence is a movement to encourage the development of cultures of peace around the world. The differences that lead to violence are often religious, but they need not be. So the search for cultures of peace reaches out not only to other religious tradition, but also to any in the community who share the hope of overcoming violence. The reader is invited to consider the Historic Peace Churches' search for cultures of peace in Asia as a contribution to the Decade to Overcome Violence.

NOTES

1. John Danforth, *Faith and Politics* (New York: Viking Penguin, 2006).
2. See Appendix IV.
3. A. A. Yewangoe, *Theological Crucis di Asia* (Jakarta, Ind, 1983), 1
4. Pratyusha Basu,. *Villages, Women, and the Success of Dairy Cooperatives in India: Making Place for Rural Development* (Amherst, N.Y.: Cambria Press), 2009.

AN INTRODUCTION TO INJUSTICE, RELIGIOUS PLURALISM, AND POVERTY IN ASIA

DANIEL LISTIJABUDI

Aloysius Pieris, a Christian theologian from Sri Lanka, describes the Asian reality as an interplay between religiosity and poverty,[1] two realities with which churches in Asia must deal so that they can be truly in Asia and also from Asia.[2] Andreas Yewangoe, an Indonesian theologian and currently president of the Communion of Churches in Indonesia, summarizes the significance of Pieris' point of view in this way:

> Though poverty and poor people can be found everywhere in the world, not to mention in the First World . . . more than three-quarters of the poor live in Asia. In addition, poverty usually has a strong connection with human religiosity. . . . Not only because most of the world religions originated in Asia . . . but also because Asian people, in their search of comprehending and overcoming their poverty, will generally relate it with their religiosity.[3]

Now, the connection between poverty and religious pluralism is such that it can be destructive or constructive. While human religious practice should bring personal and social liberation and enlightenment to people, ungrounded religious interpretation may serve only to provide fatalistic answers to the lives of the poor and oppressed.

Indeed, it is well known that religious pluralism can create destructive conflicts for human life in general. When religious conflict is exploited by those with political and military power—power that is often influenced by fundamentalist thinking and practice—arbitrary thinking surfaces to exacerbate already volatile situations and create barriers between one religion and another or between societal/ethnic groups.

In Asia, therefore, a clear and deep understanding of these issues is essential particularly among the churches and especially those involved in this conference. After all, the Historic Peace Churches often declare themselves to be agents of the kingdom. They too, must seek this understanding.

Poverty and religious pluralism, of course, are not the only issues in Asia. Many countries witness varying forms of political, social, economic, and military upheaval. And in a globalized world we are ever more inter-connected. The conflict in the Middle East, for instance, often has a significant impact on Southeast Asia as well as Asia in general. In Indonesia, for example, military and social crises are sometimes directly related to issues originating in the Middle East. And when the situation in the Middle East is related to Western cultural and military hegemony, it creates further issues of injustice for key individuals and institutions in Indonesia. This condition becomes more complicated when such issues are related to religious attempts to verify, defend, reject, or justify individual or group interests and interpretations of the Truth.

At times religious principles contradict common understandings of human rights, such as between Middle Eastern religious concepts and Western humanism. Certain patriarchal cultural values among orthodox religions often restrict cultural and socio-economic freedoms, especially for women. All in all, multi-dimensional repression and violence against the powerless is fact of life in Asia.

In this book, these three issues are presented creatively and actively as we work toward enunciating a peace theology, a peace orthopraxis. Perry Yoder has explored how

> biblical peace, shalom, refers first of all to well-being and material prosperity, signified by the presence of physical well-being and the absence of the threat of war, disease, or famine (Jer. 33:6, 9). Second, peace refers to just relationships signified by the right relation between people and between nations, as well as to social order and harmony in which there is no oppression or exclusion in any form (Isa. 54:13, 14). Third, peace also refers to the moral integrity of a person in whom there is straightforwardness or no

deceit, fault, or blame (Ps. 34:13, 14). In the New Testament, peace (*eirene*) receives yet another nuance. It is related to God and the good news from God. Notice the expression "the God of peace." (Rom. 15:33; 2 Cor. 13:11; 1 Thess. 5:23; 2 Thess. 3:16; Heb. 13:20)[4]

Peace is indispensable for all; it is something for which we all hunger. Although "peace" can be interpreted in many ways, is it not the ultimate goal of human civilization? In other words, there is a calling for people to realize the value of peace in the multi-dimensional human network. In this case, the Historic Peace Churches should be able to garner their historical momentum to share their profound experience, their record of innovation and knowledge. Since peace is both a personal and social issue that includes the cognitive, affective, psychological, physical, and even systemic dimensions of life, we should be aware that the calling to bring peace in the Asian context includes addressing issues of poverty, religious plurality, and injustice.

Consequently, there is a need for an ongoing conversation that addresses the relationship between concepts and creative action. The values and practical involvements of such a conversation should be shared and tested. Although humanitarian conflicts in various forms and contexts keep taking place, we must remain committed to contributing to the individual and collective conscience of the world through deep, inspiring and continuous empathy and advocacy toward the even-new horizon of the kingdom. For this reason, the call to the church is to be rooted in the world yet devoted always to God's will: "Blessed are the peacemakers, for they will be called children of God."

NOTES

1. Aloysius Pieris, S.J., *An Asian Theology of Liberation* (New York: Paulist Press, 1988), 124.

2. Aloysius Pieris, S.J., "Toward An Asian Theology of Liberation: Some Religio-Cultural Guidelines," in *Asia's Struggle for Full Humanity*, ed. Virginia Fabella (New York: Orbis Books, 1980), 80.

3. Andreas Yewangoe, *Theologia Crusis di Asia*, (Jakarta:1983), p. 1.

4. Perry Yoder, *Shalom: The Bible's Word for Salvation, Justice, and Peace* (Newton, Kan.: Faith and Life Press, 1987), 10-16, as quoted in Alan Kreider, Eleanor Kreider, and Paulus Widjaja, *A Culture of Peace: God's Vision for the Church* (Intercourse, Pa.: Good Books, 2005), 28.

Historic Peace Churches International Conference—Peace in Our Land

Welcome By Solo City Mayor Widodo
Solo, Indonesia, December 2-7, 2007

WHEN I FIRST BECAME MAYOR of the city of Solo, immediately a demonstration came to the city hall. So I began to ask why there was a demonstration in the city of Solo almost every day. I observed that the demonstrators were quite engaged when the gate of the city was closed and the police and security guards were stationed there. Then demonstrations would become very, very intense. Pushing and shoving between the demonstrators and the security guards would occur. So the reporters were happy. The TV media people were happy. And the demonstrators were happy because they got the demonstration on the news and on TV. So everybody was happy.

So I changed the strategy. I opened the gate. Whenever there was a demonstration, I invited those people to come into my room. I even provided snacks and lunch for them. We sat together and discussed together. I asked them what they wanted, what they were thinking, and what they were demanding. Since I did that, the rate of demonstrations in Solo has decreased by sixty percent. I think this year it will decrease again by eighty percent.

To have open dialogue and communication is also something I would like to do between the different religious groups in Solo. As has been observed, in Solo we have soft-liners, middle-liners, and hard-liners. If you are not able to get along with all three of those attitudes, then unexpected things will happen. So I have intentionally invited that kind of communication, sometimes once a month, and sometime bimonthly. I have observed that relationships between the different religious groups in the last two years have been peaceful, cordial, and enjoyable.

I also believe that through open communication and dialogue different religious groups will gain the understanding and rational thought to become more aware of, and more knowledgeable about, the other groups. Thereby the misperception between different groups can be avoided. We can prevent being caught in an attitude of narrow exclusivism, the sense of superiority that sees our own group as superior to all other people. This attitude can be prevented, and all kinds of prejudices can be avoided. I believe that a good relationship between different religions becomes a foundation for peace in the whole world.

Part I
ENGAGING VIOLENCE

Chapter 1

THE HISTORIC PEACE CHURCHES IN THE ASIAN CONTEXT

Donald Eugene Miller

TO APPRECIATE A TWENTY-FIRST CENTURY discussion of the Asian Historic Peace Church about overcoming violence, we must look back a decade or more. The WCC adopted The Decade to Overcome Violence (2001-2010) at its 1998 Eighth World Assembly in Harare, Zimbabwe. The Decade is an extension of the Program to Overcome Violence adopted in 1994 by the Central Committee of the World Council at a meeting South Africa shortly before apartheid was overturned in that country. The setting in Johannesburg, South Africa, was the opening worship service of the Central Committee of the World Council. The speaker was South African Methodist Bishop Stanley Mogoba. The scene was a gala, ceremonial worship, with festive banners and glorious music. The atmosphere of many languages and many Christian traditions was everywhere present.

The great sense of anticipation at that worship service was due largely to the impending election, only a few months away, at which time it was certain that apartheid in South Africa would be overturned at the ballot box. One could feel the joy and expectancy. At the same time one could hear the gun shots in the distance from those resisting the change. The freedom movement had struggled for many years in South Africa to come to this moment, at great cost in human suffering and death. The WCC had been very much engaged in this struggle through its Program to Combat Racism. Bishop Tutu and Nelson Mandela were among those who credited the World Council for being a major force in bringing about an end to apartheid.

Standing before that festive gathering, Bishop Mogoba acknowledged the historic significance of this meeting. He spoke of the Program to Combat Racism and of its role in bringing apartheid to an end. Then he went on to say that at this dramatic moment, another historic movement should be initiated. In view of the widespread violence in many places around the world, needed was a program to combat violence. The proposal was a passing suggestion, not one dwelt upon in his sermon. But the seed was planted in the hearing of the body of worshipers that evening.

With the help of two Quakers, a member of the Church of the Brethren brought to the Central Committee of the World Council a motion that a Program to Overcome Violence be adopted. After an extended discussion, the motion was approved. The text of the motion included these phrases:

> (That) the WCC establish a Programme to Overcome Violence, with the purpose of challenging and transforming the global culture of violence in the direction of a culture of just peace. . . .
>
> (That) in view of the need to confront and overcome the "spirit, logic and practice of war" and to develop new theological approaches, consonant with the teachings of Christ, which start not with war and move to peace, but with the need for justice, this may be a time when the churches together, should face the challenge to give up any theological or other justification of the use of military power and to become a koinonia dedicated to the pursuit of a just peace.[1]

It was not the first time that the Council had addressed the question of violence. Indeed the First World Assembly of the World Council of Churches (Amsterdam, 1948), on the occasion of its founding shortly after World War II, declared, "War as a method of settling disputes is incompatible with the teaching and example of our Lord Jesus Christ. The part which war plays in our present international life is a sin against God and a degradation of (humanity)."[2]

In its publications the World Council of Churches acknowledges,

> The modern-day ecumenical movement has its roots deep in the church peace union movement of the late nineteenth and early twentieth centuries. Though that movement was comprised of a

fairly broad spectrum of Protestant churches, the theological option for pacifism, nonviolence, and/or active nonviolent action for justice has been advocated most consistently and persistently by the "Historic Peace Churches" (Quakers, Brethren, or Mennonites) of the Anabaptist traditions.[3]

The name *Historic Peace Churches* was first used in a conference in Newton, Kansas, October 31-November 2, 1935, at a gathering of representative Friends, Mennonites, Brethren, and other interested groups to consider their "absolute opposition to war." The Mennonite leaders who called the Newton, Kansas, conference offered the name. Likely it was to impress the government and others that each church had held to peace beliefs since its founding. The name has endured and is well recognized by the other church bodies.

Between 1955 and 1962 the Historic Peace Churches invited other churches to a series of four major discussions challenging the morality of atomic weapons.[4] Known as the Puidoux Conferences because the first meeting was in Puidoux, Switzerland, these conferences, along with reaction to the assassination of Martin Luther King Jr., led the Fourth Assembly of the WCC (Uppsala, 1968) to direct its Central Committee "to explore means by which the World Council could promote studies on nonviolent methods of achieving social change."[5] That directive led to the formation of the Program to Combat Racism, which in turn led to the Program to Overcome Violence adopted in Johannesburg, South Africa, in 1994, as I have already indicated.

In 1998, four years after the Johannesburg meeting, the Eighth Assembly of the World Council was held in Harare, Zimbabwe. As the assembly approached, considerable enthusiasm for the Program to Overcome Violence had developed, but the question was how best to extend the Program. One idea was to establish a Decade to Overcome Violence that would parallel the United Nation's Decade for a Culture of Peace and Nonviolence for Children of the World (2001-2010). On perhaps three occasions delegates sent this recommendation to the rules committee, but on each occasion the rules committee withheld its approval, thus blocking the recommendation.

The last day of the World Assembly was not to include any item of business. All formal motions were out of order. It was clear that the Program to Overcome Violence was at an end. During that final session Fernando Enns, a Mennonite pastor, asked for permission to speak. When the permission was given, he referred to the remarkable work done by the Program to Overcome Violence and to the many in the Assembly who would like to see that program continued. Then he moved that a Decade to Overcome Violence be adopted.

The chair was uncertain whether the motion was in order. Turning to the parliamentarian, the chair asked, "What shall I do?" The reply came quickly, "Vote on it," So the chair took a vote. The motion passed with an overwhelming majority. The Decade to Overcome Violence was adopted.

The WCC then invited The Historic Peace Churches and the monastic movement, as well as other churches, to offer suggestions for the development of the newly authorized Decade to Overcome Violence. The Mennonites took the initiative in calling a conference in response to the invitation. Some sixty representative Friends, Brethren, and Mennonites gathered at the Mennonite seminary in Bienenberg, Switzerland, in summer 2001. For three days speakers presented papers and participants discussed the meaning of the peace witness for the new decade. These papers have been published in the volume *Seeking Cultures of Peace.*[6] When the conference was over, participants were unanimous in their opinion that a second conference should be held. However, it should take account of the perspectives of people in Africa, Latin America, and Asia—and it should be held with members from the Historic Peace Churches who were actually trying to survive and be faithful in situations of conflict and violence.

The Church of the Brethren agreed to take primary responsibility for the second Bienenberg conference, which took place in Nairobi, Africa, in August 2004. More than ninety persons attended, most of whom were African members of the Mennonites, Friends, and Brethren. The purpose was to engage in discussing how the theology of peace might be applied to the many conflicts in Africa.

The African conference featured the telling stories of violence, conflict, and reconciliation that participants brought from their home communities. The stories addressed these questions: What is the role of your faith in Christ and of the your church communities during the situations of violence and suffering? Does your faith give you hope, encourage reconciliation, and promote healing? Does belonging to a peace church tradition make any real difference to you? Does the Spirit of Christ bear you up? The stories were guided by three themes on successive days: Threats to Peace; Christian Faithfulness and the Common Good; Forgiveness and Renewal. Threats to Peace included not only warfare but also disease and poverty. The common good referred to areas where radically different religious commitments and tribal loyalties prevail. Forgiveness and Renewal focused on the role of the churches in seeking to overcome violence and in building cultures of peace. Those discussion have now been published in the book *Seeking Peace in Africa.*[7]

The first two Bienenberg conferences generated so much enthusiasm among those who participated, and so much interest among other churches, that the organizers decided to hold another such conference in Asia to focus on applying the theology of peace to the special circumstances of Asia. The background document cites Aloysius Pieris, a Christian theologian from Sri Lanka, who has declared, "The Asian reality [can be] described as interplay of Asian religiousness and poverty." Following this lead, the Steering Committee has set the sub-themes to be Religious Pluralism, Poverty, and Injustice. Together they address the overall theme, "Peace in Our Land."

Konrad Raiser has said this about our churches:

> The long-term witness of the Historic Peace Churches for nonviolence receives new relevance in the present situation. It formulates the most basic challenge to the prevailing culture of violence and is, therefore, no longer a respectable but idealistic and apolitical position, but points toward the need to develop a new form of political reason which we have to learn if humanity is to survive."[8]

Our task is fundamental to the survival of humanity. May God grant us grace, wisdom, and courage to our search.

NOTES

1. Salpy Eskidjian and Sarah Estabrooks, eds., *Overcoming Violence: WCC Statements and Actions 1994-2000* (Geneva: World Council of Churches, 2000), 25-26.

2. Eskidjian and Estabrooks, *Statement*, 6.

3. Salpy Eskidjian, ed., *Programme to Overcome Violence: An Introduction,* (Geneva: World Council of Churches 1997), 17.

4. Donald F. Durnbaugh, *On Earth Peace: Discussions on War/Peace Issues Between Friends, Mennonites, Brethren and Ruopean Churches, 1935-1975* (Elgin, Ill.: The Brethren Press, 1978).

5. Eskidjian, *Programme*, 10.

6. Fernando Enns, Scott Holland, Ann K. Riggs, eds., *Seeking Cultures of Peace: A Peace Church Conversation* (Telford, Pa.: Cascadia Publishing House, 2004; copublished with Geneva: World Council of Churches Publications; and Scottdale, Pa.: Herald Press, 2004).

7. Donald Eugene Miller, Scott Holland, Lon Fendall, and Dean Johnson, eds. *Seeking Peace in Africa: Stories from African Peacemakers* (Telford, Pa.: Cascadia Publishing House; copublished with Geneva: World Council of Churches Publications; and Scottdale, Pa.: Herald Press, 2007).

5. Eskidjian, *Programme*, 24.

Chapter 2

THE DECADE TO OVERCOME VIOLENCE

Hansulrich Gerber

I WANT TO GIVE A BRIEF OVERVIEW of the Decade to Overcome Violence and then discuss the plans for the final three years of the DOV, 2008 through 2010. We shall connect with the theme of this consultation, "Peace in our Land," and the three sub-themes, injustice, poverty, and religious pluralism. The final three years of the DOV are important and this conference may become a significant contribution to the consultative process between 2008 and 2011. A major event is being held in 2011 to evaluate the Decade and to encourage the churches in their efforts prevent and overcome violence beyond the Decade. Rather than just a closing event, it is intended to contribute to an ongoing process.

Allow me to begin with two comments. First, I assume that injustice and poverty are realities that are unacceptable and need to be changed, so we work to overcome injustice and poverty. Religious plurality on the other hand is also a reality but not necessarily to be seen as negative. So rather than try to overcome religious pluralism or plurality, we will need to learn to embrace it. God's creation is a beauty that consists of diversity, and I suggest that religious diversity is a part of that beauty. Human dignity is closely is linked to difference and diversity.

Likewise, it is often assumed by church people that conflict is bad and inevitably leads to violence. However, that is a false assumption, and unless people learn to accept conflict as natural and deal with conflict constructively, violence will not be prevented or overcome. Churches have a lot of work to do here because people feel a tremendous sense of guilt when they go through conflict. Often the words *conflict* and *violence* are used as if interchangeable. The media suggest that conflict and violence are pretty much the same, when in fact they are not the same at all.

Second, French anthropologist René Girard in his work over several decades has contributed significantly to a deeper understanding of violence and its root causes. Violence is intrinsically linked to things religious. Religion both justifies and limits or inhibits violence. Sacrificial violence is a means of redemption and peacemaking that restores community. That is the function in pretty much any religion, Girard says. However, the Bible already in the first Testament gives voice to the innocent victim. In Jesus the violent mechanism of imitation that generates ever more violence and ends in the scapegoating of an innocent victim is exposed as a myth and thus made invalid. God in Jesus Christ breaks the vicious cycle of violence, and therefore violence is not necessary to make peace and bring about redemption and reconciliation.

However, the Light has come into the darkness and the darkness has not understood it. Violence no longer works, but people still rely on it. Because violence does not work, religion has lost its limiting power over it. Violence is henceforth unleashed, out of control, and spiraling up into its extremes. In confessing Jesus Christ as redeemer and savior, the church should know this and renounce violence, but alas, it has not done so.

With these remarks I now come to the overview of the DOV. What does the Decade to Overcome Violence do for us? The Decade calls us to walk with those oppressed by violence and to act in solidarity with those struggling for justice, peace, and integrity of creation. Before the decade there was the conciliar process for justice, peace, and the integrity of creation (JPIC). Churches have been under way together in this cause for decades. The DOV now calls for churches to repent for our complicity in violence and to engage in theological reflection to overcome the logic and practice of violence. Challenging the churches to overcome the logic and practice of violence is in fact one of the goals of the DOV. Another goal is to relinquish any theological justification of violence. That is a major challenge and is a piece of hard work for the church. What we try to do through the Decade is to move the concern for justice and peace from the periphery of the church to its very center.

So in a way, when you look at the history of the ecumenical movement, the Decade to Overcome Violence is the prophetic call to everyone in response to the growing epidemic of violence that holds us in suspense between fascination and fear, passion and indifference. I think it is important that we recognize our ambivalent relationship with violence: We are both fascinated and terrified; we are both attracted and repelled. (The DOV study guide illustrates that. See www.overcomingviolence.org.)

Let us ask for a moment what has changed. Why is violence suddenly at the top of the agenda? Since the Decade began, violence has made it to the first page of the newspaper every day. That has something to do with what I mentioned above about Girard's observations on violence. The institution of war as it was practiced until the mid-twentieth century has ceased to exist. Of course there is still war, but it is no longer an institution in which one state declares war against another state. War has become much more messy than that and also much more far-reaching and threatening. Today we hear talk about war in the streets, war on the international market. Many wars going on. One could say that a world war is going on. As it has spread all over the world, war has fallen apart as an institution.

Also, no one has the monopoly on violence anymore, if anyone ever did. An illustration: In 1994 there were riots in Los Angles, United States, and the police chief went on a TV talk show to declare that the police of Los Angles were the biggest gang in the city. That is to say, everyone has the same access to and right of violence, and by the way, the same means. The threshold of resorting to violence is lower, and violence is used in a less inhibited way than before. Violence also generates counter-violence, as Dom Helder Camara reminded us when he spoke of the spiral of violence. At the same time, violence tends to increase to its extremes, just as Girard has described, tending to ultimate destruction, which is the threat of nuclear weapons.

Finally the human capacity for the destruction of oneself, both on a personal and collective level, is apparent. In Switzerland a debate is taking place on the right to suicide and the right to help someone commit suicide. This is the one end of the spectrum. On the other end, as we have already observed, is humanity's ability to destroy itself within minutes. The means are absolutely there.

Another change in reality and perception is that democracy has largely reached all human spheres except the church and the military. When Pope Benedict was elected, a prominent Catholic politician in Switzerland commented that the biggest challenge for the new pope, and actually the measure of his accomplishment, would be to bring democracy to his church. I am aware that certain churches tend to be democratic in a better sense of the term, but by and large democracy has not made its way to the churches.

Someone recently observed that globalization has affected all human activity and expression except loving kindness (*hesed* in Hebrew), justice, nonviolence, and truth speaking. These are qualities and values and activities that need to be globalized—and that is what the DOV is about.

The Decade to Overcome Violence is guided by four themes, and readers will recognize in them the themes of the articles in this book. First is *the logic and practice of violence*: Violence and war begin in people's minds and hearts. Second is *the use and misuse of power*. Third is *the issue of justice*, which has much to do with all of our themes. Fourth is *religious identity and plurality*.

At this point I won't go into how much religion is being used both to justify violence and to explain it. Yet we also know about the potential of religion for peacemaking, and to that I want to turn now. Partners for the Decade to Overcome Violence include regional and national ecumenical organizations as well as the Pontifical Council for Justice and Peace. Although the Catholic Church is not a member of the World Council of Churches, it is very much a part of the Decade to Overcome Violence, which goes beyond the membership of the WCC. Churches, denominational bodies, and Christian World Communions are involved in the DOV. We also get input from the Historic Peace Churches, which has been critical because from the beginning the Historic Peace Churches have been instrumental in getting the Decade to Overcome Violence started. The DOV partners with ecumenical networks, special ministries, church agencies, the International Coalition for the United Nations Decade for a Culture of Peace and Nonviolence for the Children of the World (which runs parallel to the DOV), the World Health Organization UNESCO, and other nongovernmental organizations.

The DOV is placed within the same time frame as the United Nations Decade, and there the World Health Organization (WHO) has done the most substantial work. I encourage the reader to go to the WHO website and look up their reports and recommendations. This information is most helpful for the work of the churches, and I have spent a lot of time and energy to encourage churches to learn from these reports and recommendations, which are based on *the World Report on Violence and Health* (2002). The World Health Assembly passed a resolution that declares violence prevention a public health priority.

If your country is a member of the World Health Organization, it is required to set up violence prevention programs. Churches can be instrumental in helping that to happen.

We won't go into the definition of violence here, but let me just say that most people are astonished by the realities portrayed by the WHO report. Violence can be individual, interpersonal, and collective. Fifty percent of the world's violence-related causalities are due to suicide—individual violence. In Europe, North America, and Western Pacific the rates are much higher. Interpersonal violence, which happens mostly within families (actually mostly among intimate partners), accounts for thirty percent of deaths caused by violence. Collective violence accounts for only twenty percent, which includes terrorism and war. So when the world powers and the media declare that terrorism is a major threat to our world, statistically speaking that is not true. People as a whole are much more at risk to be victims of interpersonal or individual violence than of terrorism or other collective violence. This is a reality that we need to understand. The reader can get more detail and find these statistics and graphs in the World Health Organization's report.

The statistics that I mentioned are based on physical violence only. The WHO differentiates between physical violence, psychological violence, sexual violence, and violence by deprivation or negligence. What we are talking about here has to do very much with psychological and sexual violence and also violence by deprivation or negligence. The biggest killer of the world is hunger. According to the UN report on the right to nutrition, one child of five years or younger dies every five seconds. This is a reality so shocking that we can't comprehend it.

Hunger is one of the consequences of the world's military priorities. Military spending has gone up in the years since the Cold War and especially since 2001. Military spending worldwide is so big now that a table calculator cannot display the dollar amount; it doesn't fit on the screen of a calculator and it doesn't fit in a person's mind. But experts tell us that one-third of the world's military spending would be sufficient to address any and all global issues in budgetary terms. It would not necessarily resolve all these problems, but it would be sufficient to address them properly. This is neither something that churches and Christians think about, nor of which they are sufficiently aware. So we need to build coalitions to change the budget priorities of our countries. Efforts in that regard suggest it may not be as impossible and complicated as one generally thinks. It is quite simple in a way. We have to understand the realities. I believe that understanding violence is a prerequisite for overcoming it. Even more significant is the understanding nonviolence.

The three things that churches are addressing most in the framework of the DOV are these: 1) domestic violence, especially violence against women; 2) economic globalization; and 3) youth and violence, including the question of child soldiers as well as entertainment violence. Generally churches are working on building a culture of peace, which means finding positive and constructive ways of handling conflict and of settling differences. Yet violence that is driven not by conflict but by entertainment or by business is a reality and also needs to be addressed.

I want to point out one important activity that we in the World Council of Churches promote, and that is praying for peace on September 21 every year on the International Day of Peace declared by the United Nations. The movement has grown over the last few years. Churches observe the International Day of Prayer for Peace in many different ways. For example in 2007 the annual focus of the DOV was on Europe, and the theme was "Make me a Channel of Your Peace," which is the first sentence of the peace prayer attributed to St. Francis of Assisi.

Let me point to a few issues and trends in the Decade to Overcome Violence. I have already mentioned several of these issues, and they are challenges which until recently were not at the top of the list of churches. They include suicide; terrorism and counter terrorism; commercialization of violence; violence as entertainment (computer games, video games, movies); gender violence; the confusion between conflict and violence; violence within the church; and on the positive side, the need of our churches and communities to tell the stories of nonviolence as peacemaking. Peace stories need to be heard and the world is becoming more and more interested. For some media a story without blood is not a good story, but that may be changing.

We want the DOV to be a worldwide, comprehensive movement, which is represented for me by a memory from the World Council of Churches General Assembly in Porto Alegre 2006. There two prominent people, Desmond Tutu and Alfonso Esquivel, led a peace march, dancing in front of the crowd following them through the streets. Neil Blough, a Mennonite theologian from France has said, "The gospel of Jesus Christ compels us to promote a culture of nonviolence." Approaching the end of the Decade, the WCC General Assembly mandated the WCC and the whole ecumenical movement to prepare a major peace convocation to take place in 2011. The theme for the convocation is "Glory to God and Peace on Earth." It is a Christmas theme in a way, but basically it says that the way believers can glorify God is by being peacemakers. The Bible presents evidence to support this view. The angels declared this announcement at the birth of Jesus. The two affirmations belong together, God's glory and peace. Unless there is peace on earth, there cannot be glory to God. This is what Christians do; this is our ministry.

The mandate of the WCC Assembly calls for two things: 1) to undertake a process of broad consultation leading to an Ecumenical Declaration on Just Peace, and 2) to mark the conclusion of the Decade to Overcome Violence by an International Ecumenical Peace Convocation (IEPC), to which I have already referred. What we are saying in the articles of this volume is very much a part of that consultative process. The ecumenical movement and the member churches of the World Council of Churches are very interested in what the Peace Churches have to say and offer, because they have much hands-on and field experience with peacemaking, both historical and current.

Here is the mission statement of the International Ecumenical Peace Convocation (IEPC):

> The IEPC aims at witnessing to the peace of God as a gift and responsibility of the whole oikumene (all the living things in the entire world). It seeks to assess and strengthen the church's position on peace, provide opportunities for networking, and deepen our common commitment to processes of reconciliation and peace.

In essence, we are trying to reverse the spiral of violence into a spiral of life and reconciliation. This is not possible unless we believe it is possible. If not, we might as well go home. It *is* possible to reverse that spiral, but as we know from the story of Jesus, it may cost us something. It doesn't come free. It takes effort and may be more risky than using violence. We have identified eight thematic streams as we work toward the International Ecumenical Peace Convocation.

1. Violent theology and theology of peace

This is where the HPC's contribution comes in. A legacy of violence is to be found in theology and in the history of the church. When I tell people what I do, they find it fabulous that I work for peace and overcoming violence. Then when they realize I work for the church and that I am a pastor, they often become more distant, especially Europeans and North Americans. They say, "You know, I have nothing against religion. I am a very religious person, but I am not interested in organized religion, especially the church." I say, "Why is that?"

Usually there are two responses: "Look at what the church has done in history, its complicity in violence. And look at how the church is divided; its members can't even talk together. They won't share communion, for instance. How could I be part of the church?" This is a standard conversation when I am traveling. The church is often seen by people as an instigator of violence and thus not trustworthy or credible.

2. Peace at heart

Peace at heart entails overcoming our self-destructive passions. I mentioned earlier suicide, the inclination to self-destruction. This addresses the destructive potential of ultimate despair. I believe suicide bombers and people who commit suicide have much in common. You know Samson's story in the Bible. In a way he was the first suicide killer. He didn't have bombs, or he would have used them when he tore apart that building.

3. Peace begins at home

Working to prevent domestic violence, learning to embrace conflict and reject violence, begins at home. These are hard lessons to learn close to home.

4 . Peace in the virtual world

Peace in the virtual world involves seriously considering and promoting alternatives to the violence provided by the entertainment industry. You cannot watch TV without seeing crime and violence, and children are exposed to that.

5. Peace in the streets

Peace in the streets calls for strengthening efforts against urban violence; giving hope to our young people; encouraging churches to work at and with civil society. Christians cannot overcome violence by themselves. We need our brothers and sisters in our society, whether they be Christian or not; and there are people who are committed, willing, and capable.

6. Peace on earth is peace with the earth

Peace on earth includes making the earth a sustainable home for all of God's creatures, promoting self-sufficiency, including alternative and renewable energy sources.

7. Peace in the marketplaces

Peace in the marketplaces requires engaging the struggle for a dignified life between the extremes of abject misery and shameless wealth. The World Council of Churches has started a program on poverty, wealth, and ecology. We are now saying that not only is poverty is a big problem in the world, but also shameless wealth is a big problem. They are related, and we need to look at them from a believer's prospective.

8. Make peace not war

Here is an old motto to be sure, but no less urgent for all that. Churches are urged to join the resistance movements against wars. Work to help with global budget priorities in favor of peace initiatives. We should celebrate the good news in this respect. We are part of a worldwide interreligious campaign, The Global Priorities Campaign. It is building constituencies to work on the issues of budget priorities, especially in regard to nuclear weapons and child survival. Many people think that the public cannot work effectively at budgets of public agencies, but they can. Projects in Brazil, India, and elsewhere have documented the power of people addressing budget issues and holding their government accountable for their promises over against their spending.

Now let us consider the Ecumenical Peace Declaration on Just Peace and its goals. In a worldwide declaration, we want to affirm what we can say together as Christians. We want to identify topics for further discussion. We want to recommend fruitful examples of promising initiatives. There are many examples in the Historic Peace Churches that can be recommended, and we want to initiate practical services for committed groups such as the Christian Peacemaker Teams.

What do we expect from the International Ecumenical Peace Convocation? We expect renewed liturgical life wherein nonviolence is being affirmed. We expect ministries of accompaniment for those at risk. We expect a new ecumenical spirituality. Rather than dogmatic or bureaucratic issues that leave the world wondering what the church is about, we expect that the concern for just peace will come to be at the heart of all churches

RESPONSES TO HANSULRICH GERBER

Quaker, Aotearoa/New Zealand)

I'm interested in the International Ecumenical Peace Convocation, and I'm not sure how to proceed in bringing young people and children into the efforts on overcoming violence for the future.

Hansulrich Gerber

We had a brainstorming meeting with our colleagues of the communications department, and we identified children and youth as our primary target audience. Not that we don't want to speak to churches or church leaders, but children and youth are where we need to do most of the work because they are the future generation. Youth have become very involved in the issues of the DOV. At both the general assembly of the World Council of Churches and in other meetings we have had significant input from youth. The ecumenical youth network worldwide has made overcoming violence one of its priorities. So youth have become very active, and we have created space for them.

Regarding children, the WCC has always said children should be involved, but that becomes more difficult because the World Council of Churches is not equipped to work with children. We do encourage churches to address issues relating to children within local communities, because children are very much affected by many of the types of violence I pointed out earlier. Children are victims of violence both at home and in war situations but also in the entertainment world. We hope to have media related activities that bring children into the process.

One idea with which we are working is to have artistic events. For example, children could be invited to do drawings of what peace looks like for them. The drawings could be in a worldwide exhibit via the internet, and also in traveling exhibits. Another idea that we're considering would be to have children's peace concerts that could be videotaped and distributed via broadcast and video. We have also been in conversation with the Media Lab at Massachusetts Institute of Technology which has developed a children's workshop, especially in Africa and Latin America, for storytelling. The program introduces children to the art of storytelling. The children are challenged to identify their own cultural heritages, since one of the factors in the eruption of violence is the loss of a sense of belonging. The Media Lab has developed internet-based tools for children to tell their stories and

make their stories part of another story. It's called "Our Global Storytelling Tree." The Armenian Church, with the background of the Armenian genocide, has done some pilot projects on global storytelling.

Quaker from Australia

In an earlier theme the World Council of Churches worked on
Justice, Peace, and the Integrity of Creation, and I think that resonated
with people at the time. I hear justice and peace appeals very strongly
in all that you've said, but I wonder whether we've forgotten about
the integrity of creation. Everything you said is very people centered,
and understandably so, but I'm concerned about looking at other
species and remembering the wholeness of creation. Also I wonder
why there is no mention of phrases such as "global warming" or "climate change," which are really the crucial issues affecting all of us as
members of the human family in relationship to all other species. We
must deal with them. While I think we're really grappling with big issues here in terms of the violence and nonviolence, I also wonder
whether there is room in our deliberations to have an overlay of
global warming and climate change.

Hansulrich Gerber

Creation and nature are very much part of the DOV. Let me
quickly point out something in response to your concern: I'm not sure
I could say environment is one of the priorities. We did realize that
within the Decade to Overcome Violence environment clearly has not
been high on the churches' agenda. It has now been put on the World
Council's agenda and is identifiable in two projects on the thematic
tracks. The WCC's project on poverty, wealth, and ecology is one of
them. The second is the ecumenical water network. Access to clean
water for everyone is part of the whole challenge of overcoming violence. These are two programmatic entities within the World Council
of Churches that are part of its work on the DOV. But you are right; I
think two agenda items that churches worldwide have had on their
agendas in the 1990s have slipped down the list. One is the environment and the other is militarism. In the DOV we have deliberately
tried to bring them back to the table.

Mennonite Bishop from the Philippines

Please elaborate on the issues and trends about gender roles and
gender violence as it relates to this issue of the Decade to Overcome
Violence.

Hansulrich Gerber

I'm not sure where to start because this is such a big topic. Evidence shows that the majority of victims of interpersonal violence are women. Clearly this is a gender issue. In my work with the churches, I often find women more responsive to the challenges of violence than men, and this is a gender issue as well. I'm not saying that men are more violent than women. I leave that up to you, for that's a whole discussion in itself.

One particular issue comes up often. At the assembly of the World Council of Churches in Porto Alegre, Brazil, a number of women came to us saying, "When will you address the issue of violence of clergy against women in the church? Why is the church quiet?" I had the same experience in Spain when women came and said that with the changes taking place in society, violence against women has become a major plague. Yet the church remains silent. This is a gender issue, and the church needs to deal with it.

Our gender roles in modern society in the globalized world are in conflict. A striking trend is evident in countries where women have had a clearly defined traditional role until the last generation. The new generation of women starting to go outside the house to work experience severe violence both at home and in the street. This trend needs to be explored and addressed. In Guatemala alone in the last year, over 600 women were killed on the street on their way to or from work. These killings go practically unreported and with almost complete impunity. It is not right that women are suffering because they are women. The church proclaims Christ to be our savior, lord, and unifier, and we affirm that in Christ there is neither female nor male. We need to work at the meaning of that biblical prophetical statement in light of what happens to women in the world. I know some are men are being beaten up by their wives, and although it is a growing number, it is statistically a small number compared to the women being maltreated by men.

At the same time, in North America the average prison inmate is a black, twenty-four-year-old male. The average victim of violent crime is a black, twenty-four-year-old male. There is a race as well as a gender issue here, aside from matters of justice and prevention. Most victims of physical violence at home are female, and that's a gender issue. Most inmates of prisons as well as most offenders of street crime are young black men, and that's also a gender issue. Churches have a prophetic ministry of reconciliation, specifically of raising awareness and working at prevention. The World Council of Churches does not have solutions, but we want to encourage churches to address these issues in a fraternal, open and Jesus-like way.

Member of the Evangelical Friends Church, Philippines

What can the Decade to Overcome Violence do in regard to women and men being killed by clandestine actors? When these events happen and are reported, I think the media contributes more to promoting violence than to preventing it. So what can we do to prevent the media from promoting or advertising violent events in such situations?

Hansulrich Gerber

I'm not certain about what we should do. On the one hand we are called to publicize such violence. People tell us that the whole world needs to know how wrong such violence is, and that we should spread the news. Others say such violence shouldn't be given publicity because that is part of the strategy of such killings. Why do terrorists do what they do? The attack on the World Trade Center in New York in 2001 was not done so much to punish people who were in that building or to disable the power of the U.S. It was done so the whole world could see this center of world injustice fall apart. Publicity is what it was all about, but that's also part of the dilemma and tension with which we struggle. My question is how we can spread the news to the community of faith so it can intercede. Our churches need to know that church people in the Philippines are being killed. At the same time, we don't want media news because it gives a notoriety that this kind of act doesn't deserve. So we have to work with the tension.

I don't know exactly what we are to do, but I do realize the secular media have less interest now in church events and church statements than they did twenty or thirty years ago. Young journalists I meet from North America and Europe don't know that the World Council of Churches exists. They know almost nothing about the church unless they've been trained to work on these issues. The media thrives, of course, on spectacular or scandalous news. It's a big problem for us, and I don't have answers. But I take your question as encouragement for us to not publicize these incidents because publicity could hurt the people in danger even more. I think it's an important concern for us to consider.

Mennonite from Indonesia

The reality is that most of our church people are struggling to make a living. Most of them do not even know if they are going to live tomorrow. The types of issues the DOV raises may seem far away for them. My question is how we can bring these types of people into the struggle for justice, peace and nonviolence.

Hansulrich Gerber

I believe they are already onboard. They may not be aware of it, but they are a part of what is going on because their daily struggle is to survive. It is not in vain that we prefer to speak of *survivors* rather than *victims* of violence. People have long struggled to survive in situations that could potentially kill them. Part of the reality I see—and again, I hope I have been clear enough in stating this—is the close relationship between hunger and violence. Hunger is the world's biggest killer and it is a form of violence. It is well documented that suicide rate in Asia, in the Pacific, is going up steeply among people who are in utter despair, especially women who don't know how to feed their children the next day or the next week. In the past, at least enough food for the immediate future was available, but that is less and less the case. So extreme poverty is a part of the new reality. At the same time, people don't know how to spend their money, not only in Switzerland or the U.S. but also all over the world. You have both extremes in the same countries and even in the same cities.

The people who struggle for survival on a daily basis are actually at the heart of the movement for peace, reconciliation, and overcoming violence. Part of purpose of the Decade to Overcome Violence is to get the church to give a listening ear, to be more informed, and therefore to draw closer to the reality of these people.

Sometimes when we list global problems, they may seem very far away. But these global problems for people on the local level take very specific concrete forms. Global warming has become a very real threat to the people in the southern Pacific because they know that in next several years their land may be gone. Their issue is not "peace in our land." Rather, their questions are, "Where will our land be in a few years, and where will we live?" These questions are a real part of their daily struggle.

What approaches can we find in the ecumenical movement and also in the Historic Peace Churches to make these people feel at home in our corporate efforts? In gatherings of theologians, peace activists, church leaders, and also ecumenical bureaucrats like myself, we are sometimes quite removed from the hands-on level. We need to find ways to be better listeners and better partners to people who are struggling daily to survive. I like my job partly because I have the opportunity to meet and interact with these people. I think that such encounters are the key to church and ecumenical theology and programs.

Brethren from India

I would like to know if the World Council of Churches has developed specific programs for local churches, the grass roots. This is crucial because we want to reach and interact with society at the local level. Has the World Council of Churches provided or developed specific programs for local churches?

Hansulrich Gerber

When I started working for the World Council of Churches, I spoke with my colleague who is active in interreligious dialogue, now renamed interreligious dialogue and cooperation. I asked, "What is being done for local churches to have tools and learn the skills needed to carry out WCC programs?" His answer was, "We are working on the worldwide level and the local contexts are very specific. We can't have a tailored program that does justice to every local situation. That's not really our role in the World Council of Churches." The World Council of Churches works at the global level. It has been equipping, and is accustomed to working with, church representatives and church leaders.

Eventually the programs trickled down to the grassroots level. When the Decade to Overcome Violence was initiated, the WCC General Assembly said that this should be a grassroots movement. They want this to be a movement in the church at the grassroots level, and that includes the people in the pews. This effort has been a struggle for the World Council because it is not really equipped to offer hands-on practical programs. The WCC has been moving very, very slowly in that direction because it does not have the instruments to work at the grassroots level.

What the World Council of Churches can do is to encourage local or regional initiatives by specialized partners who develop such tools. One of the most successful tools was the DOV Study Guide, which was translated into fifteen languages and well over 100,000 copies were distributed. In terms of violence prevention, tools and programs for local groups, churches in Germany have developed excellent educational tools. Churches in many parts of the world have developed very good tools for youth, catechists, teachers, families, and pastors. Also excellent tools have been developed on interreligious encounters, dialogue, and cooperation, but much more is needed on the local level. Sometimes we know about these programs and can refer you to them, but we don't have the capacity or the expertise to develop tools for the local context.

However we do realize that in a globalized world—and that is the beauty of the globalized world—we can exchange such experiences, tools, programs, and stories as a way of encouraging and learning from each other.

Part II
INJUSTICE

Chapter 3

BETWEEN RETRIBUTION AND RESTORATION: A REFLECTION ON THE MEANING OF INJUSTICE IN THE ASIAN CONTEXT

Atsuhiro Katano

A PRIMARY THOUGHT ON BASIC CONFERENCE THEMES

In the articles of this book we are focusing on three subjects to develop a peace theology in the Asian context. They are religious pluralism, poverty, and injustice. Since I have been interested in social sciences and international relations from religious perspectives, the three issues for these articles remind me of the human pursuit of world peace in the twentieth century. I am particularly reminded of the development of the United Nations in three major categories of work. These are security, economy, and human rights.

The development of these three areas of the United Nations activity can be summarized as follows. When the UN was founded, its primary concern was the prevention of war and maintenance of security. Making the Security Council resolutions legally binding strengthened the system of collective security. But this security system was paralyzed by the Cold War, an ideological confrontation between Soviet Union and the United States. The United Nations failed to establish the so-called UN military force, and major security issues were dealt with outside of the UN.

The UN's inability to resolve security issues did not mean doing nothing. The UN did work very hard during the Cold War in the area of economic and social issues. In addition to the Economic-Social Council, many specialized agencies such as World Health Organization (WHO), United Nations Education, Science and Culture Organization (UNESCO), International Fund for Agricultural Development (IFAD), and International Labor Organization (ILO) were established to work for economic and social welfare especially for the developing nations.

The third area of the UN activity is human rights issues. On the one hand, human rights issues were recognized as war and security issues. The tragedy of the Holocaust exemplified that the massive violation of human rights was actually a destruction of peace. The connection between human rights and war led to the development of a series of international humanitarian laws. The captives should not be tortured, prohibited weapons should not be used, and civilians and refugees must be protected.

On the other hand, human rights issues were recognized as economic and social issues too. Access to clean water and sufficient food is essential for the right for life. Children should not be put in exploitative labor, but the right for education should be secured. In this way, the UN activity on human rights issues stands in the middle, making a bridge between security issues and economy issues.

I would like to suggest that these three areas of UN activity are roughly identical to the three topics being discussed in this book. The theme of religious pluralism seems to remind us of the various aspects of security issues in personal, social, national, and global dimensions. In the world today, security is not all about military and war. As Mary Kaldor, a British political scientist has argued, the contemporary war is of a new type, the war based on what she calls "identity politics."[1]

In short, the motive for lethal violence has become so private that the personal sense of belonging and excluding others plays as a major driving force to war. Frequent terrorist incidents have shown that military forces are no more monopolized by the official governments but privatized by the international network of terrorists through the arms trade. In Japan, religions are regarded as a major motive for such violence and thus an obstacle for peace, even among academic people.

Whether we are for or against Samuel Huntington's provocative hypothesis of "the clash of civilizations," our thoughts on religious pluralism cannot but address security in today's world.[2]

The worldwide economic issues seem to appear inevitable when we discuss the issues of poverty. On the one hand, we have been benefited from the expansion of human transportation and the development of information technology. We should admit that this conference owes much to these advancements. On the other hand, the emergence of the global market has restructured the world economy so fast that we are thrown into the waves of rapid changes and severe competitions for survival.

One of the characteristics of globalization can be the disappearance of the wall between "domestic" and "foreign." We used to assume that poverty exists between the rich countries and the poor countries. It was seen as an "international" problem, a problem between nations. However, the poverty issue has now become more complicated. While the gap between the rich and the poor is becoming a substantive problem in the rich countries, the poor countries are stratified according to the international competitiveness. It seems to me that poverty has become a universal issue as the world becomes flat without walls.

My suggestion will be, therefore, that the remaining theme of injustice should address the dimension of human rights. Here I would like simply to reaffirm the freedom of religion as the source of human rights of liberty. Georg Jellinek, a German legal scholar, once pointed out that human rights originated among free church Puritans in England rather than in the French revolution and modern Enlightenment thinking. He especially looked at Roger Williams, who emphasized the internal freedom of thought, creed, and conscience. Williams also argued that the church and the state should be separated. From this internal freedom, many other kinds of freedom emerged. For example the freedom of speech was called for originally as the freedom to preach. The freedom of assembly was initially addressed as the right to gather for worship. The freedom of association was the right to organize the church. The freedom of press was the right to publish one's religious conviction without being censored. Religious freedom is the source of other freedoms.

Just as the human rights issues have become a hub for other issues in the UN, the theme of injustice seems to be a connecting point of the articles in this book. Injustice is a wide theme. Religious intolerance and economic exploitation are forms of oppression and thus significant portions of injustice. But I cannot address everything here. So let us remind ourselves that these three themes are closely inter-twined, affecting each other.

RECENT DEVELOPMENT OF THE CONCEPT OF JUSTICE

It seems to me that many people, including Christians, are inter-ested in the conceptual shift of the images of justice. Let me review very briefly how Mennonites came to get more interest in concepts and issues of justice. The primary theological position of the six-teenth-century Anabaptists is often called "two-kingdom theology," based on the distinction between the realm of God's reign and the realm of the worldly powers. As exemplified in the so-called Schlei-theim Confession, things related to the governmental authority are regarded as "outside of the perfection of Christ." Thus the early Anabaptists put justice issues in the realm of the world, whereas they placed love as the virtue to prevail within their community of faith.

This perspective, a theological ethic of two kingdoms, one of love and the other of justice, gradually changed as the Anabaptist-Mennonite groups were tolerated and came to occupy a certain room in the larger society. As a part of the civil society, they could not but face the issues related to social justice. For example, some of them emigrated to a new country to establish colonies, and then they had to do the justice work, such as policing and managing prisons, by themselves. Another group refused to be conscripted to be conscien-tious objectors and was engaged in alternative service at places like mental hospitals. There they saw the abusive situation of the men-tally disabled, deprived of human dignity. This experience encour-aged Mennonites to work later for the welfare of those with mental difficulties. Along with many theological influences from outside, such the civil rights movement, the second wave of feminism, and the liberation theologies, the experiences of social involvement have led Mennonites to work on a theology of justice.

So far we have seen some developments and expansion of the concept of justice. That is from retribution to restoration. It is said that the concept of restorative justice was born and developed among North American Mennonites during the 1970s. The term be-came globally known when the international society observed the pi-oneering work of the Truth and Reconciliation Commission (TRC) in the post-apartheid South Africa. Desmond Tutu, then chair of TRC, describes the concept's meaning in the African context:

We contend that there is another kind of justice, restorative justice, which was characteristic of traditional African jurisprudence. Here the central concern in not retribution or punishment. In the spirit of *ubuntu*, the central concern is the healing of breaches, the redressing of imbalances, the restoration of broken relationships, a seeking to rehabilitate both the victim and the perpetrator, who should be given the opportunity to be reintegrated into the community he has injured by his offense.[3]

The development of restorative justice concept can be put in the context of the resurgence of traditional wisdoms to right the wrongs. The biblical tradition is by no means an exception. For example, Chris Marshall, a biblical scholar in New Zealand, argues that "biblical justice is all about creating and sustaining healthy, constant, and life-giving relationships between parties," and that "when wrongdoing occurs, the fundamental concern of biblical justice is restitution and restoration of what has been damaged."[4]

The Bible not only describes the reign of God, the ideal society where there is no conflict and enemy, but also presupposes the conflict among human beings in the fallen world. The Bible is full of stories to tell how easily and how frequently our relationships are damaged and broken. On this recognition, the Bible illustrates how the broken relationships were and could be restored.

The shift from retribution to restoration is well exemplified in Jesus' teaching on retaliation in the gospel of Matthew: "You have heard that it was said, 'An eye for an eye and a tooth for a tooth.' But I say to you, Do not resist an evildoer" (5:38-39). In this passage the part about "An eye for an eye and a tooth for a tooth" is called in Latin *lex talionis*, a traditional embodiment of retributive justice. In this concept, justice is achieved by returning the equivalent harm to the initial evil done. This is not just an ancient custom but a widely shared concept of justice even in the twenty-first century. Retributive justice is not all about punishment, but rather it supports the idea that a person should be rewarded proportionally to the good she or he has done. And of course, the criminal justice system in our society is primarily based on retributive justice.

But Jesus said, "Do not resist an evildoer." He told an alternative "way of nonviolent, sacrificial, peacemaking love" (Marshall, 61). We should notice that the alternative is shown in the context of Jesus' proclamation that "unless your righteousness exceeds that of the scribes and Pharisees, you will never enter the kingdom of heaven" (Matt. 5:20). This righteousness or justice, which exceeds that of the Jewish religious leaders, is restorative justice, a justice based on the restoration of broken relationship, between God and humanity, between human beings including neighbors and enemies, and between humanity and other portions of the creation.

AN ANALYSIS OF JAPAN'S PAST WRONGS FROM A BIBLICAL JUSTICE PERSPECTIVE

Let me move on to a specific example from the East Asian context, namely Japan's responsibility for the past invasion and colonization. As a Japanese person involved in peace studies, I believe that the issue is great enough to be inescapable. However, despite its inevitability, I often feel too diffident to address it. The reason seems clear: because any kind of argument on this issue draws emotional reactions. Even for a comment such as, "Since this is a serious issue, we all have to discuss with a cool mind," I am accused of not being sympathetic enough to the victims of colonial rule.

Generally speaking it is unthinkable that those who differ in opinions succeed in resolving conflict quickly because they all get emotional. When emotional words shower a person, she or he is deprived of the will to think through the issue and continue an effort to dialogue. The more people are deprived of opportunities for dialogue, the more the resolution will be pushed back.

I used to think that this issue gets emotional despite the necessity of calm and rational attitude. But my thought is changing. What if "getting emotional" itself has become the goal of argument? The only logical explanation I can imagine is that the issue is a kind of problem from which people can extract more interest as long as it is unresolved. The longer the issue is protracted, the more benefit can be obtained.

It is obvious that Japan is responsible for the past wrongs. Japanese are obliged to answer the issue of reconciliation and peaceful coexistence in East Asia. Japan's answers are evaluated by the standard of how much the Japanese regret the past wrongs and how much effort they make for compensation. So far, all the answers have failed. One of the reasons is obviously because Japan has not felt and expressed sufficient remorse. But we need to consider another possible reason: because more can be gained from the issue being protracted than being answered correctly.

I got this insight from the field of political philosophy. The goal of political philosophy is to understand social relations from the perspective of power. Debates on Japan's responsibility for the past colonial rule can be seen as a relation of political power. Namely, the structure of the issue is the relation between questioner and answerer. This is a power relation, since the questioner always holds the position of evaluator, while the answerer is kept in a passive position of being questioned, examined, and judged.

I said earlier that I feel diffident whenever I talk about the issue of Japan's past wrongs because I know that my answer will never pass this exam. And please do not get me wrong; I do not think this is unfair and unjust. That is exactly what the Japanese had done to the people of Taiwan and Korea. We asked them in what way they would show their loyalty to the Japanese empire. They changed their names into Japanese ones. They spoke Japanese and taught their children in Japanese. They worshiped the Japanese emperor. But we appraised their answers and kept on putting zero on them. The evaluation was always the same: unsatisfactory. What a humiliation! What a pain! What a terror!

Now we have come back to the justice issue. My analysis is this: The dynamism of the debate over Japan's past colonialism and militarism is based on the concept of retributive justice. As long as we stand on the principle of retribution, Japan's abuse of colonial power must be retributed by the use of the same power upon it. Humiliation for humiliation, pain for pain, appraisal for appraisal, accusation for accusation. *Lex talionis*, indeed.

Again, I am not talking about injustice. Retributive justice is not withstanding a justice. Retribution has been a way of doing justice. It is fatally flawed, however. Retribution can cause another retribution, as no one can assure the completion of retribution. As long as humiliation is sought to repay the past humiliation, nobody can claim that Japan has paid everything back.

There are those who say, "That's the way it should be. There is no other way for the Japanese to compensate the past sins." Well, I admit that such a claim has a historical ground. But I also question whether it should be the only way for the future. As long as we stick to seeking retribution for the past pains, it is difficult to see the sense of trust, respect, and reciprocity emerge from it. If we really desire reconciliation and convivial fraternity, I suppose that there must be a point of "changing lenses" from retributive justice to restorative justice.

REAFFIRMING INJUSTICE AS OUR COMMON GROUND

Where and how can we go from here? One possibility is to explore the process of moving from retribution to restoration. But we have to reconsider our assumption that there is a sharp contrast between retributive justice and restorative justice. For example, Howard Zehr, "the grandfather of restorative justice," warned that the distinction between the two concepts would be misleading, hiding important similarities.[5] He affirms that "a primary goal of both retributive theory and restorative theory is to vindicate through reciprocity, by evening the score" (Zehr, 58). While retribution holds that "pain will vindicate," "That is often counterproductive for both victim and offender," whereas restoration tries to vindicate through "acknowledgment of victim's harms and needs, combined with an active effort to encourage offenders to take responsibility, make right the wrongs, and address the causes of their behavior" (Zehr, 59). From his explanation, it seems to me that one of the key elements of the change is the shift of attention from what is to be done for justice to what has been done as injustice.

Since I was initially assigned to offer some conceptual exploration on injustice, I thought I would begin with a general overview of the concept. There came a second thought to me, "Why injustice, why not justice?"

As you may speculate, there are many articles on justice in the dictionaries and encyclopedias, but it is very hard to find an independent entry on injustice. It seems understandable to me, since it is widely assumed that to know what injustice is, we have to know what justice is. As far as I remember, one of the motives for Mahatma Gandhi to invent the term *satyagraha* (holding onto truth, hence truth-force) was that he did not want to define his philosophy in negative terms, such as nonviolence.

So, a typical flow of ideas seems to take a shift to defining justice so as to clarify its absence or denial, that is, injustice. But my second thought did not take such an ordinary quick shift of attention. Rather, I was somehow drawn to stick to the original term, injustice, and to make sense of thinking about injustice rather than justice.

I would like to draw a clue to such exploration by some arguments on suffering. Peter Dula, a Mennonite educator, has argued that

> opening ourselves to the pain of the sufferer is exactly what we usually want to avoid. One reason, I think, why we might want quick answers to the problem of suffering is because of the burdens suffering . . . places on us. But a faithful Christian response to the problem of suffering will always direct us toward more intense engagement with suffering. A Christian response will keep in mind that the most severe problem we face with regard to suffering is not "How can it coexist alongside a good God?" but

"How can we bring ourselves to face it, to stop avoiding it, in ourselves and in others?"[6]

Japanese philosopher Tatsuru Uchida argues that a definition of a term does not necessarily help define its negation.[7] We are tempted to overestimate the objectivity of "what we know." Too often, without evidence, we tend to say, "If I know this, others must know it, too." But the truth is the other way around. It is much more often the case that "what I don't know, neither do others know." Why? Uchida explains that human beings shut their eyes only from the things related to the human ontological nature. Thus what we glance at with curiosity differs depending on social groups, but what we desperately glance away from does not change. In other words, human beings share much more universality on "what we do not know" and "what we cannot do," than "what we know" and "what we can do (Uchida, 39).

Uchida's argument is not very unique. For example, Edward Said often argued that the crime of the Holocaust was so serious that the distinction between Jews and Gentiles has become meaningless. Therefore he commented that both Palestinians and Jews were basically the same in practice. Palestinians are victims today and occasionally offenders of terrorism, and Jews used to be victims and offenders today (and occasionally victims of terrorism). Although they confront each other, they actually share a common ground, that is, the way they suffer. This can be called "the universality of suffering."[8]

This point is worth further exploration. Since the tragedy of 9-11, we have heard many claims of the universality of one's own justice, and most of them are beyond all help. But what if we claim instead the universality of injustice? Perhaps there are not multiple different tragedies on each side but one big tragedy covering all parties. Such recognition may provide a common ground for peace, forgiveness, and reconciliation.

RESPONSES TO THE PRESENTATION BY ATSUHIRO KATANO, MENNONITE PROFESSOR IN JAPAN

Mennonite from Indonesia

Atsuhiro has focused three provocative issues for me. One is the idea that human rights stem from religious freedom. Second, he proposed the idea of restorative justice and its interplay—not opposition to—but its interplay with retributive justice. And third is the definition of justice. He proposed that we define justice from the universality of suffering.

Quaker from Aotearoa/New Zealand

I have been working in Palestine, and I would just like to make a comment regarding what you have just said about the universality of suffering. The most moving group of people I have met there are the bereaved families circle in Israel. They are both Palestinians and Israelis who have suffered the loss of very close relatives from the violence of the other side. Together they have taken the difficult path of recognizing their common suffering and saying, "We must rise above retaliation. We do not want this suffering to happen to anybody else. We need to work together, to embrace one another as brothers and sisters," as they do when they talk publicly together. Their example is most inspiring and humbling. .

Atsuhiro Katano

I just want to make an additional comment to what I had in mind when I wrote about this topic, especially the universality of suffering. As Japanese, we have shared the common experience of the atomic bombing by the United States. Fortunately after the war we somehow succeeded in understanding that tragic experience as something more universal than the perpetration of war crimes against a particular nation, the Japanese. Somehow we tried to understand that nobody would want that kind of experience of being bombed, and it should not happen again anywhere in the world.

It is not just Japan accusing the United States of war crimes based on human law, or the Geneva convention, or whatever. Rather somehow we transferred that experience into the gate of the universality of suffering. Nobody would want that experience. It is not just for the United States and Japan. It is a topic for everybody. The disaster is for everybody. One other conviction is a heritage for me as a Japanese person, namely not always seeking retribution or compensation to regain what has been lost. These were some thoughts in my mind as I wrote.

Mennnonite from WCC, Geneva, Switzerland

I want to make a comment related to your words in regard to more gain coming out of unresolved issues than out of resolved issues. Often there is deliberate resistance on the part of victims against their suffering being made universal. You see that in the Jewish history. You also see that in Mennonite history. You know we Mennonites are the biggest victims of persecution. To take our own history as an example, our resistance is linked to what you said about more being gained out of unresolved issues. Perhaps if this gets resolved, if our suffering gets to be universal, then we don't have a point any more. In fact we might even lose our sense of identity. I remember a friend in Northern Ireland saying, "People are complaining about the violence and the troubles, but they don't necessarily want peace. With peace they may lose their identity of being those who are as opposed to their opponents." What you said about interests also applies to identity. There is identity in being the victim or the enemy of someone else. That plays an important role not only in politics but also in personal stories.

Atsuhiro Katano

You say not only interest, but also identity. It is a good insight, and I want to think through it in a deeper way. One thought in my mind as I composed these arguments was about family relations. In your observations about global violence, you mentioned that the major portion of such violence occurs daily in domestic situations, in casual individual and intimate relationships on an interpersonal level. I began to think about managing families and about family relationships in the development of children. As a father who has an eight-year-old daughter, I sometimes reflect on how I manage this role as a father. I was amazed to discover that I tend to stand in the position of questioning rather than answering my eight-year-old daughter. And I said, "Why?" Maybe it is comfortable. I can obtain a position of sympathy, like those who pose questions rather than those who passively answer the questions.

I definitely agree with you that this is not only an issue of interest but also includes identity issues. In what position in this interaction would we put ourselves? That affects our understanding of power and powerlessness as well as our own sense of belonging. It also affects our sense of making or counteracting relationships with others, of superiority or inferiority. So yes, I think it is an identity issue always. I hope that I am quite aware that what I am trying to say could be a challenge for the victims and those who are harmed, especially those who see their experience as something particular and very unique. Sometimes the practice of making one's experience too unique or too particular simply shuts the eyes of the victim to wider realities of the world. So I sometimes try to be provocative to those who are harmed as well as those who are harming.

Member of the Evangelical Friends, Philippines

Perhaps you are aware of the so called "comfort women" during World War II. Perhaps you do not understand who the comfort women were. These were women who were forced to engage in prostitution with Japanese soldiers. Perhaps you are aware that we were under the Japanese soldiers for four and one half years during World War II. Also I believe that the Japanese are trying to give retributive and restorative justice to our people. They give money for our infrastructure. But from time to time I see these women are still living today, many in the streets calling for retributive and restorative justice for themselves. Could you tell us what the Japanese and the Japanese government are doing today to give retributive and restorative justice to these women, who are still crying for justice because they are victims of a violation of human rights.

Atsuhiro Katano

I have to confess that I am not fully aware of the new situations of this particular issue, for I have not been following it carefully. So my comment will be very general. As far as I understand, the Japanese government is working on this issue in terms of compensation. They try to compensate for this situation with some kind of funding, both publicly and privately. There are also private groups and non-government organizations that try to work on this issue as well. When it comes to compensation, or anything beyond compensation, there is an argument among Japanese about whether the situation at that time was governmentally organized or was a more spontaneous event that happened coincidentally in many places. Some of the Japanese are quite unwilling to accept accusation that the Japanese military were responsible for such an organizational and institutional violation of human rights. The discussion is ongoing.

My personal position is that there was actual enslavement of women by the Japanese military. But I am somewhat hopeful that the meaning of that situation would be that there are people who are very hesitant to admit the reality, because once they admit, they cannot justify it any more. In this sense, those people are quite aware that sexual violence during wartime is a crime. Therefore I believe there is a common ground. The fact is that actual stories have been discovered many times. This means that we should work further, and I am somewhat hopeful that will happen, although it may take some time.

Member of the Evangelical Friends, Philippines

Do you think that the Japanese government would be willing to accept the children that were produced as a result of that practice during World War II? These Filipinos are half-Japanese. Do you think that the Japanese government would accept these children living in your country because of the extreme poverty of these families in our country?

Atsuhiro Katano

Immigration comes into this question. When it comes to immigration, I think the Japanese government should be more friendly to the Asian immigrants than it is. We in the churches are pushing for greater openness to Asia immigrants, but most Japanese are hesitant. The Japanese people are not aware of situations like this. We are so dependent upon the information and the resources from outside of Japan. The people are not really informed about how much we are interconnected and interdependent with other countries in Asia.

Basically the Japanese government will be very, very careful before accepting any claim concerning Japanese nationality on the basis of the biological constitution of the Philippine population, especially when it comes to allowing those who claim to have some Japanese blood to come more easily to Japan. They are going to be very, very critical and very careful. There must be some Japanese who are pushing for that argument, not necessarily because they have half-blooded inter-Japanese nationality. We are not that racially oriented. We are not that caught up with the actual blood which is flowing inside our bodies but rather with how we should manage the international relations among other nations.

What about our international neighborhoods in terms of refugees and immigrants? We have Japanese activists who are into the immigration and human rights issues of those who come from a foreign country to work in Japan, but perhaps such activists are not really aware of this Filipino claim for immigration to Japan, or of the historical reasons for it.

Mennonite bishop from the Philippines

I am very impressed with your presentation. But listening to your presentation, I am wondering, and you owe me an answer to this: How can a nation experience peace when its circumstances threaten its people with worry, frustrations, and fear?

Mennonite from Japan

You talked about the universality of suffering. That is the very thing that a visitor from the Korean Anabaptist Center said after he visited Hiroshima. What is happening now is that the Hiroshima Center and the Korean Anabaptist Center are visiting one another. A Quaker group, I believe, started the exchange program with the Hiroshima Friendship Center. When the people of Hiroshima visited Korea, some of them were victims of the A-bomb. When Japanese people visit Korea, we always go to the house of sharing where the comfort women, the victims of World War II, live together. Now they are very old. I was not there, but I was told that the Japanese victims of the A-bomb and the Korean victims of the Japanese sex slavery embraced each other. That was really appealing, not just to those who were there, but that story was so inspiring to the Mennonites in Korea.

I wonder whether you could give me some insight. Sure, immediate victims can interact with one another. Sure everyone participates in the universality of suffering. But I have to deal with my own generation. I am not an immediate victim of anything. I remember one time an American Mennonite, a young lady, talked to me. She expressed how sorry she is about America dropping the bombs on Nagasaki and Hiroshima. I am not from Hiroshima. I know it from the textbooks. I couldn't just say "Apology accepted," or anything like that. It would be totally phony and fake. I notice that some of the young Korean members of the church just have a good time with other young members of the Korean church. I wonder whether we should always bring up the justice issue and try to relearn the history. In what framework is it possible? How can we really relate to each other when neither of us is an immediate victim of injustice? Rather we are representative members of two countries who have a terrible history.

Atsuhiro Katano

As I listen to Ambrosio and Nika commenting on my presentation, one of the things that comes to my mind is that injustice itself is a negative term. I simply said something about sticking to this negative concept, injustice, rather than easily jumping to the positive concept of justice. As we share the common experiences of injustice and oppression, perhaps the challenge for me is to find any common ground for human being and experience and see what would emerge after that.

Nika's comment reminded me of the difficulty of dialogue. As I was educated in the United States in a conflict transformation program, one of the attitudes I was hesitant to learn from this Western or

American way of thinking was that dialogue solves everything. Can it solve everything? There may be some point where we have to acknowledge that we just can't dialogue. We just can't communicate anymore. That is one of the most fundamental experiences of my study in the United States, speaking English with friends, and taking English courses, and writing English papers, and reading English books. I learned a lot; it was a blessing for me. But still there was the matter of my identity. I had good friends, but still there are things I just could not communicate. So my experience was somehow the recognition of our limit, our weakness. We just can't verbalize everything. We just can't communicate everything.

When it comes to loss of experience, I'm not quite sure whether it will help you or not, but I have a thought. What about common experience? For example, let's say, what about weeping together? Sometimes it is very easy to have fun together, or smile together, or work together for something constructive, something enjoyable. Praising together, singing together, dancing together, whatever. Constructing houses together, feeding the hungry together. They are enjoyable things. If we are to get into a deeper dimension, there may be a time when we will weep together. And that kind of experience may become another breakthrough into a deeper human relationship. That is my thought.

Mennonite from Indonesia

Related to injustice issues which you have expressed before, I would like to speak about Indonesians. As Indonesian people, or even other Asian people, we live in injustice. As Christians who live in Indonesia, so often we feel that we are second-class citizens. Because we are a minority in Indonesia, so often we have difficulties dealing with our faith. How do we actualize our faith in freedom, worship our God in freedom? Very often and in many places we cannot do that.

As I see it, the majority who live in Indonesia don't simply work on their own. They work hand-in-hand with other people around the world, which gives them the power to pressure the minority who live in Indonesia. But as the body of Christ, can we not do the same thing? Maybe working with people from other countries will give us the resources to share together, show Christ's love, and build the kingdom.

As we talk about Indonesian issues of poverty and justice, maybe you can see persecution of the minority on television. We talk about "peace in our land" in the context of Asia. If we can do that, how do we deal with those issues in Asia? The general issue in Asia is that we have problems like poverty, injustice, and pluralism. But the basis of our problem is that we don't care about one another. We need other hands, your hands, brothers and sisters in Christ. By doing that, many people will resolve, "Oh, yes," and they will recognize that we are their brothers and sisters. It won't then seem like being alone living in our own country. My question is, Can we as Christians in the body of Christ work together to pursue our goal to implement the love of Christ in our lives, as we live daily in Asia?

Atsuhiro Katano

My comments have been general in character and abstract in content, and I am not aware of particular situations other than my own context. I would just like to remember that I am thinking of myself as being in a process of learning, and having responses from you both personally and publicly is also a part of learning. Let's remind ourselves that we are all in the process of learning. We should keep on being open and being insightful, encouraging, empowering each other, and working together.

Mennonite from Australia

Someone has said that we have to live with injustice. It's there, and we just have to live with it. I disagree. As Christians we shouldn't have to live with injustice. When we see an injustice, we need to come up with a solution to that injustice. Whether the injustice be large or small, I don't believe we should live with it at all. Jesus didn't live with it. When he saw the injustice of the people selling in the temple, he went over and threw them out. We should follow his example and not live with the injustices that we are accepting.

The brother over there said that if their country is invaded by another country and they just submit, they are giving in to injustice. Sorry, I also don't agree with that. If you are submitting to someone, if someone comes and hits you with a stick and you give back love, that's not submitting to injustice. That's being Jesus Christ. If someone hits you again, you give love back, that's being Jesus Christ.

It's the same whether it be country versus country, religion versus religion, Christian versus Christian. If we as Historic Peace Churches who are against injustice don't stand against injustice, then we betray ourselves. As Christians we shouldn't have to live with injustice. We should stand up and fight against those injustices no matter where they show up.

Mennonite bishop from the Philippines

Hallelujah! I want to make a supplement to the last statement. First I want to throw out a question. How peaceful are we with God? How peaceful are we with our neighbors? How peaceful are we with our own selves? If we can answer that practically, then we are really on the way to being pacifists. It appears that most people want not to have war, to maintain peace. Nevertheless I want to tell you, if that should be the case, if we want really to prevent any nuclear development, it will not hinder the prophecy of the Bible that during the last days all these things will happen.

Mennonite from Indonesia

Even though I can't say I'm from Indonesia, neither can I say I'm from America. I'm from both worlds. I see the issue of injustice permeated through the Indonesian school system. Imagine a boy going to school in his uniform, coming into the classroom and being asked to sit down. Now he listens to what the teacher has to say. If he starts to question the premises or the issues that the teacher brings up, he gets whacked on the head. So what do you think will happen to this child? His perception of violence and of what he should be doing when he grows up is learned from the teacher. That's the norm, and that's the way to do things. So in my family, if my son disobeys me, the right thing to do is to give him a nice whack on the head, and that should be sufficient; that should be good. Peace now prevails in my family. Peace now prevails in my school.

My concern is how we as parents communicate peace to our children. I know personally that when I come home from work, I get very impatient and say things that I probably should not say to my children. After seeing kids in Aceh, as a father I think quite often about how they were treated. The Acehnese have a culture in which the kids are expected to be satisfied with whatever they are told. The parents also follow the old rule. So if the kids start to intervene in family discussions, they should just be satisfied to be quiet. The exclusion or the alienation of a child—a little person, but still a person—starts at an early age. I can imagine when an Acehnese child grows up, he will perceive that the only way to deal with issues of conflict between him and his family or his neighbors is to alienate them, because this is what he has been taught.

Church of the Brethren Member from India

So many questions have been raised that I want to give an answer according to the Bible. According to Matthew 24: 6-8,

And you will hear of wars and rumors of wars; see that you are
not alarmed; for this must take place, but the end is not yet. For
nation will rise against nation, and kingdom against kingdom,
and there will be famines and earthquakes in various places: all
this is but the beginning of the birth pangs.

Mennonite from Indonesia

We in Indonesia have experienced many injustices. Injustice expresses itself as violence not only in matter of religion, where there are
majority and minority; but also I believe injustice has expressed itself
where there are so-called communists and ex-communists in Indonesia. In 1965 and 1966 between 500,000 and three million people
throughout Indonesia were killed to establish the new regime of President Suharto. I think it was very, very unjust, because to erect or establish a new regime, there were very many murder victims, communists, and ex-communists.

What is the role of the church in the Indonesian context? Antonio
Gramsci was an Italian Marxist imprisoned by Benito Mussolini, but I
think some of his ideas are helpful. We know Gramsci developed the
idea of civil society in relation to the ruling class. In every society
there are the ruling class and civil society. The ruling class has the
power and exerts its power through influential ideology or by oppressive means. The churches are a part of civil society. In Gramscian
thinking, the civil society can take three steps to stand against the ruling class that promotes injustice. First, civil society can make cultural
hegemony; second, civil society can make opposition; and third is
revolution.

I think the relevance of Gramscian thinking is the first two steps
of his opinion—cultural hegemony and opposition. What do I mean
by these? In cultural hegemony the church as a part of civil society can
develop and promote Christian influence, Christian values in the
spirit of Jesus: love, peace, justice, and truth. In opposition the church
can promote unity between the church and anyone in society who has
good will. A saying of our former President Sukarno was to unite
everyone who has good will to influence society, the government, and
ruling class, so that we can hope for a better society, a more peaceful
society, and a more just society.

Quaker from Australia

An injustice that troubles me greatly in my own country, and I am
part of it, is our attitude toward the indigenous people of our own

country. There is such injustice in Australia based on the dispossession of aboriginal people. We don't deserve to have peace in our land until we sort out that the injustice. It is fundamental, really fundamental, and it is very deep. It is a big scar for us in our country.

Dr. Krisetya's sermon reminded us about the sword that we may be wearing. I found myself realizing that I am certainly wearing a sword because I'm part of the powerful elite about which our friend just spoke. That power elite includes those who have comfort, wealth, and power. These are all swords, all swords, and we were invited to think about turning them into plowshares. The work that I'm intent on doing, as you have already heard, is about the swords others are wearing, but I have to look at the sword that I'm wearing. That sword is about some privilege, education, and some power, so it is a sword that I must readdress.

I've been troubled by this issue over many years. It doesn't leave me and it won't leave me until we as a nation can actually set things right with the indigenous people of our country. That is going to take some doing, but I think it is in my heart, and I think it is in the hearts of many more Australians now. So I hope I can work with other people to turn that particular sword into a plowshare.

Quaker from Australia

I want to tell a story about an effort toward restorative justice in Papua, New Guinea. It's a difficult story in Indonesia because Papua is part of Indonesia. In the past under the colonial rule, it was semi-separate, and some people in Papua still feel separated from the country of Indonesia. An armed independence struggle is ongoing in Papua, and there are many Papuan refugees around the world who feel strongly about the issues. Equally, there are people in Indonesia who say we should avoid another Aceh.

So the Australian Center for Peace and Conflict Studies supported a coming together of people from Papua—people from the armed conflict, people from the churches, people from youth groups, people from outside, and the people who have spoken on behalf of Papua. First they came together in Madang in Papua, and they've come together twice more to see if they can come to a common understanding of where they want Papua to go. One of the outcomes of those meetings has been a statement for Papua as a peaceful country, for working together to come to a common solution to Papua's problems. One positive outcome is that when the Indonesian government wishes to have a dialogue with Papua, informed people can speak on behalf of Papua.

Dialogue with people you don't know is really difficult. In Jakarta there is a Forum Papua composed of Indonesian ex-public servants and journalists who want to encourage the process of dialogue. So there are many exciting things going on in Indonesia. The message that I want to emphasize is "networking." Get to know to one other; get to know what other people are doing, people outside as well as people inside.

NOTES

1. Mary Kaldor, *New and Old Wars: Organized Violence in a Global Age* (Stanford, Calif.: Stanford University Press, 1999).

2. Samuel P. Huntington, *The Clash of Civilizations and the New World Order* (New York: Simon and Schuster Inc., 1997).

3. Desmond Tutu, *No Future without Forgiveness* (New York: Doubleday, 1999), 54-55.

4. Chris Marshall, *The Little Book of Biblical Justice: A Fresh Approach to the Bible's Teachings on Justice* (Intercourse, Pa.: Good Books, 2005), 66-7.

5. Howard Zehr, *The Little Book of Restorative Justice* (Intercourse, Pa.: Good Books, 2002), 74.

6. Peter Dula, "Questions, Answers, Stories: Speaking of God and Suffering," *Vision: A Journal for Church and Theology* 8.2 (Fall 2007): 15.

7. Tatsuru Uchida, *Murakami Haruki no Goyohjin* (Tokyo: Artes Publishing, 2007), 39.

8. Toshiki Mogami, *Kikkyo naki Heiwa ni* (Tokyo: Misuzu Shobo, 2006),10.

Chapter 4

INVITATION TO POETIC PROPHETIC WITNESS

Jarrod McKenna and Jo Vallentine

JARED MCKENNA

Jo Valentine is an incredible woman. If you are pursuing women's studies in Australia, Jo Valentine is in many current textbooks. Jo was named one of Western Australia's 100 most influential people throughout the state's history. She was a co-nominee for a joint Nobel Peace Prize. All of this has come out of Jo's deep faith. Jo is a brilliant example of the form of spiritual engagement that the peace churches have always held, and that Christian engagement is found in the non-violence of the cross. Almost like the early Anabaptist women, Jo has been someone so filled with the Spirit that she has gone into many places ranting of a world transformed, and in so doing, so threatened the patriarchal powers that she has provoked at least the desire of some to see her share the fiery fate or watery grave of those early Anabaptist sisters. But none of this has dampened her passion or fire. This passion saw Jo elected as Western Australia's first Greens senator in Australia. She has campaigned tirelessly on peace, on justice, and on a safe environment.

JO VALENTINE

Jarrod McKenna is an exceptional young man who is fired by the Light of Jesus Christ, and it is wonderful to be working with him. We did an amazing thirty-day workshop from full moon to full moon several years ago with an amazing teacher—Joanna Macy—a deep ecologist, systems theorist, and anti-nuclear activist. And we looked at the plight of our planet and *our* place in it. The work was very deep, very meaningful, but joyful because there is so much to be grateful for.

Jarrod does amazing work with young people in schools through an organization he started, Empowering Peacemakers in Your Community (EPYC). Together we went to Pine Gap, a huge American military base in the middle Australia's glorious and living desert. Orders for war are transmitted through that Pine Gap base, so it's crucial to the United States military. We went on a pilgrimage there, out into the desert, and it was wonderful. Jarrod has chosen voluntary poverty by living in a small community, the Peace Tree Community, in one of Perth's least salubrious suburbs, and that is commendable too.

JARROD MCKENNA

We don't call our lifestyle "voluntary poverty." We call it "shared prosperity of the early church." I live on the same rate that you would get if you on the dole in Australia, which puts me in the top eight percent of the wealthiest people in the world. So I'm not going to claim any poverty at all. We are trying to deepen ourselves in the narrative of Scripture and in what happened through Jesus, how we have moved from protest as activists to something more, something of a poetic and prophetic witness, something which is embodied. Both of us on various campaigns have experienced a sense that our identity is often formed simply against something else, and we need to find our identity in the nonviolent Messiah.

One of those experiences for me was at the Baxter detention center. As you may know, Australia has an embarrassing and shameful history of racist policies and how it treats refugees. At Peace Tree Community we practice hospitality for people who need a place to stay, and also often for people who live on the streets or are refugees. One of our friends was locked up in this prison that we call a detention center for four and a half years. His only crime was fleeing his war-torn country and trying to make another start. So our Christian commune, inspired by the Historic Peace Churches, traveled together to the Baxter detention center to hold worship services outside these gates of Jericho, to pray for their injustice to fall. We had amazing and moving experiences that even brought hardened Socialists to tears.

What happened the next day, and what was screened on international TV, was me being smacked in the head by a very angry police officer. He was wearing riot gear that made him look like he was playing ice hockey, but since he and the others were in the middle of the desert, it must have been very hot. Maybe that's why they were so angry. Amid that, and amid being beaten up, violence broke out between these 600 protesters and these riot cops. The cops retreated behind a large concrete water pipe—only this separated the angry protesters and the angry riot cops.

We had angry protesters on one side just yelling, and violence had already broken out. I was standing squashed against this water pipe right in front of four rows of riot cops. The first cop was standing with her hand open, as if waiting to give a command. Behind the first row of riot cops every police officer had their batons drawn.

So I did what anyone would do—I started praying! "What am I going to do!" And I heard the still small voice that even now continues to speak the Word when we are attentive. I knew what I needed to do, to cross the water pipe and pray in the luminal space between the protestors and the riot cops.

But I didn't even know how I was going to do that. I couldn't get over the water pipe; I was sandwiched between it and a mass of people pushing behind me. So I literally got down on my hands and knees and crawled under the water pipe on the red desert dirt. Before the police could run at me I took the position of prayer that I take at home in the mornings. Knees on the ground, palms lifted open in praise at chest level. In this position of prayer, between hundreds of riot cops with batos drawn, with hundreds of angry protesters behind us, I experienced something beyond protest, something of prophetic witness. Again kneeling there, what was I to do? And clear as anything, I started singing some of the songs we felt that we were given in worship as a community. Simple songs, songs like

> Easter means freedom,
> Free the refugees.
> Easter means freedom,
> Free the refugees.

Something incredible happened. Protesters started singing this song. This is in the Australian post-Christendom context, angry protesters stop yelling and start singing, *"Easter means freedom, free the refugees."* Then something else amazing happened. The police put their batons away. Not only was the violence deescalated, the focus moved from who we are against to the suffering of these people and the God of the Easter Exodus whose Spirit is moving to liberate creation from domination. Doxology is dangerous when it dares to be sung with our lives at the gates of hell. Something of what happened to me in this experience has opened me to a new way of engaging, to what Paul Alexander calls "pro-testifying." Beyond protest *against* to a prophetic, poetic witness *for* God's New World.

JO VALENTINE

My story is about Brussels. The Hague Appeal for Peace was a big international conference in The Hague in 1999. Thousands of people were there, and I get worried when I am with thousands of people. I'm not very good in big crowds. But the Hague Appeal for Peace brought together of an amazing group of people, all seeking peace at the deepest levels. Some people chose to walk from The Hague to Brussels, and I went with them, camping out along the way for a couple of weeks. It was a good pilgrimage walk. Along the way we practiced what we would do when we got to the gates of NATO, because that was our destination. We wanted to ask NATO to stop the bombings that were then raging in former Yugoslavia. We also wanted to be a citizens inspection team to find out about nuclear weapons, because NATO is very involved with the nuclear weapons of Britain, France, the United States.

We had planned all kinds of routines to guide what we would do when we got to the gates. And a team was delegated go inside to speak to the commanders of the base about nuclear weapons, about peace generally, and about stopping the bombing in particular.

When we arrived at the gates of NATO, we were suddenly outmaneuvered by the military on horseback, water cannons, and barbed wire fences, so that we were gradually moved into a smaller and smaller space. We were pushed into a very nasty uncomfortable triangle. No exit. We weren't military strategists, but it was clear to us that the people inside NATO had us all sorted out well before we got there. It looked like it might turn very ugly with people being dragged out over the barbed wire fences. I had been in a little affinity group between The Hague and Brussels, and we had practiced a very special dance that Joanna Macy had taught us. So I said to my affinity group, "Let's dance!" That's what we *had* to do in the face of this violence. I'd never before actually experienced water cannon and horses coming very, very close. I felt sorry for the horses as well as the people on their backs.

So, we started our dance, the Elm dance. It's a spiritual meditative dance that I've used in many situations. I have done it in the marble hallways of a mining company, in a forest when we were trying to stop the desecration of the forest, and there again at the gates of NATO. Once we started this dance, the military, or the NATO officials, were perplexed. They didn't know what to do. This happens every time. They sensed there was something spiritual going on there. They were not sure what it was, but it confounded them. So they sort of stood back. We danced and danced for hours in the hot sun, and no more arrests were happening. In the end I said, "We've got to change the dance." So every time we went into the center, I'd say, "Okay, let's change the dance." Two or three entries later we would change the dance and do something different.

Finally we were all quite exhausted and more or less inviting arrest, which then happened. We were held in very bad conditions, all bunched up into the Brussels watch house. Yet it happened in a much more peaceful way than what otherwise would have occurred. Nobody was injured going over barbed wire, the horses trampled nobody, and we had conversations with the arresting officers. So the dance made a big difference in how this event played out. That's my little story of transforming a situation through dance, through movement, through the Spirit—not through shouting and protests.

JARROD MCKENNA

We in the Peace Tree Community, inspired by many different elements from the Historic Peace Churches, have moved into one of the lowest socio-economic areas in our city to seek to be a community of God's peace, which for us often looks like practicing hospitality for people in need and urban permaculture gardening to empower ourselves alongside local people. In prayer we feel God has opened to us what has been lost in many of our churches, the art of lament and its importance for us today. If we cannot enter into God's grief for our world, our ability to experience the joy of the transfiguration of our world will be seriously crippled.

The world is facing an ecological crisis which is unprecedented. Since 1970 we have destroyed thirty percent of creation—living water systems, forests, and the oceans. This is happening at a rate that is not slowing down. Somehow today the practicality of Jesus' eschatological message has been taken from us and our imaginations. Maybe these ecological disasters and the end of oil that we are facing can actually waken us up to lament, to enter into our pain and the pain of the world, trusting in Resurrection power.

So we have been gathering with the Friends, with our community, and with some other people, as we wait on God. This is a little bit of what has come out of our waiting. We call it "An Invitation." What I'd invite you to do now, as I perform the theopoetic piece I wrote, is to close your eyes and enter into the poetics of the biblical narrative, which are too easily abstracted away in theology instead of bringing us into doxology.

The Vine and Fig Tree Planters—Our Invitation

We woke to a sound as distant,
as distant as we are from the earth,
from each other,
from ourselves,
from the Spirit of all life.

A sound audible when the imperial legions of appliances, plasma TVs, iPods, computers, mobiles,
microwaves that occupy our hearts and imaginations
with their pervasive hum gave way to the wildness of
what *is*.

Gave way to the wild melodic stillness and wonder of
the stars, the redemption songs of crickets and frogs,
of the wind dancing with a thousand leaves. Gave
way to the untamed gratitude and joy at the extrava-
gant "given-ness" of the world. Exiled in the manu-
factured milieu of the suburbs, the offices, the shopping centers, the media, the market, the institutions
which foster escapist spiritualities to accompany the
destruction of creation. We heard an "untamed-ness"
as foreign to us in these places as we are to ourselves,
as alien as we are from our places in,
and as,
and not above,
creation.

Ambushed by worshipful wonder, at the sheer goodness
of what is, of wildness and its dangerous expectant

doxology, we at first could not interpret the tongues
of that living which was other than ourselves. We
presumed silence despite the rocks crying out.
Yet Pentecost has become our own.

We've been found with ears to hear that,
mixed with a symphony of praise from wild animals,
undomesticated forests and waterways,
a groaning and a growing lament is heard,
a lament that we are deaf to the cries of the suffering and
      numb to the pain that would transform us,
if we would only stop running.

We have become, we've become so fearful.
We cannot face the reality of the end of oil.
We cannot face an unprecedented ecological crisis.
We cannot face the fact that we live in a world where our
      world governments in one year spent $1.4 trillion on
      weapons whose sole purpose is to take human life.
      One point four trillion dollars,
twenty-six times the amount of money we need to end
      absolute poverty around the world.

We've hidden in endless home improvements, in reality
      TV shows, in Indonesian or Australian or American
      Idol, in our overflowing shopping carts, in our unwa-
      vering faith that the market will sort everything out
      and will bring our salvation.

Yet some of us are haunted by a hope that we have
      encountered in the Gospels that these cries will be
      and have been answered. A dream so crazy it is
      uttered only by the prophets: *God will justly arbitrate
      between many peoples and will settle disputes for strong
      nations far and wide. They will beat their swords into
      plowshares and their spears into pruning hooks, nation
      shall not take up sword against nation, nor will they train
      for war any more. Everyone, everyone will sit underneath
      their own vine and fig tree. And no one shall make them
      afraid for God Almighty has spoken.*
This moves us past protest to the invitational witness of
      the nonviolent glory that will one day flood the earth

like the waters of the seas, that has started gushing
into reality in the person of Jesus. So we've been
moved to enact the heretical orthodoxy of walking in
the resurrection,
of embodying the foolishness of the cross,
of strange acts offered as signs to wonder.
We will witness to the transformation of armories into
Eden,
the planting of vines and fig trees at military bases as a
concrete sign of hope.
All members of these bases are invited to put down their
weapons and pick up spades and help join us in
planting these signs of stable peaceful fertile future . . .
what the Gospel of Matthew calls the kingdom of
heaven, of Luke calls the kingdom, that Paul calls the
new creation, that John calls life everlasting or the
New Jerusalem.
These actions are not simply inspired by some timeless
ideal or the simple invitation of abstract ethic, for in
Jesus, God's dream for creation has become our wak-
ing reality.

These cries are being answered,
And creation's groans for us to witness what has broken
into history.
His is a name so safe in the mouth of the preacher promising fire and insurance of the afterlife and threatening
hell;
yet dangerous,
so dangerous when embodied by people who know what
time it is and through this Messiah who rejects the
sword,
the transformation of all things has rushed into this
moment,
into this moment,
into *this* moment.

The time has come, and now the world is not just possible—it's here in our midst waiting for us to simply
repent,
to change,
to step into *metanoia* and to live into it.

It's a reality lying in dynamic dormancy in the earth,
just below the insanity of our current way of life.
It's an invitation,
an invitation to a party where those who come are the
    right ones to welcome this new world by the way we
    joyfully live our lives,
live this grace,
live this gift.

This is the dream that became the lived reality of the
    early church and the prophetic communities through-
    out history, and of the Historic Peace Churches.

Jesus, we pray that you plough our weapons back to the
    earth so that we might walk in, and depend on, your
    Resurrection power.
This is an open invitation to which we long to say . . .
    "Yes."

Our danger that Isaiah's call to turn swords into plow-
    shares gets turned into timeless truths and ideals, and
    then we don't hear the Gospel invitation to pull
    down heaven, right now, "on earth"! Jesus in Mark
    1:15 says, "The time has come." We need to ask our-
    selves, "What time?" The time to go to heaven? That's
    not the Jewish hope. The Hebraic hope of the New
    Testament is that through Jesus, uniquely through
    Jesus like none other, heaven is crashing oppression's
    party. So we must go through a shift in our under-
    standing when we hear Jesus say, the time has come,
    and it is the time of which the prophets spoke. "God's
    dream for creation," as Desmond Tutu puts it—I love
    Desmond Tutu—God's dream for creation has broken
    into reality and is close. It is at hand, as Jesus says.
    Not out of reach, it's right here if we grasp it. If we
    would just live into it, if we would find our identity
    in Christ, we could have imaginations that could see
    everything come under the nonviolent lordship of
    Jesus.

That is our invitation.

Chapter 5

THE ELEPHANT AND THE RHINOCEROS

Jo Vallentine

WHAT I AM ABOUT TO DISCUSS is with some advice from the Medical Association for the Prevention of War, one of our great allies in Australia doing wonderful work on getting rid of nuclear weapons. I want you now to think about a big room that we're in, but an elephant is in it, and the elephant is climate change. Now, we want to address that elephant in the room, climate change, which is really been talked about a lot more, but it seems to have slipped a little bit lower on the World Council of Churches agenda. As well as an elephant in the room, there is also a rhinoceros—two big things to deal with—and the rhinoceros represents the nuclear industry with all of its ghastly nuclear weapons.

So, either climate change, the elephant, or all of the nuclear industry with all of its nuclear weapons, the rhinoceros, has the capacity to change things beyond recognition on our planet. I've worked on the nuclear industry for thirty years; for it is part of my life's work to shut down that industry. Now we're going to focus on the elephant, but I want you to remember in the back of your mind there is also a rhinoceros.

What has our group been doing as we've been preparing all this year to become the vine and fig tree planters, as Jarrod referred to them in the beautiful invitation in the previous chapter? We want to connect the global issue of climate change with militarism. Not too many people have done this, although we have started to find them as we've been talking about it. We find there is a group in Sweden and Norway who have been doing something similar, planting life giving plants instead of focusing on the negatives of militarism.

We have a big question for the groups that are or will be working on climate change, and I hope that all people will send their spiritual energies and their very, very deep prayers to them. Those groups so far have not mentioned militarism. They have mentioned everything else you can think of on the face of the planet that is contributing to global warming, but not militarism. It's an enormous gap in their deliberations. Even if the military don't fire a weapon, they are contributing *hugely* to global warming already with their preparations for war, and with the theft of the millions and *trillions* of dollars that go into preparations for war, whether weapons are used or not. The amount of money that is spent on the military is disgusting.

That's just money though. What all of that money does is to embed energy into the weapons they make, the tanks they make, and the delivery platforms they make. All are embedded energy that has produced carbon emissions. It's all going into the atmosphere already even if they don't fire a shot, and unfortunately many shots are being fired. Here is a huge contribution to global warming that nobody is really talking about!

We know there is a huge contribution to climate change from militarism. However, we want to get beyond thinking about the military only as being negative. What we will need in the coming years is cooperation like the world has never seen before. We're going to have nations in the Pacific disappearing because they live so close to the ocean with rising sea levels caused by global warming. Nations are disappearing. Vanuatu is already preparing for massive evacuation. They can't come to Australia—or they might because we've had a change of government. Vanuatu has asked the New Zealand and the Australian governments, "Could you help us begin to talk about what we might do when our island disappears? It's not safe for us to live here any more." The New Zealand government said, "Let's talk about it," but the Australian government said, "Go away." Dreadful! Since Australia has changed governments, we can do what is right.

So what would we like to invite military forces around the global to do? A military force is in nearly every country. Lots of money is being wasted now on military weapons systems. We'd like to invite them to lay down their weapons. Cut out the killing. A negotiated peace settlement follows after every war, so why don't we do just that straight away. Cut out all of the killing in between. Who really wants to kill other human beings? Most people in the armed forces don't actually want to do that. When they do peacebuilding work and disaster relief, they feel so empowered because they're doing something useful for the community.

Indeed, they're very good at that. I really like it when the Australian defense forces go to help in the wake of the tsunami for example, or to help in a situation where there's been some other kind of disaster. They're good at doing that work, and in the future that work is what we are going to need very much. We're will need their expertise. They are good at transport and engineering. They have great medical teams, many resources, and infrastructure like we wouldn't dream about.

Our churches are always struggling to meet the poor and to deal with poverty issues. We could have huge resources available if we could invite the military to be transformed. However, they can't do that on their own. They are subject to their political masters. So actually it's up to us to invite our political masters to let this transformation happen. As environmental refugees start flocking to our shores, let us see the security of the world not in terms of keeping people out but rather in terms of working together as a global community. That's what we must do. That's what I believe we are called to do; that is part of our Christian witness.

The transformation is possible if we make this invitation to bring out the good in the defense forces and really create our defense forces to be forces for the defense of the Earth. That is our invitation, but it will have to come through all of you, your governments, your churches.

CHURCH OF THE BRETHREN MEMBER FROM INDIA

Jo, my question is: Should we support our Indian government's decision to develop nuclear power for energy, or not? Is that a good decision or not?

JO VALLENTINE

The argument for developing nuclear power for energy is very much the same for India and China as well: a booming economy, desperate for energy. We in Australia have a government of change, but even the new government is in favor of Australian uranium being sent to India, a country that is not a signatory to the nonproliferation treaty. So those of us in the peace movement oppose that totally.

China is a signatory, but we still oppose it. This is the nuclear industry's last gasp to try and present itself as credible in any way, shape, or form.

Anyone who is pro-nuclear will have an argument with me. I am not in favor of nuclear power being an answer in any way for the energy requirements of emerging nations, fast-growing nations, or as a solution, even a part-solution, to global warming. It is very slow, extremely dangerous, and extraordinarily expensive, while other renewable energy sources are not being investigated and promoted.

There are two main reasons to my objection to nuclear energy. One is the proliferation of nuclear weapons, and I am afraid of nuclear weapons. We worry about India and Pakistan quite a lot because of their propensity to test their nuclear weapons. The other reason which is absolutely global is that there is no answer as to what to do with the nuclear waste. No answer. No country has that sorted out. The United States has tried very hard with the Yucca Mountain. No deal. No country in the world has found a way to store radioactive waste safely. So we are leaving already a terrible legacy to future generations. For me, that is a great regret. The future generations are already stuck with our folly. I call it a twentieth-century failure. It's an industry that can't clean up its own garbage. It has no place in the twenty-first century.

MENNONITE FROM INDONESIA

I am from Indonesian and my question is addressed to Jo. Right now in Indonesia there is a big issue about nuclear energy and the government's plan to build a nuclear power plant. It's close to our area. We as Christians know the results of nuclear power, but we cannot do anything. Is there something I can do in our area right now as a Christian leader? We are mobilizing people to have a kind of dialogue with the government and also to discuss the positive and negative impact of the nuclear energy. However, until now we have not found the way to do that. There's another group ready to resist the nuclear power plant that the government will build in our area.

My question to you: Do you have any suggestions for me? Is there something we can do in practical way? It is really dangerous now. When I was in Germany, I discussed nuclear power with many people. They said, "No, we can not use it for human beings because it is too dangerous." Now we need your suggestions for us because this is our first time to deal with this kind of issue in our country, and specifically in our area, the Muria area.

JO VALLENTINE

For many years there have been plans to build nuclear power stations in Indonesia. Maybe this is the first time it has been in your area. But since I have been involved in the issue, Indonesia has been on the agenda, and we keep talking about earthquakes. It is not clever to build nuclear power stations on the Pacific Ring of Fire, the scene of continuous earthquakes and volcanic eruptions, although it has been done before. The Diablo reactor on the west coast of California is right on a fault line (and since this writing we are aware of the devastating Japanese tsunami effects on the Fukushima plant).

So people do really stupid things, especially when it comes to nuclear issues, because the nuclear lobby internationally is extraordinarily powerful. The global nuclear energy partnership which George Bush had on the agenda is the last gasp of a nuclear industry to legitimize itself. And unfortunately, the Australian outgoing government has signed up for that partnership. It means that they want to try to keep the industry going, and they want to build more reactors all over the world.

We must resist that effort. For you locally, I would suggest that you find nongovernmental organizations that are already working on this question, such as Friends of the Earth here in Indonesia. If you know which company is going to build the atomic reactor, then we can look at doing an economic campaign internationally about the particular company. Only a few companies are promoting the technology that is now not popular at all in the West, and it is unmercifully being promoted here.

The only thing that I can suggest is mobilization of people power. Getting masses of people to write letters to the government saying you don't want power to come from a nuclear source because it is inherently dangerous. The big issue to deal with is the danger of nuclear energy. It is about people power. What really counts in all of these arguments that you have with government is people power. Eventually governments must either hear the people or be ousted. They might build a nuclear reactor as the Philippines did during the time of the Marcos government. But it was never switched on because they realized after they built it that it was on an earthquake fault. Millions and millions of dollars wasted, but it has never been switched on. There is an example of failure. I can give you lots of examples of failure to help with the argument.

MENNONITE FROM INDONESIA

I am interested in education and your response about engaging the military. So far as I'm aware, military education itself promotes violence. What are your suggesting? Do you have any programs that actually try to engage military educators about how to teach nonviolence in the military?

JO VALLENTINE

We know from conversations with the military in our own country that they are not unreasonable people. I was actually on a defense subcommittee when I was in the Parliament. It was a privilege for me to go to many military bases, to talk with people in the military, and to give presentations at the military academy. I learned that there are many good people in the military, which was important for me to learn. There are many bright people, and there are many good people. You never want to throw the baby out with the bath water. From my perspective as a Quaker, I never give up on anybody. There is always some goodness that you can find in everybody. We have to admit that in some people it is more hidden than in others, but you can find it.

I think that when you can engage with the military person-to-person, you can find that there are good people. As Sieneke Martin said, they love doing this other work that is not about killing. I know they have a culture that they have to maintain. They have to pump people up to get them to go and do the killing. That is true even if it is from an aircraft, where their target is way below, and they do not actually have the face-to-face experience of the destruction. But I do believe that we can engage with them on a person-to-person level.

We can also talk to ex-military people. Ex-military people, particularly generals, are wonderful. Generals for peace are all over the place. They make very good sense when they leave the military. They realize it's a terrible, terrible game they are playing with people's lives and with the world itself. Some very, very good ex-military people who are great thinkers still have influence with their colleagues back in the military.

We don't have a program all worked out yet. We are at the beginning, like the seed, literally. We are planting a seed with this idea of the vine and fig tree planters. We know that there are other people doing good research who can begin to develop plans, educators who can begin to work out particular programs. I believe that we will find very fertile ground for the seeds to fall upon.

Already in our recent election in Australia we had an ex-military man from the Special Air Services (SAS). The SAS are like a special terrorist training group. They have trained the Philippines' military to put down their own people. I had quite a conversion this man about our ideas and he said, "Yes, yes, yes," to every point. He really liked our ideas of a defense force for the earth, but he hadn't thought of the ideas about the carbon emissions that the military is already producing and pumping into the atmosphere. I know there is fertile ground in the military, and I have great hope that we can find support from many of them.

I think that our bigger argument, much bigger argument, will be with our political masters. Quite frankly, they are not as clever as the people in the military, for they are always thinking short term. Military people are starting to realize that the security issues accompanying global warming are going to mean a lot of hard work for them. They are thinking farther ahead about this issue than the politicians are thinking at the moment.

ANOTHER QUESTION

My question may sound obvious to us as peace churches: However, before we can ask anything of the military, are we discipling each other in the way of Jesus? Do our communities speak of nonviolence? Ron Sider talks about how we sometimes end up asking government to do what we can't do in our congregations yet.

JO VALLENTINE

We need to start with ourselves. As Gandhi says, we must be the change we want to see in the world. But as people, our story must be the combination which is in Jesus. We must be in the world what God longs for the world to be. Or we must be in the world what the world will be, and that was started in Jesus. This is our very practical basis before we engage anyone.

One of the things we can do is practice hospitality. In our town we have American sailors coming, so sometimes we have American sailors around for dinner. We do that because we know where we stand on these issues. It's important that we not be naive when we're dealing with principalities and powers. The early Christians didn't live in Barney's World. It wasn't "I love you, you love me." They knew that I love you, and I get crucified. We need to be serious that we are following Jesus who says, "Pick up your cross and follow me."

That is what we should expect. But we do it in joyful participation, not as heroic individuals, but as recovering sinners in communities with one another. That is what church must be.

I find it really interesting to consider the witness of those early Christians who we know were in the military, because the records we have indicate that they were all killed. We know from these records that they refused to wear the amulet, which was a sign of worship to Caesar, and they also refused to carry the sword. That's what our invitation should be. Maybe shockingly to some of us, they stayed in these places, still believing that these places too would come under the nonviolent lordship of Messiah Jesus.

We must encourage our people to that kind of fearless engagement. Then we will not run into the trouble that we sometimes run into as peace churches, when we forget our particular prophetic identity, and end up in an evangelical malaise that plays chaplain to the fallen systems of our world.

On the other hand, we sometimes hide out away from everything where we become holy huddles and aren't ever actually facing the roughness of being blessed for being persecuted. We must remember, as Walter Wink has summed up beautifully what John Howard Yoder said decades before, that the powers are created good, but they have fallen. That is what we would like to emphasize.

Our challenge is that powers will be redeemed. Therefore we must enter more deeply into our narrative and make sure we are schooling our people, particularly our young people, in the narrative of Scripture as understood by the early Christians and the peace church tradition. Most of their spiritual formation is actually happening when they go home from church and turn on the TV. We need to be awake to the fact that most of our spiritual formation doesn't happen on Sunday morning when we gather for meeting or Wednesday night at Bible study. Rather, it happens as we engage in the world and forget what time it is.

QUAKER FROM ENGLAND

Let me add something to that. Though we actually don't talk about it, in Britain we certainly know from the budget that our Quaker peace and social witness committee is involved in running military training courses in nonviolence, often for officers. It is possible to do that sort of thing?

JO VALLENTINE

I would also want to draw your attention to the great resource which the churches have in their women. The resource that women have, and particularly older women, is being physically weak and powerless. Women have to learn how to make their way in the world without being a threat to anyone. Men would do well to learn that from women. One of the things discovered by Quaker relief teams in Sri Lanka was that when the lorries with relief supplies were driven by older, gray-haired women, they got through safely because the women were no threat.

PART III

RELIGIOUS PLURALISM

Chapter 6

PEACE AND RELIGIOUS PLURALISM AS A WORLDVIEW

Aristarchus Sukarto

I WOULD LIKE TO INTRODUCE MYSELF. I am the moderator of a synod of Mennonite churches in Indonesia. I was appointed chair of the synod from 2004 until 2009. But I'm also the former president of the Christian University of Jakarta, which is owned by twelve churches including Mennonites. Now I am the president of the Jakarta Christian University owned by the Presbyterian church. I am also a pastor of the Mennonite church. I no longer pastor a particular congregation, but my congregations are spread all over Indonesia.

I graduated from the law faculty, and then I took my theological course under the Reformed churches, taking Old Testament studies under the Anglican and Presbyterians in Indonesia. Next I took my Ph.D. at the Lutheran Theological Seminary in Chicago and Catholic Theological Union. So I have many traditions within myself. I am Javanese by birth because my parents were Javanese, although they have already passed away. My wife is Chinese by birth, so there is also a mixture of cultures within my family. I was Muslim until I was twenty-one years old, when I converted to be Christian. I have a Muslim background and my father and my grandfather wanted me to study in Egypt, but then something went wrong. I did not go to Egypt, but I took a theological course in Indonesia instead.

I would like to talk about peace and pluralism as a worldview. My views are based on my Indonesian experience, of course, but also on all that I have learned. My academic field is theology and culture. The well-known Catholic professor and author Robert Schreiter was my supervisor. I also studied with James Scherer, the Lutheran missiologist, and Wilbert Chang from the Mennonite church. Even though I took my course from a Lutheran school of theology, my supervisor came from a different background. This probably influenced some of the thoughts that I would like to share with you.

IS THERE ANY POSSIBILITY OF HAVING PEACE IN A RELIGIOUSLY PLURALISTIC COMMUNITY?

My first question is whether there is any possibility of having peace in a religiously pluralistic community. Indonesia is known as a country that is very hospitable to many kinds of people. However, viewed from inside the country, peace is not an actual reality, a real peace, but rather a surface appearance. Sometimes we grumble about the treatment that we get from others, but actually we treat them the same way. I believe if we Christians were the majority, the pattern would be the same. We should not blame Muslim majority for being hostile or harmful, because our pattern of thought is still the same. If we were the majority we would do the same thing. Our Christian brothers and sisters in an area that is almost 100 percent Christian are refusing to allow the building of a mosque. It is the same pattern, the same way of thinking.

That's why I question whether there's any possibility of peace in this religious, pluralistic country. Indonesia claims to be a pluralistic community with at least five religions, not to mention local religions. The official religions are Catholic, Protestant, Buddhist, Hindu, and Muslim. They are the five officially recognized religions, but there are also some other religions. Indonesia has shown the world community that it is tolerant country, that it is very hospitable, and that religious communities are living together harmoniously. We are not like the Balkan area, nor are we are like the Middle East. We are a happy country with compassion for all peoples in Indonesia.

So why do I say that the reality is far different from what has just been described? The tension between one religious group and another happens frequently, especially between Muslims and Christians. The persecution of the Ahmadiyah people by other Muslims because of different opinions and different doctrine is an example. Such differences have happened frequently not only among Muslims, but also among Christians throughout the history of Christianity. The restricted building permits given to the Christian community are another example of how the apparently harmonious life in Indonesia can be regarded as a pseudo-peaceful community. The seemingly peaceful community occurs because the minority group do not want, or do not dare, to challenge the majority.

So we are living in an enclosed hut, not an open assembly, because Christians are not a majority, not a large proportion of the people, and not able to speak. We are shouting within our own walls. Many Christian intellectuals are saying privately what I have said, but they are not willing or not able to say it publicly. They are saying this within the church, within their conferences, but they are not saying it openly.

We are a diverse country with so many ethnic groups, socioeconomic groups, and religious groups. In expecting to have a peaceful Indonesian country, our forefathers have formulated our nation's vision as diversity in unity within our Pancasila ideology. Yet today, this vision is being challenged and questioned. Some groups are suffering because the idea of unity is not that clear. Unity is seen as uniformity according to majority. Ideologically, politically, or economically, unity is conformity for the sake of the majority or for the sake of those who are holding power. It is not seen as unity with freedom and a happy atmosphere to be united. It is not a real unity with freedom—but unity by force. In the old days the force was by the president, and now all must obey the majority opinion, but it is still the old pattern.

Indonesian religious life is more complicated. Every religious group claims that they are the only ones holding the truth. So we Christians are also doing the same. Muslim friends declare, "We are the right religion"; Christians also say, "We are the only ones who know about selflessness"; and Buddhists say, "We are the only people who have a peaceful community." So everyone claims to belong to the only true religion.

How can these absolute religions live within religious plurality? If we are claiming that we are the only true religion, and they are claiming that they are the only true religion, how can we live together in peace? We may not be in open conflict if we have no power, but if we do have power, we will be fighting because of underlying conflicts. Can we live together integrally, peacefully, with respect for one other, without compromising our own faith and convictions within a particular community or country? If we have these feelings, these underlying conflicts, then our peace is only on the surface, and we do not live in a genuinely peaceful reality.

RELIGIOUS RELATIVISM MAY
CREATE A PSEUDO-COMMUNITY

Religious relativism may create a pseudo-peace community. To achieve peace in our life of religious diversity, we may adopt religious relativism. According to the notion of religious relativism, every religion is just the same. My community may say that religion is just like clothing. Everyone has different clothing; but as human beings, they are the same. Religion is seen as a way, not a purpose of life, but one way among others. It is a wagon, a vehicle. We may get to Solo city by using one or another vehicle. Each religion is seen as a different way leading to the same end, which is God. That is relativism.

Religious relativism does not solve any existing problem. It just covers a bit but doesn't solve the problem. It doesn't give genuine peace in a pluralistic religious community because it does not pay attention to revelation and the nature of religion. Relativism is the notion that you are there, but that's you; and it has nothing to do with me. I walk in my way and you walk in yours, but we have nothing to do with each other. But these religions maintain that they are the truth given by God for all human beings. As the given truth, they see themselves as absolute reality. For Christians Jesus is the Word of God, not simply one of the spiritual leaders. For Muslims the Koran is not one of the holy Scriptures but the only complete revelation given by God. Again, religious relativism does not deal with these absolute claims. In the relativist view, you may go with your own conviction and your own claim, as long as you're not disturbing me and I'm not disturbing you. But this is not real peace because when anything happens, it is very easy to get friction.

We may not suppose that we are able to solve religious conflicts caused by these absolute claims by saying that religion is concerned only about the eternal world, worship, and acts of charity, while all other worldly matters are the state's business. If relativism is being refused, then we use John Locke's view that religion deals with eternal life and heavenly things while other things should be handled by the state. That view has influenced the American conviction that religion has nothing to do with government. I believe that Indonesia also would like to move toward that view.

Whenever I consider the declining influence of religion, I too am attracted to that view. Why do we have to give religious education in the public school? It is of no use because almost all of the intellectual disciplines are corrupt. Religious education as a support for Indonesian morality is declining according to Muslim teachers (Ulama) and Christian pastors. So religious education in the schools is of no use.

Why not agree to say that religion is the business of the church or the mosque, not of the state-operated school? Some intellectuals in Indonesia have accepted this view.

There are many different understandings of the role of religion within life of the society, but almost every religion agrees that its religious life is not limited to its place of worship or day of worship only. They agree that their task is to embrace or enfold every aspect of human life, including what we eat, how we do business, and whatever.

But all religious life would like to split off from everyday life, and the church itself is also spreading this split. The intellectuals are not alone in proposing this split between the religious and the secular. The church teaches that it is a good thing to be a pastor in the church, but it is not as good to be a doctor with a Christian heart. This understanding of one's calling is Lockian. The best thing is to be a pastor, a deacon at church, or some other church official—but to be a trader, a doctor, or something other than a church official is not as good. I guarantee that more than eighty percent of the churches in Indonesia think of things in this way.

That's why being a politician is prohibited. Yet the politicians are the people controlling public policy, including policies about nuclear power. The churches say that is not their business but the world's business. Such splitting is Lockian, for it follows John Locke's teaching about religions. We are not able to create a peaceful community in that way. So every religion deals with both heavenly and worldly reality, both the spiritual and the material aspects of human life.

In 1983 I introduced a pension benefit for pastors in the Mennonite area. At that time I had an accident on the way to a meeting to discuss this program. Some members of the church visited me in the hospital and prayed, "Praise God, forgive this man," because I was thinking about money. Even though the money was for pastors, still it was considered to be sinful. This is still how we look at money. For me, money still has two faces. You can use money as a spiritual teacher if you have money and you would like to organize for the welfare of the community. That's a spiritual journey, and you are not being corrupt because of money. That is power, but you don't want to use that power because you want to serve, and that's good.

However, Luke 16:8 says that "the children of this age are more shrewd in dealing with their own generation than are the children of light," for the children of this age are willing to share, whereas the children of light would like to collect all the time. I would like to say that we are trying to separate reality into the heavenly and the worldly. The world is getting worse and worse because all of us would rather have our own inner peace by ourselves, and we are not willing actively to work at the peace of the community through sharing material things.

When I was studying at the United States in 1988 to 1993, many friends from United Church of Christ and Baptist were discussing the sharing of wealth. They were blaming my president and saying how corrupt he was. Then I said, "You are also bad. Why? Because in my present position I am being paid only two hundred dollars a month and you are receiving four thousand dollars. Are you ready to share with me? If you re not ready to share, then I don't want to hear your criticism of my president."

That was just what I felt. Sharing peace is not just sharing an idea or sharing a spiritual experience. It is also sharing wealth at the same time. If you are not doing these things, then there is no peace. The poor people live or die, and it doesn't matter because there is nothing to lose. Rich people are afraid of dying because of what they possess. That's why radicals say, "No problem. We are willing to die. No problem. We don't have anything to be afraid of."

PLURALISM AS A WORLDVIEW

I would like to introduce the idea of Christian pluralism as worldview. If we want to have a peace, genuine peace, within the religious community, then we should consider pluralism as a worldview. I would like to introduce pluralism as worldview, as a Christian worldview, and this will require a discussion of Christology. First I want to distinguish between pluralism and plurality. You are American; I am Indonesian. You are Indian; I am Korean. That's plurality, not pluralism. The fact that we are different is plurality. Indonesia is very plural, and we have a very plural reality. But not every Indonesian has plurality as a worldview or a way to see things. We can see the differences, the many realities, but if we are not seeing these differences from pluralism as a worldview, then nothing will happen.

We in Indonesia are facing a global culture. We are accepting bad things like consumerism, capitalism, social violence, and materialism as a part of global culture. Why would so many Indonesian pastors like to be a pastor in the United States? The old missionaries moved from their palaces in New York to Papua, New Guinea. But the modern missionaries are moving from Papua to New York. Of course, in New York are some people don't believe in Christ, but what are these modern missionaries looking for? I also studied in the U.S. I lived in

Indonesia from 1972 up to 1980, and then I was a pastor. In 1980 I became a lecturer at the Evangelical Reformed Theological Seminary in the U.S., and in my surroundings were missionaries studying in the United States.

What I want to say is that we are facing a global culture with negative aspects as well as positive aspects. Global culture brings worldwide human community and equality, even though there are negative aspects like consumerism, materialism, social violence.

Nevertheless we have to understand our culture here in Indonesia. Part of my culture is Javanese, one-hundred percent Javanese. I don't want to say that because I was outside Indonesia for brief periods, I know world culture. I was in India for one month, in Japan for a week, and in Egypt for three months, but that doesn't help me really understand the world community. That's why I would like to say that I am only Indonesian. According to the old tradition, the old realities, we do things in our relationships with others, and what we do also influences our religious life. One group is an in-group and the other is an out-group. We are Christians; you are not Christians. We are Javanese; you are not Javanese. So this attitude, this social category of being in or out, is very strong in our lives, even in the life of the church in Indonesia. It creates tension. Indonesian traditional culture is actually compelling the out-group to submit to our in-group. This is a war, even though we do not realize it.

The new global cultural reality should be that we are all human beings. We are all the same. If you pinch me, I am hurt; and if I pinch you, you are hurt also. We are human beings. This is the new global culture. But at the same time we are also creating very strong feelings of inside and outside groups.

The problem is also that nearly no religion in Indonesia is aware of this. We as Christians are universal. We are all brothers and sisters. But when we see Muslims, we ask, "Are you my brothers and sisters?" and the answer is, "No." I can say to you as an Indian, American, Canadian, or Filipino, "You are my brother sand sisters" because you are Christians. But when my Christian friends see Iraqi people or Palestinians in Gaza as refugees, my friends say, "They are Muslim. No, I don't want to accept them because they are not Christians." In fact some are Christians, different from us of course, but they are Christians. This feeling is very strong. Religious people do not follow their own doctrines of behavior. They are following a different interpretation. If you see people of other beliefs, you have to convert them.

What does this mean? What are the consequences of this view? An Indonesian with a small salary would like to become a Christian and work in a multinational company because many multinational companies are saying, "Are you Muslim or Christian? If Christian, we will hire you. If Muslim, you are out." If I'm a Christian and go to the government for work, they say, "Oh, you are Christian. You should be Muslim." These practices are not good, but they are reality. So each religion's primary teaching is this: Do not change this insider and outsider group feeling between religions. The religions maintain this social attitude. However, this doctrine of separation is not the teaching of the Bible, for it does not create a peaceful life. As long as churches, or religions, or religious life continue this kind of understanding, they are not going to create peace.

This new situation is not ideology against ideology. We are not talking about capitalism against communism anymore. We are not talking about religion against capitalism or religion against communism anymore. Today we are talking about other religions as though they were ideology. When American friends were visiting us in Jakarta, one of them told me, "You are lucky you are Christians. Many Indonesians are complaining because it is very difficult to get a visa, especially if you have a very thick beard, which is regarded as a mark of the Middle East." This is not ideology versus ideology but religion being used against other religions. It may be political, but it is reality. What I want to suggest is, as has just been stated, that peace can not be achieved through a notion of religious relativism, a notion of not distinguishing between religions, but dealing only with the reality of life and death. We have to find a new way of thinking to solve these problems.

Many theologians and social scientists today propose the idea of having pluralism as a worldview. Pluralism as a worldview is more than the view that one's own religion is not the exclusive source of truth, thus recognizing that some level of truth and value exist in at least some other religions. I am not simply saying that you are Muslim, you are Buddhist; and each of you has your own identity. To say that you have some truth in your religion and I have some truth in mine is not pluralism. It is not a loosely defined term concerning peaceful correlation between different religions, or religious tolerance as a condition of harmonious coexistence between adherences of different religions. It is not just an attitude of tolerance. It is not just peaceful relations. Religious pluralism is the worldview that all views of reality are diverse and each has its own unique identity, and yet they are related in a dynamic way so as to create a new energetic force renewing self and the whole of reality. Pluralism enables me to see the uniqueness of the worldviews of others but also the uniqueness of my own worldview. These two uniquenesses playing together create a new understanding of God.

Consider how Jacob came to understand God better. Did Jacob go to the temple and pray, "Oh God, you are the only one and my own source of life!"? No! Did Jacob go to a church or temple and declare, "Ah, this is the grace of God!" and, "Now I recognize how big, how powerful God is." No! When Jacob build a temple at Bethel, he was still a man who loved cheating. How could he know God better after seeing Esau, who is regarded by most Christians as a sinner because he was part of a people who were turned away by God? But Jacob was able to see God better, which occurred through the uniqueness of Esau, even though the two were of different convictions. Jacob's encounter with Esau enlightened Jacob to know his God better, and that is pluralism (Gen. 32-33).

How we can understand our religious uniqueness so as to develop our beliefs in a powerful and dynamic way? Pluralism is the energetic engagement with diversity. It is not tolerance, but an active seeking of understanding across grand differences. It is an encounter of commitments without monopolizing and without throwing away our own identity. So a pluralistic worldview influences my understanding of what mission is.

Tolerance is a passive way of dealing with diversity. It may offer a harmonious situation but without any drive to create a dynamic peaceful reality. Becoming tolerant does not mean that someone understands diversity, is able to respect diversity, or may be able to create something new out of diversity. For me tolerance is passive, but pluralism is an energetic engagement with diversity. Tolerance knows that we are different but moves away from our diversity. Within pluralism you have something to say to me and I have something to say to you. Pluralism does not say, "Your reality is not the same as my reality and you must conform to my reality."

In 1983 I was doing evangelism in a Javanese village. One of the village people was a Muslim who prayed in a Muslim way. He paid honor to all in his daily prayer like the Javanese do according to the Koran. His prayer was that he would be a chief of the village. But when he failed to get what he prayed for, he converted to become a Christian and prayed in the name of Christ. For what was he now praying? He continued to pray to be a chief of the village. Is that conversion? Is it not just changing clothes? It is the same tolerance with diversity. He will see my faith, my belief, my Christian value. I will speak about this value and he probably will hear and change to create a new idea, not necessarily to be like me but to be himself in a particular way. Such tolerance is passive way of dealing with diversity. It may give a pseudo-harmonious condition but without any drive to create a dynamic peaceful reality. Becoming tolerant does not mean someone understands and is able to respect diversity or make something out of diversity. Peace is not a static condition or reality. Peace is always developing dynamically, as are human beings and culture. So religious pluralism, as understood above, may help to bring peace in a dynamic sense.

ACHIEVING A PLURALISTIC WORLDVIEW

1. Overcoming an absolute claim of the truth

How can we achieve this kind of worldview? How can we see diversity within our own uniqueness but also be able to create a dynamic way forward? First, I would like to say that we have to overcome our claim to the absolute truth of our own view. Essentially religion always has divine and human elements. God reveals himself or his will, and human beings make a response by faith. The revelation of God is the absolute element of religion, while human faith is not. Human faith in it's various forms—worship, prayer, and teaching—reflects the divine revelation, but the revelation is limited within the human cognition and culture. Since faith expression is culturally bound, it is not absolute.

Suppose I carefully read to you aloud from the Bible, say the Gospel according to Luke. After I have finished reading and you have heard the witness from those who knew Christ, I look to you and ask, "This is the gospel, isn't it?" In fact it is the gospel within Luke's culture, isn't it? That's why Luke's theology is different from Matthew's theology, which is different from Paul's theology. The accounts are conformed to the writer's culture. The revelation is absolute. However, our confession, including the apostolic confession and doctrine, comes to us in a cultural form. The cultural form can and does change from age to age, but the revelation is still absolute.

I prefer to read the authors who say that the Bible is a carrier of revelation. The languages and translations are constantly changing, but the revelation is absolute and unchanging. The early revelation is absolute, but the language of Paul to explain that revelation is not. So worship, teaching, and interpretation reflect a continual development, for they are limited within human cognition and culture. To put it another way, the faith expression is culturally bound and thus is not absolute. Our witness is culturally bound, so that I can catch and touch the absolute only through my eyeglasses, my own perspective. I can receive the witness of an American friend or an Indonesian friend about how the cross of Christ Jesus is experienced within his life. But I cannot accept his expression as final because I have different culture. The message, the revelation of how Christ Jesus suffered, was crucified, and offers forgiveness to human beings, I can understand, I can feel, I can acknowledge, I can accept, and I can put into my life.

I read the Bible before I became a Christian because my uncle was an assistant pastor of the Javanese church. He gave me the Bible and I read every sentence, but I didn't comprehend. I became a Christian because someone expressed to me how he as a city person was willing to go to the village to share Christ's love. I asked him, "Why do you do this?" I wanted to study law to get rich. Life as a lawyer is very easy, with no harm and much money. My dream was to be rich, powerful, and honored by those around me. My ego was so large that I wanted only to pay attention to myself. Then my life changed. I was a follower of the Javanese meditation. At that time I was taught how to heal people and how to understand people hundred kilometers from my presence. By mediation I could see my father's bed, observe what he was doing. Then I thought, "Why are you doing that?"

Suddenly everything changed. I was changed by a witness, not by a set of convictions, but by how this man expressed his faith as he witnessed to others. That's why I say that the expression is culturally bound but the content, the revelation, is absolute. You can see through your eyeglasses your vantage point. For this reason no religion should claim to be the only religion having the only truth. Every religion is a culturally bound faith expression of God's revelation. Lutherans, Mennonites, Presbyterians: all are culturally bound. We aren't able to claim that we are the only ones to know the truth. We accept God's revelation and would like to witness how this revelation affects our life and may affect others.

2. Be humble and throw away triumphalist faith

"Our God is more powerful than your God!" was the claim of ancient Israel. But the Palestinians defeated the Israelites, according to 1 Samuel 4. In this culturally bound religious life, the triumphalist worldview tends to be universal. The worldview of religious pluralism is not natural to anyone. Humanly speaking, none of us are able to see the identities of other to be as good as our own. Therefore the religious journey of people, as described in the Bible, has always been filled with an attitude of triumphalism. The defeat and exile of Israel led to a crisis of identity. The reformation brought about by Jesus is a reformation of self-identity. The great commandment is to love God with one's whole heart and to love one's neighbor as oneself.

After recognizing that all religious experience is culturally bound, the next step toward a stance of religious pluralism is to be humble. Religious people who believe in the Majesty of God should be people who know their own limitations. They are people who do not feel right in claiming God's righteousness. They are people who do not see themselves as better than others, and they do not see the religious claims of others as inferior to their own. They hand over such evaluations into the hand of the Lord. Being humble about their own religious claims, they are able to move toward a worldview of religious pluralism.

3. Sharing love is the meaning of religious mission

Every religion has a mission mandate to its adherents. This religious mission is commonly understood as overcoming others, or making others willing to be members of their religious group. People tend to love themselves by admiring their own strength, and they prefer to see others as subordinate. Religious pluralism as a worldview sees others within their own identity, and sees others as partners in obedience. In Christianity the religious mission is to bring people to recognize and to accept God as their God and thereby to recognize God's love and forgiveness and their love and forgiveness. Sharing love is the meaning of religious mission. That is my understanding of mission. If we understand the meaning of religious pluralism as a worldview, then we can see that it helps us to know the meaning of our missionary call.

When Jonah was asked to go to Nineveh, he refused. Jonah didn't want to go because he remembered that his ancestors were treated so badly by Assyrian people. I can understand this feeling. Because the Dutch treated my forefathers so badly, why I should love them? When the Dutch were living here, Javanese missionaries found it very difficult to accept them as brothers within Christ. Jonah's refusal is a common human experience. However, God teaches that love is different. God teaches us how to love people, how to share our value of love.

4. The eucharistic meal as a multidimensional dymbol

We experience love as a eucharistic meal, as a multidimensional symbol. In the Christian tradition the eucharist is the most comprehensive expression of how the divine revelation enter into human experience. The eucharist is very pluralistic. It is based on the Passover celebration. Who comes to the Passover? Everyone! Even foreigners come and share the eucharist. "The baptized only! If you are not baptized, you should not participate!" That is social differentiation. Notice that when we're talking about the eucharist, it is for all, for every sinner, not just for the disciples.

In the early church the eucharist was part of salvation history (1 Cor. 11:23-26; Mark 14:17:25; Matt. 26:20-29; Luke 22:14-23). We see in the early church's practice of eucharist that there were a variety of understandings. The Gospel of John (6:31-58) portrays Jesus as the mediator (bread of heaven) between human beings and God. In the Egyptian eucharistic tradition (The Prayers of Serapion) emphasizes God as the Life-Giver. So the Roman, Egyptian, and Jewish Christians practiced the ceremony, but with different interpretations.

Javanese have what we call Selamatan, the name of a communal feast, adopting all reality: God, human being, and others. In the old days Selamatan was held in the village and everyone—Muslin, Hindus, Javanese, and all others—was invited to the meal. But now at Selamatan people say, "Ah! This is for Muslims, not us." Why so? Who makes the difference? We make the differentiation. So my suggestion is this: Let us adopt a new multidimensional symbol that's able to reflect our pluralistic worldview. If I am to receive the Bible, I must take the pluralistic reality in the Bible. Jesus never refuses others. According to Jesus' teaching, make friends. That seems the only way that Jesus can be known or that God can be accepted. So we human beings take offense and make a wall between ourselves so that we are not able to see the diversity of the world with the eyeglasses of pluralism.

DISCUSSION OF DR. SUKARTO'S PRESENTATION

Member of Evangelical Friends in the Philippines

I have six questions here for our speaker:

1. How can we practice religious pluralism without compromising the absolute claims of Jesus Christ? One example of this is in John 14:6, which says, "I am the way. I am the truth. I am the life. No one comes to the Father except by me." And a second example is in Revelation 1:8, which says, "I am the alpha and the omega, the beginning and the end."

2. What is the difference between religious pluralism and universalism?

3. In what practical ways we can respect and tolerate each other's

beliefs and practices without compromising our major truths based on biblical theology?

4. In religious pluralism, how do you make the gospel of Jesus Christ relevant in the lives of people in general?

5. Could you give clear distinctions between the Christian method and message and that of other religions?

6. Are you saying that we must obtain peace and harmonious living by all means at the expense of our Christian theology?

Aristachus Sukarto

John 14:6 is very unique and always cited to question my thesis about religious pluralism. But I always say to students or to church members that they should please read not just one verse but the whole passage. What does it mean for Jesus to say he is the way, the truth, and the life? What is it to be a follower? Actually the disciples were being asked to follow what Jesus did and what the work of Christ has done. The work of Christ should be expressed, should be understood and followed, in the way of life also. So the text is not just saying that because Jesus did good, we also have to do good.

What does it mean when Jesus says "I am the way the truth and the life?" Jesus means, "Be like my way, like what I am. I am the truth because I am really like this. And I'm doing good because by doing this I give freedom, I give support, and I give spirit to the people."

So I prefer to read the whole passage, and then we can see the actual difficulties. Because we are to love other people like Jesus loves, that's why Jesus is the way. Also I am to suffer for the happiness of others as Jesus did. Jesus said, "I am the way and I am the truth," because he was consistent. What he said, he was always doing. That's who Jesus is. When the whole passage is read, then this message becomes very clear. That's why I ask, How can we practice religious pluralism? I will maintain my uniqueness. But I must also develop my own uniqueness so that day by day I am able to see Christ in an ever clearer and a more perfect way, not just in the way that I have understood him yesterday. Encounters with Muslims and with Buddhists always make me better understand what Christ was doing. Why did God send him? Why and how is he the Word of God? Every encounter makes me enlarge my faith in him.

Universalism is different from pluralism. Universalism is preoccupied with the power of a notion regarded as better than all others. But pluralism says: "I admire your notion. You admire mine." Pluralism does not impose my notion as universal. So that's why my life is a journey. I don't impose the notion, "You have to believe in Christ!"

Rather I affirm, "I believe in Christ. This is my understanding. This is the way I am practicing what I understand." I am not imposing my belief. But nevertheless many of my friends accept my belief.

I was brought up in church with no members. In the place where I lived when I was student, there was no Mennonite church. We gathered together as students, and our gathering kept getting bigger and bigger. When I came to Jogjakarta, there were only a few Mennonites. Now there is a Mennonite church. When I was studying theology, I was twenty-seven and attended a church in which is most members were older than fifty-five. But I was glad because I was like a young Jacob being treated with great hospitality.

However, I didn't impose my beliefs on anyone. I just said that this is my Indonesian Christianity, and my friends accepted it. When I became a pastor, my salary was paid by all my friends. In the United States I had a gathering of 100 friends of mine. Most were American-Indonesian or Indonesian-American. Again, I didn't impose my beliefs. Some were Muslim, some were Roman Catholic, and some of them were of other traditions.

Did I say, "You should be Mennonite"? No, I just said that I am in the Mennonite tradition to understand who Jesus is. I did not say, "Mennonite is better." I have been persecuted. My Mennonite great-grandfather was persecuted. But I understand Christ through the Mennonite tradition, and my friends are welcome to understand.

That's the different between pluralism and universalism for me. Pluralism does not impose our beliefs on other persons but affirms our beliefs in such a way that we can respect and tolerate other beliefs and practices without compromising our own. That's why I try to avoid declaring that my truth is absolute, that I need only to assert it for it to be absolute by definition. My language is part of the truth, not *the* truth. I know Jesus is the truth, the only truth. However my language to bear witness to this is only part of *the* truth because what I can understand is not fully complete. I cannot understand the meaning of the cross fully. We have the eucharist because through the eucharist actually we can absolve this conflict in our reality. That's why baptism is into the suffering and into the gloriousness of Christ, not just one or the other. We have to be immersed, to feel. That's why I can't claim final understanding of the biblical truth.

I try to separate my witness, my language of witnessing, from the real truth. I do not claim that what I am saying is the truth. It is the path of my understanding of the truth. So this way is my understanding of the gospel of Jesus Christ as Christ embodied in us. Your understanding of Christ is how you actually embody the work of Christ, particularly in suffering, crucifixion, and resurrection. Their reality is the gospel. That's why there's forgiveness to this reality. I always ask of my sermons the question of whether in my life I am acting according to my understanding of this reality.

The gospel is that you are saved by this action, not that you are saved by your prayer in the name of this action. This is the gospel, the Christian method of knowing Christ. I know the difference between the Muslim message and the Christian message in seeing Jesus and in my understanding of Jesus' message. But it is not my place to say that they are wrong. That is God's judgment. I don't accept their explanation, but I don't want to judge that they are wrong.

My task is to witness to what I can understand and what I believe, not to judge their understanding. I don't want to judge, but I would like to witness that, according to the book of James, judging is God's business. My task is how to be disciple of Christ and to witness these disciplines to others, not to judge their understanding. Again, Christianology is our faith expression when it becomes fixed and culturally bound. My theology is being revised all the time, never-ending. We have to work all the time if we hold a particular theology. When you are facing reality, you are doing theology. But is there any same reality all the time? So I am not living with a finished theology. Rather, I am being reformed, being enlarged, being widened all the time by living with others.

My understanding of mission is that I am not to overcome others. My experience in many Javanese churches is that they have become so dependent. Why? Because we are destroying their life system. Culture is a system, an economic system, a social system, a life system. When we pull ten people from the village, it changes their culture. Then the system can be broken, often creating an ongoing dependency. The reason many Javanese churches are so dependent upon American or Dutch churches is that the Javanese churches are pulled from their culture without any replacement for the economic, social, and other features of their life system. That's the new mission perspective we should pay attention to, because local culture is not not devilish. It is a system, a life system.

Mennonite from Japan

I'm interested in this kind of religious pluralism. One can consider inclusivism, exclusivism, and pluralism. You said that pluralism is not relativism. Can you explain?

Aristachus Sukarto

Exclusivism is very clear. To say that I am exclusively Javanese means I believe that everything I have is best. Exclusivism gives me the feeling that because I am a Javanese, I am better than people from any other culture or civil way of life. With exclusivism, I don't want to open my gate for anything!

Inclusivism, in my view, means that I would like to include others without in any way enlarging my reality. All are included. I have a table and others are coming, but everything is mine. With inclusive, I am open, but actually it is my table to which everyone comes.

With pluralism, I admire the views of others, and they admire mine. There is a kind of dynamic encounter without changing my uniqueness. I may change my theological formulation, but not my belief in crucifixion and resurrection. This is difficult for people who won't accept the reality of change. But then, I don't accept that their view is the final expression of religion in the world. I believe that we are living beings; we are part of a living reality; we are living human lives. We are moving; we are on a never-ending journey. Almost every day we are reformulating ourselves based on our faith and the Christ events of suffering, crucifixion, and resurrection. So this is what I mean by pluralism: I accept the criticism of others, because it helps me to develop my belief, my theology, my present life.

Mennonite from Japan

For instance, Mahatma Gandhi accepted Jesus Christ, but he was not baptized. He did not become a Christian. Still, as a Hindu, he respected Jesus Christ. How do you understand or explain that?

Aristachus Sukarto

In my understanding Mahatma Gandhi had a pluralistic worldview within his own tradition. If he had converted, then he would have become a Christian. But he was still Hindu and therefore was accepting my worldview. He was not accepting 100 percent of course—only in part, which was suitable within his theological perspective.

Chapter 7

JAVANESE TRADITIONS ABOUT HARMONY

Traditional Sources

KEHIDUPAN MASA KANAK-KANAK
When we are young

**Hidupmu pandai dalam seqala hal, dari ayah dan ibu.
Namur sesungguhnya dari Tuhan YME, untuk itu kita wajib
berbakti.**
(Serat Niti Sunu—Sasono Pustoko, Karaton Surakarta)

Your life is clever is all respects, with some you received from
your father and some from your mother.
However in all truthfulness you received all from God, which
is why we should be devout.
(Serat Niti Sunu; the court's library "Sasono Pustoko").

**Hendaklah bersikap taat terhadap bimbingan ayah dan bunda.
Jangan sampai membuat kesal hati, ingatlah jasa beliau yang
selalu
berkorban bagi putra-putrinya.**
(Serat Niti Sunu—Sasono Pustoko, Karaton Surakarta)

Try to obey the guidance of your father and mother.
Don't make them feel frustrated, and remember their efforts,

124

how they always make sacrifices for their children.
(From: Serat Niti Sunu; the court's library "Sasono Pustoko").

**Kendalikan makan dan tidur, jangan suka foya-foya, lakukanlah
sewajarnya
Kejelekan orang bersuka-ria mengurangi kewaspadaan.**
(Serat Wulang Reh, ISKS Pakoe Boewono IV)

Regulate the time when you eat and sleep, don't be extrava-
gant, act truthfully.
The badness of people who live as they please decreases our
vigilance.
(From: Serat Wulang Reh; by His Highness Pakoe Boewono IV).

**Janganiah keras hati, keras kepala dan tidak melaksanakan per-
intah oran tua.
Orang muda tinggal wajib melaksanakan, tiada diperkenankan
menyimpang dari petunjuk orang tua**
(Wulang Dalem Warna Warni ISKS Pakoe Boewono IX)

Try not to be impatient and angry or stubborn, and don't dis-
obey your parents' advice.
A young person only needs to follow their guidelines, and have
no excuse for deviating from them.
(From: Wulang Dalem Warna Warni; by H.Highness Pakoe Boewono IX).

KEHIDUPAN MASA KEMAJA

When we reach puberty

**Jangan melakukan segala sesuatu secara mendadak.
Pikirkaniah sebelumnya dengan tenang**
(Wulang Dalem Warna Warni ISKS Pakoe Boewono IX)

Don't always do everything suddenly.
Think about it quietly before you act.
(From: Wulang Dalem Warni; by His Highness Pakoe Boewono IX).

**Jika enkau sedang sukar berpikir, diamlah sebentar dan bermo-
honlah
Rahmat Tuhan, maka la akan dating mengajar hai yang baik
kepadamu.**
(Wulang Dalem Warna Warni ISKS Pakoe Boewono IX)

When you have a problem to work out, be quiet for a while
and ask God's mercy,
after which He will come to you and teaches you something
good.
(From: Wulang Dalem Warni; by His Highness Pakoe Boewono IX).

**Kendalikan makan dan tidur, jangan suka foya-foya, lakukanlah
sewajarnya.**
Kejelekan orang bersuka-ria mengurangi kewaspandaan.
(Serat Wulang Reh, ISKS Pakoe Boewono IV)

Regulate the time when you eat and sleep, don't be extrava-
gant, act truthfully.
The badness of people who live as they please decreases our
vigilance.
(From: Serat Wulang Reh; by His Highness Pakoe Boewono IV).

**Orang yang sopan santun menjauhkan pertengkaran. Adapun
kepandalan itu berguna untuk mencari nafkah.**
Sedangkan adat yang baik akan membawa keselamatan dirimu.
(Serat NITI SUNU—Sasono Pustoko, Karaton Surakarta)

A polite person stays away from conflict. When you can do
this, it will become a means to earn a living. At the same
time good habits will bring you salvation.
(From: Serat Niti Sunu; in the court's library Sasono Pustoko).

**Mudah sukarnya 'sesuatu' tergantung pada kita yang akan
melaksanakan, terhadap segala yang akan kita kerjakan. . . .**
(Wuland Dalem Warna Warni ISKS Pakoe Boewono IX)

Whether something is easy or difficult depends on us who have
to do it, which we apply to everything we're going to
do. . . .
*(From: Wulang Dalem Warna Warni; by his Highness Pakoe Boewono
IX).*

**Wahai para pemuda dan pemudi, wajib mencari, menuntut ilmu
yang tinggi sampai mencapai kesempurnaan lahir dan batin.**
Batin hendaknya terisi dengan ilmu dan pengetahuan. . . .
(Serat NITI SUNU—'Sasono Pustko', Karaton Surakarta)

Hey there all of you young people, you're obliged to search and
obtain the highest knowledge, until you reach a perfect balance between your outer form and inner life. Your inner life
too should become filled with science and knowledge. . . .

(From Serat Niti Sunu; in the court's library 'Sasono Pustoko')

Orang muda jangan membiasakan kepada hal-hal yang buruk, budi pekerti angkara, jahil.
Hendaknya membiasakan rasa kasih saying, tahu diri. . . .
(Wulang Dalem Warna Warni ISKS Pakoe Boewono IX)

Young people should not get used to doing bad things, become egotistical, cruel.
Ideally you should harbor feelings of love, self-respect. . . .
(From: Wulang Dalem Warna Warni; by His Highness Pakoe Boewono IX).

Hati-hati berarti:
Menjaga lahir batin agar tiada mendapat kesalahan dalam langkah dan perbuatan. Dalam permikiran hendaklah teratur, jangan silang selishih.
(Wulang Dalem Warna Warni ISKS Pakoe Boewono IX)

'To be careful' means:
To guard your inner life and your outer appearance, so that there won't be mistakes in what you decide and what you do. Try to regulate your thinking, don't harbor conflicting insights.
(From: Wulang Dalem Warna Warni; by His Highness Pakoe Boewono IX).

Terucapkannya kata-kata hendakiah dikendalikan benar-benar.
Jangan sampai menyinggung perasaan,
Menyakitkan hati teman sepergaulan.
Usahakan menarik hati mereka handai taulan sekalian.
(Serat NITI SUNU—Sasono Pustoko, Karaton Surakarta)

Speak only those words that you really mean. Don't hurt or insult people, or make your friends' heart miserable. Always make an effort in pleasing your close friends and acquaintances alike.
(From: Serat Niti Sunu; in the court's library Sasono Pustoko).

KEHIDUPAN MASA DEWASA
When we're adults
Kami nohon kepada Tuhan Yang Maha Agung, agar mendapat kemuliaan dari awai sampai akhir jaman.

Bagi putra-putri yang menjalani perkawinan
(Wulang Dalem Warna Warni ISKS Pakoe Boewono IX)

We pray to God the Almighty for his blessings, from the earliest
    beginning
until the end of time. For our children who are getting married.
*(From: Wulang Dalem Warna Warni; by His Highness Pakoe Boewono
IX).*

Tegaknya mahligai rumah tangga
Bukan bermodalkan kecantikan atau kekayaan.
Hanya keserasian dan keterpaduan hati semata. . . .
(Serat Wulang Reh ISKS Pakoe Boewono IV)

To sustain the 'palace of one's household' we don't need beauty
    or riches.
We just need nothing other than balance and united hearts. . . .
(From Serat Wuland Reh by His Highness Pakoe Boewono IV).

Manusia itu wajib ikhtiar, hanya harus memilih jalan yang baik.
Manusia juga harus awas dan waspada agar mendapat rahmat
    Tuhan
(Serat Kaladita—Ronggowarsito)

People are obliged to make free choices, they only have to
    choose the right path.
People must also be careful and be alert, so that they will
    receive God's mercy.
(From: Serat Kalatida; by nineteenth-century court poet Ronggowarsito)

Segala sesuatu ditentukan oleh kehendak Tuhan Yang Maha
    Kuasa, tetapi
sebagai mahluk ciptaan Tuhan, janganiah mendahului kehen-
    daknya.
Manusia berusaha Tuhan yang menentukan

Everything is set by God's will, but as creatures created by
    Him, try not to
move faster than His will. Men make an effort, but it is God
    who decides.
(N.N.)

Orang berbuat baik untuk orang lain akan mendapat sesuat
    anugerah
(From: Wulang Dalem Warna Warni; by His Highness Pakoe Boewono IX).

People who do well unto others will receive God's blessing.
(From: Wulang Dalem Warna Warni; by His Highness Pakoe Boewono IX).

Siapa yang bangun pada waktu subuh dan bersyu kur kepada Tuhan,
akan mendapat rahmatNya.
(Wulang Dalelm Warna-Warni ISKS Pakoe Boewono IX)

Whoever wakes up at dawn and says thanks to God will receive His mercy.
(From: Wulang Dalem Warna Warni; by His Highness Pakoe Boewono IX).

Manusia yang ingin luhur derajatnya,
harus menjauhkan diri dari perbuatan yang rendah
(Wulang Dalem Warna Warni; by His Highness Pakoe Boewono IX).

People who wish to attain the highest should refrain from acting low.
(From: Wulang Dalem Warna Warni; by His Highness Pakoe Boewono IX).

Syarat-syarat orang menjadi luhur adalah kuat bertapa dan kurang tidur.
Selalu ingat pada tingka laku yang baik.
Jika berbicara harus Manis agar sesamanya mudah tertarik yaitu sesama manusia.
(Wulang Dalem Warna-Warni ISKS Pakoe Boewono IX)

Conditions for someone who wishes to become supreme are to meditate firmly and refrain from sleeping too much. Always remember good behavior. When one talks, one should talk sweetly, so that everyone becomes interested, as good people should.
(From: Wulang Dalem Warna Warni; by His Highness Pakoe Boewono IX).

Orang hidup itu "Beramal" demi keturunan yang ditinggalkan.
(From: Wulang Dalem Warna Warni; ISKS Pakoe Boewono IX).

People live and do well for the children they leave behind.
(From: Wulang Dalem Warna Warni; by His Highness Pakoe Boewono IX).

Segala sesuatu berasal dari satu yaitu Tuhan yang menciptakan
    segala
sesuatu didunia ini dan dari sanalah semua berasal
(Kidungan Jangkep Yasan Dalam ISKS Pakoe Boewono V)

Everything originates from one source, God, who created
    everything in this world, and everything comes from there.
*(From: Kidungan Jangkep Yasan Dalam; by His Highness Pakoe Boewono
V).*

Selalu ingat larangan Tuhan, jangan sekali-kali khawatir dan
    was-was hati
dalam menghadapi semua percobaan Tuhan baik ringan maupun
    berat,
sebab semua sudah diatur sesuai dengan kemampuannya.
Jangan sekali-kali merasa bahwa ditinggalkan oleh Tuhan, kare-
    na Tuhan
Maha Kasih dan Maha Tahu.
Penderitaan yang berat pasti diringankan dan percayalah sung-
    guh-sungguh
Dan pertebal iman
(Serat NITI SUNU—Sasono Pustoko, Karaton Surakarta)

Always remember God's restrictions, don't ever worry and be
    afraid in facing all God's ordeal, the lighter as well as the
    heavier ones, because everything is taken care of according
    to your abilities. Don't ever feel abandoned by God,
    because He always loves you and knows everything. Great
    suffering will eventually subside: believe this whole-heart-
    edly and strengthen your devotion.
(From: Serat Niti Sunu; in the court's library "Sasono Pustoko").

Chapter 8

HARRASMENT OF CHRISTIANS IN INDONESIA

Saptojoadi

SPEAKING ABOUT PEACE is easy. Anyone can say, "Peace, peace be with you; I have peace." But actually to admit what harms oneself is really hard, is it not? It is specially hard if you have a problem with someone of another group in your life or in your community. Even to say that person's name in our prayer is difficult. It is heavy just to say the name. We are to pray for our enemies, and we are to pray for any group that has done something injurious to us. It is not easy to say, "God, I love them." But as Christ's disciples, we realize that we are supposed to follow his path of love to our enemies. We are to love one another as we love ourselves.

We were born as Mennonites and grew up in Indonesia, the biggest Muslim community in the world. So every Muslim country in the world wants to see what is going on with the Muslim movement in Indonesia. What will happen with Christianity in Indonesia where the Muslim community is strong? What is the mindset of our brothers and sisters who are different from us? If we understand the Muslim mindset and also the history of the Islam, do we find that they have the same feelings that we do?

I grew up in Muslim family, and it was not easy for me to decide to become a Christian. I first decided to become a Christian and be baptized about seventeen years ago. Although I grew up in the Muslim family, and most of our Mennonite church members also grew up in the Muslim families, we are now trying to learn about the history and the mindset of our brothers and sisters who are Muslim. We are trying to be a good friends, to be good brothers and sisters and, sometimes, to be good parents for children who do not have parents in their lives.

We live in a community in which most of the members are Muslim. We don't know the theory about how to be good people. We just do simple things that Jesus commanded to do: just love one another like we love ourselves. This means that we cannot love only other Christians, but we love everybody in our community and recognize them all as brothers and sisters. We cannot say, "Oh, we are Christians. We are not your brothers." By saying that, we will create a problem. Mouthing those words plants a seed that will grow and grow, finally becoming a big problem. Our experience in the Muslim community is that while we haven't done wrong things in the community, often we are persecuted for no reason by persons who don't know us. They just persecute us. They burn a church building down close to the weekend so that we cannot use the building anymore to worship God.

This a small picture, but I would like to set a big picture. How as Christians can we be peacemakers in our society? In our daily life we play together with the Muslims and we work together. We do social things together, and sometimes we eat together from the same plate. We are not trying to be righteous or holy. We just want to share the love of Christ to them. Christ came to the earth not only for Christians, not only for a certain tribe, but for all the people, as is said in John 3:16: "God so loved the world." Christ's love is not only for Judaism, not only for Indonesia or U.S., for Canadians or Indians. It is for all people in the world. When one family in the community holds a wedding party, then all of the people who live in the community come together, work together, and help the family who is having a party. This is a part of our culture. It is not only Javanese culture, but it is also Christian culture to live by loving one another.

However, not all situations are so pleasant. In the year 2005 the church that I am pastoring was closed by the Muslims after the Easter celebrations. I was surprised, because in the afternoon of the day we celebrated Easter, I flew to attend another meeting. On the next day, Monday, people from the community came to the church compound and found it closed.

When I returned two days later, everyone said, "What can we do to deal with this problem?" Some of my church members were angry. "Let us fight! We can challenge them because we have rights as Indonesian citizens. We have the same right as they do to worship our God! We too have freedom to worship our God!"

I was quiet for a moment. Finally I said, "Brothers, just surrender. Be quiet and pray." Then I invited all the church members to begin praying and fasting.

I also invited a few of the church leaders to go to the police office, to the army office, and to other government offices to discuss the reason for closing our church. Everyone in the community knew that the church was built in 1968 and had been in the community for many years. When I had a conversation with the governmental officer, he said, "There is no way that I can help you. I have no idea how you can open your church again."

We went back home and continued to pray and fast, and God led us to engage our Muslim neighbors in a dialogue. Three of us met with the Muslim leader there. We also went door to door discussing with small radical groups in that area, sharing our belief about love. Five months after our church was closed, we still had no idea how to reopen it. We had no solution except to keep having the dialogues.

Several months later I was driving the car to take our children to a Christmas celebration in another congregation. The road at that area is quite narrow, suitable for just one car. As I drove, I was surprised to find a crowd of young people with motorcycles blocking the road. Three mothers who were accompanying their children were also in the car. They were afraid, and one of them cried. "Pastor! Let's go back to the church! I don't want to have trouble here." I said, "Please, just calm down. Let me go over and talk with these people."

I parked the car, went over, and spoke to the young men. They didn't respond to me, but just gunned their motors, *rung rung rung rung*! Some of them continued to block the road with their motorcycles. I said, "Brothers, excuse me, I just want to go through." They didn't listen to me! They ignored me. Then God led me to push the motorcycles one by one to the edge of the road. I pushed about ten motorcycles far enough aside that my car could go through. They were laughing at me. Maybe I was funny, but it didn't matter. With tears running down my cheek I said to them, "Brothers, I love you. I love you, Brothers, although you don't love me. But that is okay. I love each of you as my brother." They continued laughing and ignoring me as I drove the car past them. After the Christmas celebrations, I drove back the same way to bring the children home again.

After that incident, I continued to dialogue with the Muslim leaders. Then something miraculous happened during our dialogue. One of the Muslim leaders said, "Brother Adi, we apologize for what happened to you. We realize that what we did to you was wrong. Some of us believe that, because you are Christians, you are our enemies." A few of the church members are also the relatives of the Muslims of that area. So I just listened. He continued, "We realize that for almost eight months we have been receiving water that comes from your well," Just ten meters from our church building there is a well that supplies our water. Because we put in a pipe to send water around to the community, most of the water goes to Muslim families. During the eight months that our church was closed, the water continued running to the Muslim families. The Muslim leader recognized that and said, "Thank you very much. The water from your well gives life to our members in this community."

I said, "Oh, yes. Thank you for realizing that. This not our water. This water comes from God. Everyone can take it and use it for everything in daily life."

At the end of the conversation the Muslim leader said, "Brother, we just want to let you know that from now on you may open your church building again, and you can use it to worship your God."

Miracles open the way. We didn't do anything! Praying, fasting, dialogue, sharing the love of Christ. They recognized that love is beautiful and that love enables the peace they also feel in their lives.

I want to add a small thing. During the eight months that the church was closed, we still held the worship service on Sunday mornings outside the building in the front yard and in the backyard. Five times during these worship services a group of our brothers and sisters who disagree with our being Christian came to interrupt us. Some of them had clubs in their hands. Why the clubs? To beat us. But it was okay. At that time we said this to our church members: "Don't defend yourselves. Just be quiet and worship your God." So they left us still worshiping God.

Being a peacemaker is not easy. It's not easy in a situation like that, and I sympathize with the Christians in India. Many of the persecutions there and in Indonesia are not about a religion but about political interests. Religion is used a vehicle to cause the conflict. People say, "Oh there are Christians and Muslims fighting each other." Actually it's not about religion but about the conflict of interest in the political situation. Our culture as Indonesians is to live in peace with other religions: Muslims, Buddhists, Hindus, Confucians, and others.

Part of the task that comes from our Christian commitment is that we seek to provide peace physically and also psychologically. The people will think, *Oh yes, I feel comfortable with you; peace in my heart as well as in my mouth.* On the other hand, we also train our youth people to provide a peace program like the one in Aceh. We continue to have some six volunteers who work in Aceh with the Muslims. We don't let anyone know that we are Christian because that small island called Aceh is very fundamentalist Muslim. We don't wear our hats or bring our flags to announce that we are Christians. But in that program we share the love of Christ in their community through activities like teaching English, teaching computer skills, helping people to develop their income by planting crops, and teaching peacemaking in the school. Even though we don't say, "Oh, I'm a Christian!" they realize that the inspiration for our action comes from Jesus Christ.

We also have a peace program in the conflict area of East Timor, an area that is independent from Indonesia. We work together with a Christian organization from Korea called Frontier. We began work in East Timor in 2001 by sending young people to have a international peace camp. Every year since then we have sent our young people there. Last August I was in Indonesian on the border of East Timor, and I led the orientation training for young people. About fifty young people were in attendance from countries around the world, such as Germany, Canada, and Japan. The participants are not only Christians. Some of are atheists, Muslim, Buddhist, and Hindu. We come together with the same goal: to provide peace in the community.

One of the dangerous programs in which we are engaged is the *messenger* program. So often in the conflict area, one family is divided between two groups, and they are caught up in fighting one another. It is not easy to reconcile the two sides. One of our missionaries, a young person, was almost killed because of a misunderstanding. In the *messenger* program we make a video of a family who lives in Indonesia and longs to be reconciled to the other part of the family in East Timor. Then we bring this video tape to the other part of the family. They rejoice to see the video and say, "Oh, our family is still alive and they miss us! Why can we not not be reconciled?" Then also we take video of that family and we bring back to others.

It's wonderful when we see the family reunion. You know family reunions! They don't say, "Oh, you are our enemy." No. Rather, they say, "Oh Brother! Oh Sister!" Their eyes fill with a tears as they realize how much they have missed one another. They realize that they are still family, not enemies, even though they are caught up in the conflict of interest in that area. Some are Indonesian; others are Timorese; but they are still family. It is not easy to decide to leave East Timor and come to Indonesia. But through the *messenger* program most of the families—I would say ninety percent of them—are happy to see their family members alive. They can get together in certain places, and that's wonderful! But to arrange those meetings we sometimes have to sacrifice ourselves, like Jesus sacrificed himself on the cross just for us, just to redeem us.

We are an unholy people, day by day, every day doing the wrong thing to God. But he still loves us! He knows us more than we know ourselves. He knows everything about us: our needs, our minds, and our souls. Everything that we have done he knows, and still he cares about us. So I agree with the person who, during a discussion about how to be a peacemaker, said that if we have enemies, just surrender, for that will reduce the number of victims. Surrender doesn't mean, "Just kill me." No, it's not like that.

We have another option. The best solution is to resolve the problem, to resolve the conflict. We hope and believe the vision that peace is our culture. If peace is our culture, we're going to reach the goal. We're going to reach our main purpose of gathering together: peace in our land, peace in our family, peace in our community. Each one of us realizes that this is our task. This is our culture. This is what we want to do: love one another.

Another of our concerns is to encourage people to oppose a nuclear power plant program in our area. It's not easy just to motivate Christians to oppose a government program. Some of them say, "As citizens, we have to follow the government's policies." Even some church leaders say, "By just following the governments program, we going to have peace." My personal experience of working with Christians and people of other religions to oppose the nuclear power plant is that such work is not easy. Sometimes I am threatened by someone from the government. One time someone came to my house and asked, "Where's Adi? Will you ask Adi to stop the campaign against the nuclear power plant?" We are protesting and engaging in peace demonstrations, although it's not easy in Javanese culture to do a demonstration. It's not easy for it seems as though a big wall is in front of us, but we have to do it.

The government office that is concerned about nuclear energy in our region is trying to reach the church leaders, asking them to help them to convince people that nuclear energy is good, and that it is not dangerous. As Christians we have to give voice to the truth in helping people. We are to think not only about our selves but also about other people who live in our communities. We are to think not only about all other Christians but also about all people on the earth, including others who don't know about or care about the earth. We have to motivate them by giving them an explanation that nuclear power plants are very, very dangerous for all people.

Chapter 9

HARRASSMENT OF CHRISTIANS IN INDIA

Forum of Opinion

MENNONITE FROM INDIA

I have two messages that are disturbing. One is from south India, near Bangalore. November 25, 2007, Sunday morning a group of believers, including the pastor and some others, went to worship. The radical Hindus went there and chased them off. Some of the believers ran off in fear. Then the Hindus got hold of the pastor and two other believers, leaders of the church. They stripped them of their clothes and paraded them in the village. But then the police interfered and booked a case against the Hindus, saying that they were forcefully converting the Christians. This was in south India, near Bangalore, which happens to be a center for many Christian denominations' activities and agencies.

On December 5, 2007, early morning at 7:30, near Delhi in north India, a group of Christians were constructing a church building. The radicals went there and broke down the walls, destroying the church building. When the local people approached the Christians, they said, "We are not going to allow you to build this church here. If you happen to attempt it again, we are going to destroy it again. So please don't build the church building in this city." This was in Delhi in north India.

Father God, we know that your Spirit is grieved. We know that you see and understand more than we can possibly see or understand. We know that your Spirit works in ways that we cannot see nor understand. Lord, where you see conflict, where you see turmoil, where you see persecution, where you see hurt, we know, Father, that you hurt, that you suffer, that you weep with those who weep. Lord, through you we ask that there might be healing because we know that that you are a God of healing, a God of reconciliation, a God who yearns for and loves peace.

We lift up our sisters and brothers in India who are being subjected to what we feel is unjust and unfair treatment for doing what they believe is fair and reasonable in their hearts. We pray that there might be healing through this, that those who have inflicted the hurt might themselves see a way forward, and that they might recognize that they have responded through perhaps fear or uncertainty or of the unknown. We pray, Father, that you will enlighten them and enable them to find another way, to work together, to talk, to share, to communicate.

May your kingdom grow in ways that we could not even hope for, to bring a wonderful change that might sweep through India and enable that conflict to be transformed into a new way of relating, a new way of caring, a new way of sharing. So we pray, Father, for both the victim and the offender, that your love will encompass and transform them all through your love, through your son Jesus' name, through his ever- encompassing love. Amen.

May the peace of our Lord dwell in our hearts. I want to share with you the promise that the Lord has given us in his word in Zechariah 9:10: "He will proclaim peace for the nations and God's kingdom will extend from sea to sea and from the rivers to the ends of the earth." Amen

CHURCH OF THE BRETHREN SPEAKER FROM INDIA

I'm a primary school teacher in northern India. My story concerns a very dear friend, a committed Christian and one who was passionate about spreading the gospel for which he was forced to make severe sacrifices.

Because he was intent upon spreading the gospel, his coworkers persecuted him. He was even physically attacked. Despite all the harassment he received both in and outside his workplace, he remained loyal to the work of the Lord and continued to spread the gospel. One evening, a colleague viciously attacked him as he was going to water his fields. His assailant threw a large stone at him. It resulted in serious injuries to the left side of his face, his eyes, and his jaw, which was broken. But he didn't loose his faith and he continued his work.

However, the persecution continued, with his colleagues plotting against him. They had him transferred to another village 130 km from his home, knowing that daily transport, finding living quarters and acquiring food would prove difficult. Going to work in the new location, he was followed by people eager to take advantage of any small incident or location and attack him. They also harassed his wife, children, and even his aging parents.

On one day every year he was in the habit of taking leave from his job to attend important work at home. But even that day was not free of persecution. In fact some people had plotted against him. Some believe they hired a vehicle to injure him while making it look like an accident. These Hindu fanatics continued harassing his family, forcing his wife and children to move to yet another town, where she worked as a teacher while raising her family. Despite all the sacrifices she had made and suffered, she remained strong in her Christian faith.

CHURCH OF THE BRETHREN PASTOR FROM INDIA

I am a pastor of the Church of the Brethren in Valsad. My story goes back a few years. It's about our church in my town, but actually it's also about the church generally in Gujarat, which faces similar situations under our Hindu government. One Sunday morning we were about to go to church when news came that Hindu fanatics planned to burn Bibles in front of the building. We immediately organized an emergency community meeting with other Christians and approached the District Magistrate, a representative of the government in our city. The local member of Parliament also came. Despite being a member of the BJP (Indian People's Party), the right-wing Hindu party, he was not biased toward Christians. He mediated with the fanatics with the result that they decided not to burn the Bibles.

During this same period, however, fanatics began persecuting members of a nearby Methodist church that enjoyed close relations with us. The fanatics went to their church and pelted it with garbage and cow dung. Now, it so happens that the pastor of the church is my brother-in-law and the mob accused him and certain members of the church of "harassing their women and teenage girls." They were apprehended and taken to the police station, where the false charge was posted. We praised the Lord when they were found innocent of all charges in the subsequent court hearing.

But another church, where my father-in-law is pastor, was attacked by a mob of 300 persons. He is an old man from a family of priests. They tried to force him to chant "Ram," the name of a Hindu God and a symbol of Hindu fanaticism. But my father-in-law was defiant. "I will never say that word! You are free to kill me or do whatever you want with me!" he exclaimed. They were really taken aback by this and eventually, after some further harassment, they let him go, but not without warning him, "If you come back next Sunday we will kill you." However, as a prayerful person and a great believer in Christ, he was sure that "Christ will save me," and indeed nothing further happened.

CHURCH OF THE BRETHREN SPEAKER FROM INDIA

The place I come from, Rajpipla, was a tiny kingdom before India's independence. My story is about how we built our church. In 1991 there were only three to five families living in Rajpipla, renting a small first floor room for their worship. As time went on several more Christian families settled in the town and joined our community. In time, the elders decided to build a church, and every salaried member was asked to contribute 100 rupees for land which was eventually bought. This, however, was the beginning of our difficulties. Government bureaucracy ordered that permission had to be sought from at least twelve departments. We bought the land in 1994 and faithfully began all formalities, but even by the year 2000 we were unable to secure permission from the police department, the main department that clearly opposed the building of the church

After several failed written attempts, a delegation of the church's elders met with the police commissioner. "Why do you need a church?" he asked, adding that the government has not granted permission for a building church since 1953. He was unwilling to listen to anything said but remarked sarcastically, "If you really want to say prayers, you are invited to my home. You can have your meetings there." The elders replied, "'Just as [Hindu] temples are holy places, our church will also be a holy place where the Spirit of the Lord will work and guide us in our daily lives."

What happened next was a miracle of God. Returning from the police commissioner's office, the elders happened to meet the local assembly member, a Hindu, with whom they had good relations. He asked, "Why did you go to the police commissioner?" They told him the whole story. Then he said, "Okay, come with me to his office." So off they went to the police commissioner, who then granted permission to build.

However, this was not the end. Permission to build was needed also from the District Magistrate, the government's representative in our city. He came to inspect the proposed site and to address the leaders of the surrounding community with whom we have always lived peacefully in the spirit of Christ, being helpful whenever we could. Gathering all the people together, the District Magistrate told them about our intentions to build a church, asking them if they had objections. The answer was astonishing: "What would be a better than building a church on this place?" they said. "And if it is built here, we too will join them in prayer." Finally, in 2000 a delegation of our Church of the Brethren from the USA visited us for our opening ceremony.

Now for another story about an incident my daughter faced while in grade five. She is a brilliant child and participated in every school activity, winning medals and awards. She was also first in her class. Because of this, the Hindu girls in her class were jealous. They harassed her by hiding her belongings and throwing her bag out of the window. She would complain to us, of course, and we always prayed for her. This gave her encouragement and the strength to continue at school.

But an incident occurred which changed her. She was walking along one of the school corridors with several friends when a passing teacher asked for her bottle of water. Another girl accompanying her suddenly got hold of the teacher's hand saying, "Teacher, you can't drink that water because she's a Christian!" The teacher gave the bottle of water back to my daughter and took water from the other girl instead.

When my daughter returned home, she wept a lot. We tried to calm her down and to lead her in prayer, but she was devastated by this incident. And my little girl who used to participate in all activities, who won medals, is today a changed child. She does not perform well at school, she can't study properly, and she is unable to achieve good results. She is a very depressed child. We've approached doctors, tried to talk to her and lead her into prayer. We hope that the situation changes.

Because of this, we say that working for the Lord, having faith in him and participating in all the things taught by the Lord, we suffer. But we believe that everything will turn out for the best because we have faith in the Lord Jesus Christ.

CHURCH OF THE BRETHREN SPEAKER FROM INDIA

I'm a bank manager in my hometown in India, and my story is about blood. In India available blood is actually scarce but badly needed. When Christians undergo medical emergencies, it is often very difficult for them to acquire blood. People would indeed come to donate blood, but they turned back because they decided against giving it to Christians. We tried to find out why his was so, and when we did, we were really saddened. To confront this ignorance we held a youth gathering with tribal people who had been afraid to donate blood. We counseled them, giving them information about the harmlessness of blood donation. We told them that they would be saving our brothers and sisters who were sick and in danger of losing their lives. We also approached the blood bank but their policy was, "We will give blood only to those who return their bottle."

So we organized a blood camp where we invited Christian youth to donate blood. In the very first camp we collected 102 bottles of blood and gave them to the blood bank. We organized yet another camp and collected eighty-two. We organized still another camp, gaining seventy more bottles. We have continued to organize these camps at the same time as our annual meetings and gladly donated blood to the blood bank, who told the public that ours was the only youth group coming forward with blood.

Whenever there's a need we always give blood to anyone from whatever caste or religion. And we are always prepared to help with advice. With love we gained victory over those who opposed and persecuted us. We are, after all, helping society at large. Nowadays, we are the first to be invited whenever the blood bank organizes programs.

Part IV
RELIGIOUS RADICALISM

Chapter 10

RELATING TO RADICALISM

PAULUS HARTONO

The Indonesia Archipelago consists of more than 13,000 islands with a population of 210,000,000 people. According to the statistical data of 2006, people who live in poverty (income under $2 per day) number 30,000,000 persons and unemployment is estimated at 25,000,000 persons. Indonesia is among the countries widely known for violation of human rights. At the same time Indonesia is unique regarding the spread and development world religions within its boundaries, especially Islam and Christianity, and also regarding the degree of conflict among them.

Islam has developed significantly in many islands in Indonesia, especially in the island of Java. Consequently Islam has become the major religion in Indonesia, with about 150,000,000 followers. Catholic and other Christian groups came to Indonesia in a more organized way, and they tended to offer a more systematic religious experience. Hinduism, which came to Indonesia before other religions, introduced a system of governance in the form of kingdoms, such as in Bali, Kalimantan (Kutai), West Java (Tarumanegara), and East Java (Sriwijaya). Buddhism has left a large religious legacy, such as the Borobudur temple.

The growth and development of multiple religions in Indonesia since its beginning has been a pluralistic reality. The forefathers of Indonesia realized that the pluralism of religions could not be replaced by a single religion. Therefore they avoided determining whether the country would be secular or religious by tying Indonesia to a model called "Unity in Diversity." Under this model the nation guarantees freedom for its citizens to practice their religious traditions, including all of the five major religions. However, the model has led to numerous conflicts, and in the last ten years Indonesia has faced a great challenge in dealing with religious diversity. Churches have struggled theologically with God's calling to bring peace and prosperity to this country, (Jer. 29:7; Matt. 5:9). The conflicts in 1998, the Bali bombing, the Marriott Hotel bombing, buildings burned, churches destroyed, and bloody conflict in Ambon and Poso have become a major challenge to bringing peace to this country. The many causes of conflict, such as polarization, poverty, unemployment, corruption, and violation of human rights need to be comprehensively understood.

Polarization is a threat to pluralistic living. Polarization is the separation of two different groups until they become sharply opposed and lose their essential character. The essence of religion is to make peace and to live together with love and respect for one another. However, religion has often changed into a tool for hatred and killing other people. Theoretically churches are united and religious people are united in building a better and more just life. Unfortunately we are not an integrated unity; rather we have a fragile unity fraught by conflict. Polarization is often implicitly accompanied by exclusiveness, awkwardness, blind fanaticism, slander, aggressiveness, self-interest, willfulness, and also ideology—all of which force groups into a power struggle. Polarization affects social class differences, such as managers and employees, and groups of different national origin, such as Javanese and Chinese.

Polarization is a strong reality within the so-called radical groups, those who see their religion as an absolute, single, and final truth. Anyone outside their group is considered to be an unbeliever and lost. For instance, the members of a Muslim religious community (*Umat*) are under God's caliph and receive Islam wholly (*Kaffah*). This means that the state and the world are considered the place where only their own believers have the right to worship, and only they should be allowed to worship. Islam has to fight (*Jihad*) to build an Islamic country and also to bring God's glory into the world. An Islamic state is the only true state, and there is no other truth in this world. When there are true believers in any part of a county, the whole country needs to adopt the true religion. Therefore Islam has to be adopted by both the country and the world.

A simplistic anti-tolerance view is used to nurture *umat ul'amilin fisabilillah* (pious members and fighters in God's way). To support this view, Muslims legalize violence, take the unbelievers' property, and even kill them. They believe that they will receive a reward from God for doing these things. To die while fighting for Islam is to be a martyr and is remembered by God until the seventh generation. Martyrs will have seven beautiful angels provided to serve them in heaven. While such ideology blinds people, it is considered enlightenment in the Muslim doctrine of *Tauhid*.

Polarization happens not only in Muslim but also in Christian circles. In the middle of challenging situations of violence, Christian churches believe they are to be salt and light for the world, bringing reconciliation and peace. However, in reality churches are often guilty of not being able to bring peace within their own groups. They often struggle over theological differences about baptism, religious ceremony, church buildings, and mission. Inter-church conflicts arise around procedures for baptism, attracting congregational members, control of assets, and differences between the duty to be in mission and to be peace makers.

Issues of morality become an entry point for people to come in with radical ideas about how to solve those issues. Governmental corruption, moral crisis, poverty, unemployment, and natural disasters in Indonesia are considered to be God's curse. The radical solution is for the society to repent and build an Islamic country. The issue of poverty affects Muslims quite significantly because the majority of the poor are in Asia, and most of them are Muslim. The Indonesian statistics of 2004 indicate that there are about 36,000,000 people who are considered to be poor.

According to Islamic believers, the global economy is impoverishing the Muslim community. They consider Americans and their Jewish collaborators to be the primary cause of Muslim poverty. So Jihad in the economic sense is not just about the issues of physical violence. It is a struggle against those who benefit from the global economy, including the Chinese.

In the struggle we can see four different types of radical response in Indonesia. The first group moves into a political arena, struggling to change the constitutional law (UUD) to authorize Islamic law (*Shariah*) both in the local and central governments. The second group deals with the education. They build programs of religious education to prepare a militant younger generation, and they train some leaders to enter society through the mosques to spread the fighting spirit of Jihad. The third group works in the practical area in society. They are the defenders of morality fighting prostitution, alcoholism, pornography, and drugs. The fourth group is active in the international arena of the global Jihad movement against the super powerful countries that are considered to be dominating the world and to be doing violence to Islam. This group conducts its activities through anarchism and terrorism. They target locations popular with tourists, specifically Australians. They feel that Australia or the Australian government is the primary influence contaminating Islam. Other targets are the islands where most of the inhabitants are Christians, for example Ambon, Poso, and Papua.

Many churches in Indonesia have not done anything significant with regard to these social issues. In fact, some churches even have harsh critics of their exaggerated building renovation committees, critics who have little or no concern about answering such social problems. Such criticism leads to sharp contradictions between mission and diakonial service. Those who are eager to be engaged in mission activity consider social service to humanity to be a waste of funds. They believe that when the people repent, the nation will be revived. Likewise, those engaged in diaconal service criticize many of the mission activities. They believe that such mission activity is based upon models of dominance and is the cause for the terrible relationship between Christians and Muslims. They point out that Christianization is an issue used by Muslim groups as a reason to oppress Indonesia churches. Almost all Christian programs are suspected to be an effort to Christianize people.

The Indonesian Mennonite Church (GKMI) is struggling to find its theological presence in Indonesia through a program called *depolarization*. Depolarization is not meant to be syncretism but rather an effort to build a fair, humble, transparent, cooperative process of communication in search of a mutual understanding of one another's perspectives.

For example, GKMI wanted to visit a Muslim man in the Solo hospital. When we tried to visit him, his followers tried to block us because they were surprised that a Christian minister wanted to visit him. They asked, "What do you want? What is your business here?" We said, "We would like to come to visit him so that we can pray for his healing." We opened the dialogue as human beings who care for other human beings. As it turned out, he did not want to be prayed for, but he did want to be visited.

Depolarization encourages mutual give and take clarification in dialogues, so that religions can share with and understand each other. The goal is for misunderstanding, gossip, lies, stereotypes, and misleading accusations regarding the faith of other persons to be eliminated. So we provide an Interfaith Forum for religious leaders in the community to transform attitudes of participants from different religious traditions.

GKMI also seeks to build a community of dialogue among the religious and societal leaders through cooperatively sharing media and humanitarian relief in some disaster areas in Indonesia. With MCC and the Center for the Study and Promotion of Peace at Duta Wacana Christian University, we have tried to provide humanitarian relief in the earthquake zones in Jogjakarta. The earthquakes provided an opportunity for the youth groups from the Mennonites and the Hezbollah to work together.

Understanding between religious traditions must be built in an atmosphere of commitment and openness. Religious people need a commitment to God through faith. If genuine such commitment can lead to openness in relationship with others with the language of love expressing one's commitment to God and others: "Love the Lord your God with all of your heart and love others as you love yourself." GKMI cooperates with other churches, other religions and the palace (*Keratin*) to empower pluralism in a society that is precariously close to destroying cooperative forms of pluralism because of poverty and moral decadence, including corruption.

Mission and peacebuilding do not need to be contradictory. Some people would say that mission is more important. But other would say that peacebuilding is more important. So we try to integrate the two seemingly opposite aspects. Both need to walk hand-in-hand within a vision of peace and pluralism. If I perform peacebuilding without carrying the spirit of mission, I will soon get tired, bored, and even lose my sense of purpose. Peacebuilding can become just another commodity to promote self-interest. It can become a project that loses the values for which it struggles. If I have the spirit of mission in doing a peacebuilding program, I will hope for the best possible results by constantly listening and following God's will through his words and Holy Spirit. I will witness the love of Christ to other people, so they may see Christ and become believers.

On the other hand, to do mission without an understanding of peacebuilding is a dangerous thing in the context of Indonesia. Christianity and Islam have a terrible history of relationships fraught with disastrous communication. Many conflicts and much violence have left wounds and bitterness on both sides. So peacebuilding is greatly needed for mission.

The Indonesian Mennonite Church believes that pluralistic mission also needs global networking. Jesus called his church to be fishers of people using the casting net instead of just a hook and line (Matt. 4:19). The task of peace mission within a context of pluralism needs the energy and initiative to develop global networking. Learning and working for a peaceful community should focus on the local context, but be related to a wider spirit of global mission networking.

Peace churches such as Mennonite, Brethren, Friends need a website which can be used as a medium for sharing, information, interaction, and communication among peacebuilders.

RESPONSE TO PAULUS HARTONO

Mennonite Central Committee Researcher

I am a researcher here in Indonesia. I am researching Mennonite Central Committee and their work with their partners in Indonesia. One of their partners, as Paulus Hartono has already mentioned, is Interfaith Forum (FPLAG), of which Paulus is a member, as well as Mennonite Diakonial Services (MDS), of which Paulus is also a member. The Interfaith Forum and the MDS are quite central for the peacebuilding work that has been happening in Solo. I think it is a fascinating and exciting story. I have only just begun trying to hear the story from those involved, and to understand what is taking place.

One week ago I stayed with a member of the Interfaith Forum. His name is Pot Amunowad, and he is an Islamic leader in the Interfaith Forum. I had an opportunity to talk with him about peacebuilding and interchange with radical groups in Indonesia. I also had the opportunity to teach a little bit of English to some of these radical Islamic groups. One of things that really impressed me was the role this Interfaith Forum has in bridging the gap between the Christians and the radical Muslims. Because it has Islamic leaders in it, it is a group that has respect from the Islamic world. If it were only Muslim, or only peace churches, perhaps it would not have that same respect. So it bridges a gap between Christianity, or the West, and local Islamic groups.

One of the things that really struck me was the role of individuals in this group, people such as Pak Paulus, who has been building relationships between these groups for many years. But there are also others within the group, Muslim leaders and others, who are prepared to reach across those boundaries to form friendships, sometimes taking personal risks in doing so. It was out of this that the peacebuilding work was able to spread.

Mennonite from Indonesia and USA)

I originate from Indonesia, but I lead a church in Philadelphia, Pennsylvania, in the United States. There are 5,000 Indonesians in Philadelphia, and ten percent of them are Muslims. It has been five or six years since the Mindanaoan riots when so many Indonesians came to the United States, especially to Philadelphia. There are ten In-donesian churches but no other church has tried to communicate or build communication with the Muslims. So two years ago God gave me a sense of reaching out to the Muslims. Last year during the Ra-madan season, I called one of the Muslim leaders, the Indonesian Muslim leader. I asked, "Do you have any space to worship? If you want to use our space, you will be welcome." There was no response.

This year suddenly I received a call from that leader. He said, "Do you remember you offered us your building for prayer and worship? Can we still use your building for worship?" I replied, "Personally I am willing, but let talk to the leaders of the church, and then let me share with the members." Everybody in one accord said, "Yes. This is the time for us to reach out to the Muslims. It has been so many years, and no one from any church has tried to build a relationship." So we prepared everything, and we hosted them. About one hundred Mus-lims came to the church and had a worship service. We had a really wonderful time hosting them and providing some food for them. They worshiped, and we also broke their fast together on that day in our church basement.

The journalists, the media, and also a local newspaper covered this event. However, what I want you to know is this. A week after this event, I received a phone call from Indonesian pastors in America who think that opening a church for the Muslims is not the right thing. They are against our opening a church for the Muslims. Can you imagine? They called me and they said that the presence of God is no longer in your church. So my conclusion is this: Sometimes we talk about peace. But who are the persons who do the most to block our ef-forts to work at peace? The church, Christians themselves, according to my experience.

Mennonite Church speaker from Indonesia

In your presentation you shared that one of the groups of Mus-lims in the Interfaith Forum (FPLAG) works with the constitutional law in the governmental office to change it to the Sharia, the Muslim law. Six months ago I read in the Christian newspaper that almost twenty countries use Sharia law as their governmental law. Every-body who lives in those provinces must follow that law. My question to Paulus Hartono is this. What do you do in the Interfaith Form (FPLAG) to deal with this issue?

Paulus Hartono

Regarding the question of Sharia law and its consequences in Indonesia, FPLAG is not directly involved in the politics related to it. FPLAG encourages and opens up dialogue about these issues. So our proximity or closeness with the political leaders of Solo also gives us the opportunity to talk with them about these issues.

Church of the Brethren speaker from India

I don't have a question but only a comment about what you are doing. Holding a Muslim worship in a church, I think, is one of the best solutions we could find. We have the same problem in north India. Hindu people are in the majority there, and often tension between different communities arises. What we have done is to start celebrating Christmas along with the Hindu community and the Muslim community. It started three years ago and they are continuing to come. When we celebrate Christmas, we want to share our joy with others. People are coming, and we have started a dialogue with other communities about how we can be together this way.

Church of the Brethren speaker from India

I want to ask Paulus Hartono a question. Developing a relationship with Hezbollah must not have been an easy task. So when you took an initiative to open a dialogue with them, did they respond positively? What methods did you use to open a dialogue with them?

Paulus Hartono

It's true that building relationships with our radical friends is not easy. People are sometimes confused that I am involved in a lot of organizations; among them are Mennonite Diakonial Services (MDS), and Interfaith Forum (FBLAG). I also have the Indonesian Forum for Humanity and Humanhood (FKPI), which is an interfaith institution created to respond to national disasters in Indonesia. I cannot conduct direct transformation with my organization MDS only, so I developed FPLAG and FKPI. But the Mennonites are my inspiration and my role model.

When I entered the Hezbollah group, they rejected me. So the commander of the Hezbollah said to me directly, "Christians or anyone outside our group are *Kafir*. Because you are a Kafir, we can kill you." So we tried to open a dialogue without any type of ulterior motives, and after two years he finally began to open up. He said, "Paulus, now I know a second definition of Kafir, the Kafir that is filled with friendship. Now I can trust you and be friends with you." After five years of program and work he said, "Now I have a third definition of Kafir, Kafir as good hearted. So we have respect." Even within their community I am now considered to be one of their commanders.

With the MCC we use a personal approach to issues of livelihood because the majority of the radicals are living in dire poverty. Because of this personal approach, we hope and believe that there will be a transformation. One of them has become our staff member and is working in Bantul. So he asked me one day, "Tell me, how can I arrange my life in a much better way? Please, you have every right to do that." He learned how to manage organizational activities, savings, and personal living. We exemplify the love of Christ, but we do not tell him what he should be, because our beliefs depend upon commitment and responsibility toward God.

Mennonite MCC staff member

I am just an observer from MCC, but I wish to thank you, Paulus, because I have had the opportunity to learn from your example. For almost seven years I have watched this story unfolding, and I think I have learned that it is not program. It is relationship. What I have seen Paulus model started from an individual and personal relationship. I want you all to know the story of how it is that we are able to have this conference in Solo. In 2001 this very commander whom Paulus was talking about was so angry at the impending American invasion of Afghanistan that he and his group were conducting sweeps in the international hotels, going in military uniforms in trucks to these international hotels. This very hotel is one they came to. They demanded to see the list of international visitors to tell them, "You need to leave if you agree with the American government."

That was 2001. Now it is 2007, and the mayor of Solo knows that we are here. The Muslim leaders know we are here. They welcomed us here. I am sure that the commander and his whole group know that we are here, this whole group. They are saying "It's okay" because it is built on the beginning foundation of trust between Paulus and moderate Muslims, and I want to thank you Paulus for your example.

Mennonite WCC staff member from Switzerland

I want to emphasize what Janey just said. Paulus, thank you very much for the testimony. It was most enlightening and inspiring and encouraging too. In my work with both MCC and the World Council of Churches, the thing that really makes a difference is personal relationships and building friendships. If you want to build peace, build friendships. It will take a long time, and you won't change the world overnight. I want to reinforce that very much. We all need programs, and we need institutions; but sometimes they become obstacles. When they become obstacles to friendship and you have to choose, choose the friendship.

Another thing I want to do is to encourage us to find a way to move forward. Paulus suggested that there be an electronic platform for the Historic Peace Churches. What we are considering in these discussions makes the Historic Peace Churches today's peace churches. This kind of action, this kind of interaction, makes us peace churches. We do need a platform to share these stories. The churches, the ecumenical churches, are looking and waiting for encouraging stories like these, because it take the fear out of people, which is the best violence prevention program that you can have.

Can we find a way? If only we could find a space to imagine. I know that MCC has a website. I know that the Decade to Overcome Violence has a website, but these are institutional websites. Maybe we can find another joint platform. Maybe we need to develop one or build upon an existing one. I am not sure, but I think this is something worth pursuing, to find possibilities of sharing these stories of how the Muslims have allowed us to build open discussion together.

The right wing and populous parties are campaigning against such open discussion, even though it should be legally possible. They want to create laws to make it impossible. Sadly enough, a lot of Christian people are agreeing with the popular parties that it should not be allowed. But we need to hear these stories. Our church members need to hear these stories. That will help them have a different perspective.

Mennonite Brethren Church Speaker from India

Some of you know that Hyderabad has a strong Muslim population. In India people say Hyderabad has the largest Muslim population in the country. So the Mennonite church wanted to reach this group of people with the gospel. One of our programs is that during Christmas season, we have a friendship and dinner program. A couple of years ago I invited about sixty Muslim friends and arranged a nice meal. We wanted to share the gospel and read 1 Corinthians 13, which speaks about love and Jesus Christ.

Somehow the radicals heard that we were arranging this gathering, so they also came. Instead of the sixty people we invited, more than 120 people showed up. The radicals came in a discourteous way, shouting and trying to disturb the gathering. I was leading the program with my broken language. I come from a Turdu background, but I can speak Urdu, which is the language of the people of Hyderabad. So I tried to communicate. When they started to disturb the whole program, I myself was much disturbed. Then the Lord gave me one small thought. I said, "Brothers, why should you Muslims and we Christians have to fight? Let us remember we come from one ancestor, Abraham. We are brothers. Why should we fight? Why should we disturb each other?"

Then they said something thing about which I felt a little guilty. A few years ago the Hindu fanatics destroyed a mosque in north India. It was a very sad incident. They said, "When it happened, you Christians kept quiet. I wish you would have raised your voices. We are not saying that you are liars, but you didn't raise your voices." I said, "I give assurance that hereafter we will work together. We will meet together and settle our differences." They asked, "Are you sure?" I asked. "I can visit you anywhere in the Hyderabad area. Why should I be scared, because you are my brothers and I am your brother."

From that day onward we developed a closer fellowship. They come to our meetings. We go to their meetings. Sometimes we also have dialogue. They have their special way of doing things, but the tension is gone. Every year from that year on, either just before Christmas or just after Christmas, we have invited our Muslim friends to a festival, and they come. We share the good news. I think this is one way the church can be in dialogue with them. We give space to them so that they also can hear the gospel. They can clarify some of the misconceptions they have about us and some we have about them.

Paulus Hartono

The radicals in Indonesia are not identical with the terrorists. The radicals want Sharia to be the basis of the law. In many instances, the movements they have espoused have elements of violence. Yet it is quite difficult to define all radicals in Indonesia as terrorists.

I experienced difficulty when I applied for a visa at the United States embassy. I asked the official why I was denied the visa. I was told the American FBI was looking for a person with a similar name, similar physical features, and even a thumbprint that was ninety percent similar to mine. After three months of cross-checking and clarifying, I finally was declared a non-terrorist. Every time I have used that visa, I have been asked to enter a side room where I have been interrogated for a couple of hours.

Mennonite from Indonesia

From what I have heard from Paulus Hartono, as I reflect back on what he said, I think there are two key elements in the practicalities of religious pluralism. One is personal relationship, and I want to emphasize that personal relationship is very, very, crucial in building a dialogue, even with the radical groups. I am glad that he shared his story about how he went to these people and gained their trust. If you are Indonesian and you mention the name of the group he joined, then you know that this is very exclusive group. They have been militant, and they have a long history of excluding themselves from the other groups in Indonesia, even more so from the Christians. Paulus himself has such a good relationship with the commander that the group trusts him. The personal relationship has developed to the point that he has even conducted marriage counseling with them.

Beside personal relationship, a second element is networking. He has mentioned the Peace Center in Duta Wacana University Peace Center, of which I am the director. I do have knowledge and skill, and I have a lot of experts around me who can give the training. But all of these resources are useless unless we have a person who can build a personal relationship. Paulus opened up the way for us to come in. MCC has resources, but again these resources are useless unless a bridge can be built up between the groups so that MCC can enter in. The Mennonite church in Indonesia works at establishing a peace community. We have programs such as religious dialogue and creating a peace spirituality.

Both of these two elements are crucial for peaceful religious pluralism and cooperation. Paulus Hartono has created a good personal relationship that opens the way for others to come in, to dialogue, and to encounter Muslims, even the radical Muslims. On the other hand, if there were only Paulus Hartono's good relationship, then it would not work either. Therefore he also needs a network with many people who have the knowledge, skills, and resources for peacebuilding. So I think these are two very, very key elements.

Quaker from Britain

I want to make a comment about involving other churches in what we are doing. Obviously I come from a situation where Christianity is the majority religion. One of the things that happened some time ago was that, because of their fear of terrorism, our government wanted to pass new laws restricting the activities in mosques. The restrictions included putting lots of responsibilities upon leaders of mosques for things that would happen and allowing the police to go into mosques. The laws were framed in terms of religious buildings because not all Muslim congregations meet in mosques.

When the churches heard about this, we realized that the law was likely to apply to churches as well. So we got the churches together, though the Church of England didn't join in. The Quakers, the Reformed, the Baptists, and many of the free churches objected very strongly on the grounds of the restriction of religious freedom. Because many churches raised such a strong objection, that law fell. The government didn't pursue it. I think it is crucial when we want to build relationships with other faiths that we not leave the other Christian churches behind.

Paulus Hartono

Relationship is crucial in the process of transformation. Before we entered the radical group and before the tsunami, three negative convictions prevented them from being open. The three were anti-Christian, anti-Chinese, and anti-Javanese. When I entered their group, I had all three of the characteristics that they did not like. I am a Christian pastor, I am Chinese, and I am from Java. The process of transformation challenges us as a paradox, and Jesus has taught us a lot about paradox. Things that seem to be impossible actually carry a value that is quite meaningful.

When I asked the commander of the group, "How can I be part of you?" he said, "Paulus, the first thing you must understand in our traditional house is that the entry of the door is quite low. But when you enter the door there is this vast space without any kind of barrier or pillars. In other words, please open your heart whenever you communicate with us. Another thing is that once you are invited to a lunch or dinner with one of our families, you are a part of us. Also when you shake hands with a woman, and the woman kisses your hand, that is the point at which you are now a part of us."

As we entered and did our work, we kept in mind those three things. We visited them personally from house to house and listened to their issues and their concerns. And after one year, they finally opened up to me. Any time I go there now, when I shake hands with the women, they kiss my hand. When I ask them, "Why did you kiss my hand?" they say, "Because you come here to bring grace and peace."

Also consider this story about a lady, who after the tsunami fell into despair and wanted to commit suicide. Following trauma healing training, she revived and married a policeman who is a member of the radical group. They tried to involve me in that wedding, because I have become more like a godfather to them. That is the power of relationship and the paradox of service.

Chapter 11

MISSION AS RECONCILIATION AMID RELIGIOUS EXTREMISM: AN INDONESIAN CHRISTIAN PERSPECTIVE

Paulus S. Widjaja

QUESTIONS TO PONDER

When I think of Christian mission, I like to ponder two questions, and I hope every Christian who is involved in mission also does the same as a sort of self-evaluation practice. First, where in the world are churches growing most quickly? Second, where in the world do most brutal and bloody civil wars take place?

When the answer to both questions is the same, then we are in a very serious situation. Something is wrong with this picture. It is what the very well-respected missionary John Stott repeatedly reminds us about: the danger of *growth without depth*. The churches grow in quantity but not in quality; in numbers but not in faith maturity.

Such a situation happens, in my opinion, when Christian mission is understood only in terms of reconciliation between God and human beings. It does not include reconciliation between human beings as individuals and as groups of people. In this case, Christian mission has to do simply and, quite often, only with forgiveness of sin and a highway to heaven, but not so much with the embrace of others, especially the different others. As such, Christian mission is entrapped in *verticalism*.

With this in mind, I want to propose that we include reconciliation between human beings as an integral part of Christian mission. One such relationship that we need seriously to take into consideration in Christian mission in our day is the relationship between people of different religions.[1] How can Christian mission become a means of reconciliation between people of different religions? how can Christian mission bring redemption rather than conquest to a world torn apart by religion-inspired conflicts?

Reconciliation is, however, not as easy as it sounds. One of the biggest challenges in interreligious relationships, one that has blocked the reconciliation process between people of different religions, is *religious extremism*. We therefore need to understand the dynamics that have driven such extremism before we can even think about how to be reconciled with people engaged in religious extremism. So my intention in this paper is to try to elaborate the problem we have to deal with in Christian mission related to religious extremism.

THE PROBLEM OF RELIGIOUS EXTREMISM

Before we talk specifically about religious extremism, it is worth noting what Erich Fromm has pointed out—that human aggression has its source in the condition of *alienation*, that is, the feeling of loneliness, exclusion, or rejection.[2] This alienation, based on my observation of Indonesian society, is not related merely to social alienation where a group of people are socially excluded by the majority of society. It may well include political alienation where a group of people feel that their ideology has been marginalized and even excluded from the political life of the nation and the world, or economic alienation where a group of people feel that they have been unfairly defeated in economic competition due to the very crude capitalistic system, or cultural alienation where a group of people feel that their valued culture has been replaced by a dominating hegemonic culture of the West.

This alienation brings about two results simultaneously. On the one hand, it encourages the alienated to avenge the sense of loneliness and impotence by destroying other people through god-like acts of violence. On the other hand, it motivates the alienated to gain the sense of connection by joining people who have the same hatred toward common enemies, that is, people whom they blame as having made them alienated.[3]

Let us take a closer look at the combinations one at a time. The second part of this dynamic, namely the tight connection and solidarity among the alienated, is well supported by the findings of Max Abrahms.[4] Based on his research among groups considered to be terrorist, Abrahms came to a very interesting conclusion:

> There is comparatively strong theoretical and empirical evidence that people become terrorists not to achieve their organization's declared political agenda, but to develop strong affective ties with other terrorist members. In other words, the preponderance of evidence is that people participate in terrorist organizations for the social solidarity, not for their political return.[5]

Thus, at the individual level, the main motivation for people to join in the terrorist group is to develop strong affective ties with other terrorist members. At the organizational level, terrorist groups work hard to preserve their social unit, even when their actions impede their stated political goal. The terrorists are therefore more social solidarity seekers than political utility maximizers.

Abrahms presents facts he found in his research to support his conclusion. First, terrorist groups do not randomly recruit people to join them. They tend to recruit certain psychological types of people, namely, people who are alienated. This may include unmarried young people or widows who have no jobs before joining the terrorist group, people who are dislocated and are not assimilated in the host society they are attempting to join, and many other alienated people. It is obvious that recruitment is targeted toward these kinds of people, not primarily people who show commitment to the political goals of the group. For such people, the social tie to a particular group is more important than their ideological commitment. During interviews with members of terrorist groups Abrahms found that most of them join the terrorist group because they have some friends or relatives in the group, or they want to maintain and develop social relations with other members in the group or reduce their sense of alienation or both.

Second, terrorist groups have become attractive outlets for people seeking solidarity. The longing for solidarity matches quite well with the very strong affective ties between members of terrorist groups, which are more tight-knit than other voluntary associations precisely because of the extreme degree of dangers and costs of participation as well as the tendency of terrorist groups to violate societal norms. This explains why terrorist groups are still able to recruit new members, boost the morale of their members, and strengthen their social unit through their acts of terrorism even amid their political failure.

Third, terrorist groups that are most conducive to the development of strong affective social ties among their members become the most attractive ones. A terrorist group implodes when it ceases to be perceived as a social group worth joining.

What Abrahms has found is crucial in understanding religious extremism. As I have mentioned, the alienation experienced by a group of people brings about two results simultaneously—namely, the motivation to seek *solidarity* among people with the same feeling of alienation, and the *aggression* to avenge their feeling of loneliness by destroying the perceived enemies. The aggression aspect will be more present and intense when religion comes into play. While researchers have proposed many reasons to explain the birth of religious extremism, such as the hermeneutical problem of misinterpretation of the sacred texts, the economic problem,[6] the problem with the existence of religion itself,[7] I will consider only some that are relevant in understanding the relation between alienation and religious violence.

First of all, when religious people are disillusioned and frustrated by the reality of the world they live in, they tend to look backward instead of forward. In this process they try to find and imitate what had happened in the perceived golden era of the past history of their group because they believe that there is where they can find moral perfection. Even when these people talk about eschatology, what they mean is actually the reliving of the historical past. The new age to come is none other than the remaking of the old golden age.

This dynamic creates a sort of *romanticism*. For instance, the perceived radical Moslems in Indonesia who often engage in violent acts in the name of religion dress in the same style as they believe people in the age of the prophet Mohammed did. They imitate not only the dress code of the historical past but also the physical appearance, lifestyle, and social ruling or governance. So the men keep their beards, some put dot signs on their foreheads, some practice polygamy. They also adore and give absolute authority to persons who are believed to have a blood tie with the prophet Mohammed. In regard to national politics, they strive for the implementation of Islamic *Shariah* (law) and the Islamic Shariah economic system and so forth.

The danger of such romanticism comes when these disillusioned people become convinced that all the problems in the world will vanish should they be able to relive the golden era once more. Violence naturally lurks at the door because the history of the birth of all religions has always been a history of acceptance and resentment. It is always a history about how a religious group tried to stand for and defend its new identity, criticize the immorality of the society at large, and convert as many people as possible into the group, because the group's identity was perceived to be not only a matter of saving the society from immorality but also of saving it for heaven. Thus when such a history is to be relived, the respected religious group will have to point fingers at other groups of people as representatives of the immoral people the group's ancestors tried to defeat and convert. The struggle soon turns into one between the moral believers and the immoral unbelievers, indeed between Almighty God and the devil.

The violence of religious romanticism is further enhanced by the idea of *cosmic war*.[8] Some religious people learn to believe that there are two antagonistic forces in the universe, the good one and the evil one, that are inherently in opposition against each other.

Three crucial points must be taken into consideration related to this issue: (1) Religious people believe that the war is cosmic in nature. Therefore the war determines the identity of each human being who lives in the world. Faced with that war, everybody has to choose which force s/he belongs to; the good or the evil one. The war, in turn, determines one's dignity, and, as such, it is directly related to her/his basic need. For this reason one is willing to die and to kill to win the war, because winning is the ultimate sign that one is on the right side.

(2) In the cosmic war it is believed that what is at stake is one's own eternal life. Therefore people are willing to do just about anything to win the war. The bet is way too expensive to be taken lightly.

(3) The war is also believed to be completely finished only at the end of time. Thus as long as the world still moves on, all human beings still have to engage in that war.

When religious people buy into this idea of cosmic war, they naturally see themselves as belonging to the good force that God himself leads. It is just a matter of time before they point fingers arbitrarily at other group(s) of people as belonging to the evil force that must be fought against and even abolished. Violence naturally follows.

Consequently, the more that religious people realize the war will not be over soon, the stronger the drive within them will be to believe that they are indeed living in a cosmic war that has to be won.

Unfortunately, such an idea of cosmic war is being preached over and over again in religious precincts. This idea has influened religious people one way or the other to keep the tension between different religious groups. The idea of cosmic war can easily motivate any religious group to believe that its group represents the good force on earth that has to terminate other religious groups. The tension becomes more problematic when the religious group believes that God is on its side and therefore sees other religious groups as God's enemies.

The problem of religious extremism is further enhanced when religious people choose a *violent sacred narrative* to guide their lives. We need to understand that in such contexts lives always correlate with a decisive story that displays the virtues by which persons live. Furthermore the story is found in a community that claims one's life in a more fundamental fashion than any other institution or profession can claim.[9] Thus the difference between Confucian ethics or Islamic ethics and Christian ethics is not primarily that each prescribes different precepts but that each is based on a different narrative.[10] "One could change the story and thereby change the rule."[11]

In this light, any religious group plays an important role as a hermeneutic community within which members of the group are helped to discover the "central metaphors"[12] through which they see reality and upon which moral precepts, religious and non-religious alike, are arranged, explicated, analyzed, and interpreted. Such a narrative shows the true nature of God, human existence, and the world. Its intrinsic values necessarily connect one to the transcendent and show how morality should be shaped for the human life project because they indicate what really counts for human life.[13] Any religious injunction in this sense is not only information about a religious value. In a fundamental way it also tells about what counts for that respected value.[14] It provides basic convictions that are decisive, normative, and ultimate since they help one to see reality "under the mode of the divine."[15]

The problem emerges when the central metaphors through which a group of people see, understand, and interpret reality are violent ones. Such metaphors will provide justification for these religious people to use violence to terminate other groups of people.

CHRISTIAN MISSION AS RECONCILIATION

We have seen that human aggression is often rooted in the condition of alienation. This alienation brings a twofold dynamic: the longing for solidarity with those who experience the same fate and aggression toward those whom are perceived to have alienated them. This condition of alienation becomes very dangerous when it is experienced by people trapped in religious extremism. It can be very destructive indeed, especially when the respective religious group is so influenced by religious romanticism, the religious cosmic war idea, and a violent, religious narrative. Amid such a problem Christian mission has to be done as reconciliation that includes both reconciliation between God and human beings as well as reconciliation between people of different religions. But how can we do that?

In my article "Recognizing the Other's Insecurity: Experiences of Christian-Moslem Relations in Indonesia" (in *At Peace and Unafraid: Public Order, Security, and the Wisdom of the Cross*), I pointed out that it is crucial for Christians to validate the other's interest to understand why some people behave as they do.[16] This is the first step toward peace and reconciliation between Christians and other religious groups, especially amid the religious extremism elaborated above.

Let us take an example. Suppose we are Moslems who live in Indonesia. We compose the majority religious group in Indonesia. Our number is even bigger than the number of all Moslems in the Middle East combined. Yet, the data from the Department of Religion about the increase of the number of religious buildings shows that the number of mosques increased by only 64% in the last 27 years, compared to 131% for Protestant churches and 152% for Catholic churches in the same period.

Religion	1977	2004	% Increase
Islam	392,044	643,834	64.22
Protestantism	18,977	43,909	131.38
Catholicism	4,934	12,473	152.80
Hinduism	4,247	24,431	475.25
Buddhism	1,523	7,129	368.09
T o t a l	421,725	731,776	238.35

Sources: The Jogjakarta Regional Office of the Department of Religion. The data have been verified by Director General of Islamic Society Guidance and the Hajj . . . (penyelenggaraan), Director General of Christian Society Guidance, Director General of Catholic Society Guidance, and Director General of Hindus and Buddhist Society Guidance (March 1 and 7, 2005; April 18, 2006).

How do we feel when we see such figures? Are we not feeling threatened? Are we not anxiously thinking of the danger that one day we will be marginalized, that one day we will become minority? Is it not troublesome when we see that the number of churches in our city, both Protestant and Catholic, has more than doubled in the last three decades? It is true that the total number of mosques still far exceeds the total number of all other religious buildings combined, but the popping up of churches almost everywhere in Indonesia certainly creates great anxiety among Moslems. Therefore validating their interest and anxiety becomes crucial. Unless we take such anxiety into account when we talk about and engage in Christian mission, we will never establish peaceful relationships with Moslems.

Doing such a mission, however, presupposes certain qualities as requirements. Three of those qualities are worth mentioning here, namely, vulnerability, humility, and hope.[17]

Vulnerability is a virtue I define as the willingness to be open and wounded. We have to realize every human relationship is an open one. As such, there is always a possibility of conflict in that relationship, even in a very intimate one. No one can guarantee that any given relationship will end happily. We may end up by being happy. But we may also end up by being hurt and wounded. The crucial question in human relationships is not whether we can avoid conflict. No one can do that. The real issue we have to deal with is how we can solve and transform conflict when it arises and whether we are willing to take risks with one another when we do get hurt.[18] That is the nature of human relationship, and that is why we need the virtue of vulnerability.

Now if religious extremism is a combination of a longing for intimacy and religion-based violence, then Christian mission has to aim toward the creation of peaceful, affectionate, and empathetic relationships with those alienated people. In such mission we need to show our sincere desire to embrace and befriend them, to redeem their feeling of loneliness; and we need to show we are not in any way posing a threat to them. But to embrace the alienated, we have to make ourselves vulnerable. We have to first open our arms so that we can make space for these people. Yet it is precisely because we open our arms that we become vulnerable. Without vulnerability we will never be able to embrace people of other faiths, let alone those alienated people disillusioned by religious romanticism, distorted by the cosmic war idea, and motivated by a violent narrative.

To be vulnerable, however, we need to *empty* ourselves, especially from power of any kind. Reconciliation with people of other faiths can never happen when we are busy protecting, keeping, and fulfilling our power.[19] This kind of self emptying practice is what apostle Paul said about Jesus Christ in Philippians 2:5-8:

> Let the same mind be in you that was in Christ Jesus, who, though he was in the form of God, did not regard equality with God as something to be exploited, but emptied himself, taking the form of a slave, being born in human likeness. And being found in human form, he humbled himself and became obedient to the point of death—even death on a cross.[20]

It is precisely through the recognition of our vulnerability that we are able to share our life with others in the deepest sense, whereby we affect as well as are affected by others. It is such a vulnerability that has been demonstrated by Jesus.

> [Jesus] taught us that the way to salvation lies through vulnerability. So it is that when he was alive he walked vulnerably among Romans and tax collectors and other unfitting characters (which included women in his sexist culture), among outcasts and foreigners, Canaanites and Samaritans, among the diseased, the demoniacs, and lepers, and infectious. And when the time came that he should die, he vulnerably submitted himself to the killing wounds of the entrenched Establishment of his day.[21]

Humility is a virtue by which we acknowledge the truth of others while at the same time we realize that we are not the sole holders of truth. Related to faith, the virtue of humility enables us to understand that none of us is able to see the whole truth of God, let alone to see the whole of it simultaneously at the same time. God's truth is always bigger than we have yet seen, and ultimately we cannot see it without the other. While it is true that God's truth (ontology) is unlimited and absolute, our understanding of that truth (epistemology) is always relative, subjectively and culturally constructed, and thus limited. Therefore we simply cannot and should not impose our perspective about God's truth upon others and force them to comply with it.

Furthermore, we need to remember that the nature of religious language is that it is always a confessional language. And confessional language is none other than love language, which is very subjective. When I say that my mother is the best mother in the whole world, I am using confessional language based on my experience with my mother. It is love language. As such, it is true for me, not an illusion.

That confession, however, does not squarely mean that other mothers in the world are simply not good. The confession that I make about my mother is a subjective one. I may share with other people about what the good mother is based on my experience with my mother, but I cannot judge from the outset that the other mothers are simply bad.

Of course, we cannot simply apply this metaphor to our understanding of God and our relation with him as if there were many gods in the universe and each religious group adheres one of them. I just want to say that confessional language is always a love language that is subjective. Therefore I can only engage in sharing with people of other faiths if I humble myself.

This does not mean, however, that we have to simply give up our perspective and submit ourselves to others. Both attitudes are destructive because we either oppress others (forcing) or we oppress ourselves (giving up). What we should do is to collaborate with others in humility. We need to remember God has called us to the biblical virtue of forbearance: "[Love] bears all things, believes all things, hopes all things, endures all things" (1 Cor. 13:7).

The Greek word *hupomon* in this verse carries a very rich meaning. It refers to a virtue that enables us not only to forebear the difficulties but even to transform the difficulties into joy. It is such humility that will enable us to walk with people of other faiths, even the radical ones, in the search for transformation. Perhaps we do not see any immediate concrete solution to the problem of relationships between different religious groups before us, yet we are willing to walk with the others and share the pain. We do not give up on them, just like Jesus never gives up on us. This kind of attitude can win the hearts of those alienated.

Hope is a virtue that enables us to believe that God is at work making peace and reconciliation, even amid difficult tensions between Christians and other religious groups. We also believe that God has a vision for the church and the world that is bigger and more profound than we can imagine. So we do not give up to despair; neither do we surrender to cynicism. We do not revert to violence, including verbal violence by which demean other religious groups, thinking all other ways to transform tense relations between Christians and other religious groups into peaceful relations are useless.

Violence is actually a form of self-justification by which we give meaning to human life. After all, our mission as Christians is not primarily to bring solutions to the world's problems but to bring hope for redemption. We believe that Jesus is Lord of all, and that his lordship can express itself in surprising ways—and in the most unlikely of places. We believe that the Holy Spirit is at work and that all kinds of creativity can break loose—if we pray trustingly and if we vulnerably open ourselves to the Spirit's work.

Hope is a crucial virtue because many people, even religious people, quite often come to believe violence is something so engrafted in human life that we can do nothing to prevent it, let alone to stop it. Many of them are hopeless and powerless when they see the reality of violence in the world. In their opinion, human beings seem to have been destined to fight against each other and there is nothing we can do to change this destiny. *Que sera sera*, whatever will be will be. It is related to this matter that we need to cultivate the power of imagination that is based on hope.

We have seen before that one of the dangers related to religious extremism is romanticism. To overcome the problem of romanticism we need to bring imagination into our mission. While romanticism tends to look backward, imagination invites us to look forward. The intention is not to relive past history but to construct a future where people from different religious groups can live side by side without terminating each other.

EPILOGUE

Brian McLaren,[22] during the Billy Graham Center 2004 Evangelism Roundtable, correctly warned that churches today need a radical rethinking in regard to our understanding and practice of evangelism. He proposed five points:

(1) We have to admit that we may not actually understand the good news and that we therefore need to rediscover it. We need to understand that the gospel is not first of all "information on how one goes to heaven after death . . . but rather a vision of what life can be in *all* its dimensions." The Christian gospel is a way of life to bring that vision into reality. The battle line is thus "between salvation beyond history from hell by grace versus salvation within history from sin by grace—with *sin* including both personal and social dimensions."

(2) We have to redefine what a disciple is, bearing in mind that evangelism is not about recruiting refugees from earth to heaven,

but recruiting revolutionaries who are willing to compassionately "bring the good and healing will of heaven to earth in all its crises."

(3) We have to do good works. We need more Christians who move, not away from, but into the world to love their neighbors. The great commission has to be carried out hand in hand with the Great Commandment. There was a time in history when one could only become Christian because one actually *knew* a Christian. That was the only evidence of the gospel that people of the world could see.

(4) We have to decrease the amount of time spent on church attendance and work more to deploy Christians into communities and neighborhoods. Christians need to spend less time in the church and more time in the world to interact lovingly with their neighbors.

(5) We have to start new "hives" of Christianity, which is more honoring and receiving than protesting and rejecting other models of living as the church. These new hives will focus on spreading the good news about God who has sent his Son to save the world, not to condemn it, and promoting individual transformation through spiritual practices to be a transforming community.

When we look at the Bible, we will find this idea at work in the stories of Jesus' table fellowship, especially with those considered outcasts and sinners. Through his table fellowship Jesus has demonstrated that he is willing to embrace the outcasts and sinners and turn human statuses and roles upside down. Unlike the Pharisees, he makes clear that the kingdom is an inclusive community where there is "open commensality"[23] that includes people who are considered outcasts and sinners. Jesus has demonstrated that the invitation to the messianic banquet that symbolizes the New Age brought in him is unrestrained. Everyone is invited regardless of social standing and religious labeling. There is no social ostracism that can hinder God from extending his favor. No one is excluded at the outset. Jesus' table fellowship is no less than divine revelation to the outcasts and sinners that God has accepted them. Jesus has demonstrated that salvation is achieved through association, not segregation.

In his table fellowship, Jesus embraced outcasts and sinners before inviting their unity with him, not the other way around. Unlike the Pharisees who demand that everybody be alike first before they can embrace others, Jesus embraces the outcasts and the sinners even when they are still sinners and before they make any commitment to him. Jesus' "*will to embrace* precedes any 'truth' about others and any construction of their 'justice.' This will is absolutely indiscriminate and strictly immutable; it transcends the moral mapping of the social world into 'good' and 'evil'."[24] Jesus' table fellowship thus manifests a "cultural protest" that is concerned not with a temporary yielding of the existing norms but with a total transformation of the norms.[25]

Jesus has demonstrated that in him the Messiah has indeed come and the New Age has indeed broken in. The kingdom that humankind is longing for is no longer a future hope. It has become a present reality. There is now a new life, a whole new world where Christians and other religious groups can embrace each other and live together in peace and joy. May we all not only sing out the hymn of peace but also live it out in our lives, "Let there be peace on earth, and let it begin with me."

NOTES

1. I intentionally use the term *religion* in order to distinguish it from "faith" or "spirituality." While different faiths or spiritualities may not necessarily create tensions between people of different faiths/spiritualities, religion is something else. Religion is institutionalized faith/spirituality. As such it almost always creates tension between people of different religions; because when people speak about institution they will inevitably speak about who has the authority to determine which is the right interpretation of a sacred text. They speak about who can be in and who should be out, that is, about membership. They also speak about budget, fund raising, and so forth, that is, about money. All these tend to create tension between people of different religions.

2. As mentioned in Seyom Brown, *The Causes and Prevention of War*, 2nd. ed. (New York: St. Martin's Press, 1994), 12.

3. Brown, 12.

4. Max Abrahms, "What Terrorists Really Want: Terrorist Motives and Counterterrorism Strategy," *International Security* 32.4 (Spring 2008): 78-105.

5. Abrahms, 94.

6. Laurence R. Iannaccone and Eli Berman, "Religious Extremism: The Good, the Bad, and the Deadly," *Public Choice* (2006), 109-129.

7. Hector Avalos, "Previous Theories of Religious Violence," in *Fighting Words: The Origins of Religious Violence* (Amherst, N.Y. Prometheus Books, 2005), 75-86.

8. Mark Juergensmeyer, *Terror in The Mind of God: The Global Rise of Religious Violence* (University of California Press, 2000), 145-163.

9. Stanley Hauerwas, *A Community of Character: Toward a Constructive Christian Social Ethics* (Notre Dame: University of Notre Dame Press, 1981), 125-127, 151; Harry Huebner, "A Community of Virtues," in *Church As Parable: Whatever Happened to Ethics?* ed. Harry Huebner and David Schroeder (Winnipeg, Man.: CMBC Publications, 1993), 177.

10. Stanley Hauerwas, *Vision and Virtue: Essays in Christian Ethical Reflection* (Notre Dame: Fides Publishers, 1974), 71-72; see also James Wm. McClendon Jr., *Systematic Theology: Ethics, Volume I* (Nashville, Tenn.: Abingdon Press, 1986), 171-172.

11. Hauerwas, *Vision*, 88.

12. The term *central metaphors* comes from Hauerwas, *Vision*, 29.

13. Robert Bellah, Richard Madsen, William M. Sullivan, Ann Swidler, and Steven M. Tipton, eds., *Habits of the Heart: Individualism and Commitment in American Life*, First California paperback edition (Berkeley: University of California Press, 1996), ix; Hauerwas, *Vision*, 1, 27-29, 30-31; *Community*, 91.

14. Hauerwas, *Vision*, 29.

15. Hauerwas, *Vision*, 46.

16. For a complete elaboration of this issue, see Paulus S. Widjaja, "Recognizing the Other's Insecurity: Experiences of Christian-Moslem Relations in Indonesia," in *At Peace and Unafraid: Public Order, Security, and the Wisdom of the Cross*, ed. Duane K. Friesen and Gerald W. Schlabach (Scottdale, Pa. and Waterloo, Ont.: Herald Press, 2005), 261-274.

17. For detailed elaboration of these virtues and some more others see Alan Kreider, Eleanor Kreider, and Paulus S. Widjaja, *A Culture of Peace: God's Vision for the Church* (Intercourse, Pa.: Good Books, 2005), 69-94.

18. Ron Kraybill, "The Cycle of Reconciliation," in *MCS Mediation and Facilitation Training Manual*, 4th. ed.

19. In my article "Recognizing the Other's Insecurity" (see Kreider, Kreider, and Widjaja, 2005), I have shown some examples of power cultivation done by some groups of Christians in Indonesia that can easily be perceived as posing a threat to other religious groups.

20. It is very interesting to see that all major religions in the world know and even encourage such self-emptying practices. Thus, while Christians believe in *kenosis*, Moslems believe in *jihad*, Hindus believe in *ahimsa*, and Buddhists believe in *tapa*.

21. M. Scott Peck, *The Different Drum: Community Making and Peace*, Touchtone Books, 2nd. Touchtone ed. (New York: Simon and Schuster, 1998), 227, cf. 231.

22. Brian McLaren, "A Radical Rethinking of Our Evangelistic Strategy," *Theology, News and Notes* (Fall 2004): 4-6, 22.

23. Marcus J. Borg, *Jesus In Contemporary Scholarship* (Valley Forge, Pa.: Trinity Press International, 1994), 109-111.

24. Miroslav Volf, *Exclusion and Embrace: A Theological Exploration of Identity, Otherness, and Reconciliation* (Nashville, Tennessee: Abingdon Press, 1996), 29.

25. Marcus J. Borg, *Conflict, Holiness and Politics in The Teachings of Jesus*, Studies in the Bible and Early Christianity, vol. 5 (New York: Edwin Mellen, 1984), 75-78, 123; Bruce Chilton, *A Feast of Meanings: Eucharistic Theologies from Jesus through Johannine Circles*, Supplements to Novum Testamentum, vol. LXXII (Leiden: E. J. Brill, 1994), 29.

Part V
POVERTY

Chapter 12

POVERTY IN INDIA

Ashok Solanky

EXPLOITATION

I would like to tell you something about poverty in India, a nation primarily dependent on agriculture. Most farmers are very poor. There are two types of farmers—big farmers and very small farmers. The small farmers toil away in the hope of good harvest but they do not receive the profits or other monies needed to sell their produce. The traders take the lion's share of the profits. Hence without just returns these small farmers stay poor. Many of the rich farmers have used violence to protect their profits and have even tried to kill small farmers. These rich farmers also grab the land of poor people, whose lack of awareness leads them to believe that their thumbprints placed on legal documents will protect them. It does not. This is a contributing factor to poverty in India. What India needs a new approach, or else the same patterns followed by previous generations will continue.

LACK OF EDUCATION AND UNEMPLOYMENT

Poverty and unemployment in certain parts of India is largely the result of a lack of education, and without money the poor are unable to get proper education. As they continue to live in very bad conditions, they are unaware that different and better possibilities exist. It is the youth who lack employment because they don't have a good education. And because of this they have to work as laborers, working hard for up to sixty or seventy rupees a day. This is the poverty trap.

LIMITED ASSISTANCE SYSTEMS

The financial institutions are such that they are unable to reach the rural or religious areas where their presence is most needed. The government and financial institutions have programs for the poor, but farmers and laborers are generally unaware of them simply because they lack education and the know-how to gather the right information. But slowly, slowly, these people are gaining in awareness about such programs.

TRADITIONAL SOCIAL PATTERNS

However, the social structure prevents helpful programs from reaching rural people and so these poor people are unable to fulfill their responsibilities toward their families. This means that the young are always thinking about migrating to other areas to get money for their families. This is always on their mind. And if they don't do that then they tend to fall into violence. In some parts of India these people have taken up weapons to fight injustice and poverty. They have been doing this for quite a while. In one incident they shot at twenty-one police officers. So, what can we do as a church to uplift these poor people?

What does the Bible say? Let me cite Mathew 25: 35- 40:

> "For I was hungry and you gave me food, I was thirsty and you gave me something to drink, I was a stranger and you welcomed me, I was naked and you gave me clothing, I was sick and you took care of me, I was in prison and you visited me. Then the righteous will answer him, 'Lord, when was it that we saw we you hungry and gave you food, or thirsty and gave you something to drink? And when was it that we saw you a stranger and welcomed you, or naked and gave you clothing? And when was it that we saw you sick or in prison and visited you? And the king will answer them, 'Truly I tell you, just as you did it to one of the least of these who are members of my family, you did it to me."

What we are discussing here is economic poverty. However, it is not because we lack money that we are poor. The Bible says that human beings need food, clothes to wear, and a house in which to live. But the Bible above all teaches us about *love*. And service cannot be done without love. Mathew 25:40 says that just as you have helped the very lowest in society, you have thereby also done it to me.

Let me tell you a story about Dr. Rev. Wilbur B. Stover who came to us in 1894 as a missionary. On an old building in Bulsar he hoisted a banner in Gujarati saying "God is love." This attracted to him people who asked him to explain the meaning of this sentence. In 1896 there was a huge famine in our state, and he showed God's love to thousands of people by helping them to find food and clothing. He helped them dig ponds, educated them, and gave them vocational training. Learning from him, we developed similar programs to help the poor. Mathew 22:35-39 says that love of God is first. Then we love our neighbors as ourselves, and then we also love our enemies. This love will bring us together and it will help us combat poverty. We read similar things in the Old Testament. We need the blessings of the Lord effectively to bring hope to the people. The Lord Jesus Christ says that you show your love by your actions.

I met a Brahman who, despite being upper caste, worked as a janitor cleaning toilets for a measly 3,500 rupees a month. This man held a masters degree but was unable to find work without bribing government officials. This is how the social structure in our society discriminates against the poor. Unless the entire social structure is changed or improved, this situation will continue.

So we need to give hope to the poor just like the Protestant and Catholic missionaries who established many schools in India. Eight years ago I went to a wedding in a poor area where many of the houses were made of mud and bamboo. Here I met a young man who told me that he was neither Hindu nor Christian, but he intended to become a Christian because he had become a government official. Puzzled, I asked him to explain. He said if the missionaries had not established schools in his village, he would have been unable to receive the education that eventually led to his present work and ability to build a house. He said because of this he and others from the bottom of the social structure have been able to match the income of the upper classes. If it were not for the missionaries, he would still be downtrodden and poor.

This is how God gives this responsibility to the church. You will find that wherever a church has been planted, missionaries have established schools and hospitals. This is true for all India. These services have uplifted downtrodden people. The early missionaries simply followed the teachings of Christ. As Christians, we should also follow their example particularly through education and medical institutions for the betterment of society. The Church of the Brethren accepts this philosophy, and my church in Bulsar helps the poor both financially and spiritually.

While we are not equipped to work directly with the poor, we make donations to all those institutions that do. For instance, there are orphaned and blind children in a nearby center, together with an association for the blind in Madras and the Every Home Crusade. We make financial contributions to programs of churches that preach the gospel. Not only do we help them economically, but we uplift their spirits and thus bring the gospel of Christ to them. We have several rural churches in communion with our own, so we like to help those congregations that are poor. We also help the poor churches by distributing notebooks for their schools. And for those poor people even within our own church, widows for instance, we provide financial help, parcels of food, and gifts at Christmas.

So, the first thing we need to as a church is to abolish poverty within our own communities. Unless we deal with the poverty that exists within our own churches, we won't be a real church. We start with our own churches and gradually reach out into the surrounding community, the region, the whole country, and then the world. Sometimes when we enjoy good salaries, we tend to spend most of it on ourselves for worldly enjoyments, and perhaps we fall into debt. Therefore, we should work within our limits, even those of us who are quite well off. It sets a good example and keeps us from also falling into poverty. We know of many instances where families have become impoverished in this way.

These are my thoughts, and they have been inspired by the Bible. There is hope for everyone in the Bible. The Lord said that he would always be there for us even if we are economically poor. And if we lead our lives by following the Bible, by having complete faith in it, we will have the blessing of the Lord. We should all live with the fear and teachings of God.

QUESTIONS AND COMMENTS

Quaker from Australia

I was glad to hear our friend talk about cooperation between the different churches in India in working to combat poverty. I think one of the things that needs emphasizing is the effect of globalization and multi-national corporations that are doing their *best* to keep people in poverty while concentrating on their profits. For example, Monsanto and its control of the seed bank in India in particular. I met Indian farmers many years ago who were campaigning against Monsanto, and I know they had a big up-hill battle.

I would also like to mention the secular non-government organizations. It's not only Christians who are doing something about poverty globally. For example, organizations like the Hunger Project and Oxfam do amazing work in a non-Christian or a non-church way. I hope we will work cooperatively with them, too, because they have considerable resources and come from a deep place of humanitarian concern for people everywhere. The Bible is not our only source for this work, although I appreciate that such a statement might upset some people.

One of the things I would like to mention, and I think it would help other people to hear me say this, is the role of women. The Grameen Bank is a good example. Its founder, Muhammad Yunus, won the Nobel Peace Prize in 2006 for its low-cost financial assistance to people. It has had a considerable effect. I'm sure it's very hard to get news of such a program out to villages, as our friend said, but the bank continues to do exactly that.

However, the role of women is another thing. If they are taught to read, how much more can they change things, from the grassroots up? I support an organization called the International Women's Development Agency which organizes programs for women only. I think its approach is utterly essential, and I would be interested in hearing responses to the question of women's literacy.

Ashok Solanky

That bank is found in Bangladesh. It created a model for providing micro credit to very poor people at the worst levels of society so that recipients of cash loans can set up their own small enterprises. There are some in India working on a similar project. Concerning women: In Gujarat we have an organization called Self-Employed Women's Association (SEWA) that works with women and helps them acquire loans. They've set up a cooperative bank which provides credit to women only to support businesses like handicrafts.

Quaker from India

I'm grateful to the friend who spoke about the poverty in India and the lack of awareness of village people. But there are *so* many reasons for the poverty. First, population growth—that is a crucial factor! Since my childhood, I have seen lots of improvement throughout India. Previously, I used to ride a bicycle. Now I have a scooter. My son has a motorcycle. In my house, I have many modern appliances. Forty or fifty years ago they didn't exist. So population, illiteracy, corruption—these are also reasons for the poverty.

Mennonite from WCC staff in Switzerland

I agree that population is a very big contributing factor toward poverty in India. I'd like to add one comment regarding women. It is proven that women are better agents in overcoming poverty than men. I just want to highlight that! Women are *crucial* to overcoming poverty. However, I wish to refer to my presentation in which I mentioned the increase in suicide in the global south among women, especially in India. The increase is directly linked to acute poverty in rural areas. I would like to hear some more about that.

We've often said over the past ten to twenty years that we need to move from charity to policymaking. Charity may be good but not enough. I mean, you don't give a fish to a poor man or family; you teach them how to fish instead. It occurred to me that you were reaffirming the role of charity.

Ashok Solanky

We have vocational training courses for people, a vocational training college that was established in 1924, which also gives vocational guidance. The training fosters awareness about how tools can help people earn their living. That is what is important! I meant to say that we are not seeking charity but education, awareness, and tools to alleviate the social position of the poor instead.

Quaker from Australia

Hansulrich was asking about women and suicide and suicide related to poverty. Can you comment on that?

Ashok Solanky

There have been several incidences of suicide in Gujarat. I will tell you about an incident that happened recently. In a city just 100 km away from our town, a businessman in real financial difficulty killed himself after poisoning his wife and daughter. There are incidences where women burn themselves or they lie on the railroad tracks because they believe they can no longer provide for their families. It's a big issue in Gujarat. In another state some 400-450 farmers committed suicide last year in one place alone. Suicide is a very big issue in India because even after farmers get loans from the government institutions for their lands, they are unable to pay back the money because they can't meet their basic expenses. They constantly run at a loss, and when they can't repay the money, then they commit suicide. So it's not just about lending credit but the whole social and economic structure.

Speaker from India

With women the biggest reason for poverty is the dowry system. In India, the parents of a prospective bride often cannot pay the requirements set down by the groom's family.

Ashok Solanky

The dowry is a major factor in female suicide. The usual manner of death is self-burning, and even in-laws are sometimes responsible for burning the women who don't bring in the money the in-laws have been asking for. There are severe strict penalties for people who indulge in the dowry system. In India today, if a woman complains about her prospective in-laws demanding a dowry, the police jail the in-laws and the case will be registered for a court hearing. I have no statistics showing whether this has contributed to reducing dowry debts. But there is a negative aspect to this, too—women can use situations such as this to blackmail their in-laws. So it remains an issue.

Quaker from Britain

What does the *church* do about dowries? Is there not power in refusing to marry people if they demand a dowry? I also wonder what else the church is doing to improve the position of women.

Ashok Solanky

As a church, whether the Church of the Brethren or otherwise, we do not have the problem of dowries. Maybe the problem is relevant to some churches in south or in north India, where they still have the dowry system. In Gujarat the dowry is not a problem for us.

Speaker from India

I come from Hyderabad in the south of India, where the dowry system is very strong. But let me give you the positive side of the dowry. I come from a family of eight—five brothers and three sisters.

We had some property which my dad divided among his sons. Nothing was given to the girls. Is this justice or injustice? It is injustice. This is exactly what the dowry entails. Often it is misused and people exaggerate its effects. In southern India, parents want to give equal shares to all their children. Probably the land is more important in India. Somehow they don't want to give property to the girls. So instead of giving property, parents compensate the girls with money. That is the origin of the dowry. But you know, we are sinners; and we can exploit the situation however good it can be. As we have just heard, there are some cases where the groom exploits the situation and demands more.

With regard to suicide, in my state we have many suicides. Let me tell you the reason for this. Our annual rainfall has fallen to below average, nor do we have many canals or dams to help cultivation. We depend on seasonal rains. Now, people have become very greedy. They want to earn a lot of money. Instead of raising or producing the traditional crops, they want to raise cash crops and especially cotton, which is lucrative. The traditional beans, millet, and other foodstuffs are rejected because they are not lucrative. Cash crops like cotton mean investing a lot of *money* and receiving ample *rain*. But nature is not always cooperative. When there is little rain, naturally the crops dry up. Debts accumulate, leading some to commit suicide. I ask people, "Why do you grow so many expensive crops? Why don't you go for something like Castor beans that don't need much water, pesticides, or manure?" I think one of the main causes of suicide is greediness, which even the Bible says leads to debt.

Speaker from India

The dowry has been around for hundreds of years and, as the brother has just said, it may have provided something for daughters. But whenever the dowry is seen as a right or a gift, it has been misused more often than not. In fact, it has *always* been misused, and the women are the victims. I would like to give an example of how even educated people can act in ways beyond our comprehension. This is the story of a Christian family from India. This man from a well-educated family married a girl from a similar family. His family demanded a dowry from the wife. He was assigned to a position in another country, so he and his wife both moved there. He also invited his family to come to that country with them.

When his family arrived, they demanded a dowry from her. She made desperate phone calls to her parents for money, saying, "If you don't give me money, I'll be in trouble." Her parents were unable to do anything about it, and so the groom's family turned on this girl. Traveling on a motorway one day, they threw her out of the car traveling at eighty miles per hour and left her on the road. She suffered multiple injuries to her head, back, and shoulders. Someone spotted her and called for medical help; she was taken to hospital. As soon as they learned of her condition, her parents came to be with her. At first, she was traumatized to the point that she was unable to speak and thus could not tell her story. After a month and a half she was finally able to tell her parents. This is the ugly face of the dowry system. I don't think we need to justify dowries. They create far more ill than good.

Speaker from India

I want to tell you about my personal experience with the dowry. When the marriage of my daughter was fixed, I called my son-in-law-to-be. I told him, if you ask for a dowry, this marriage is canceled. Then I called the parents and his uncles after we settled the marriage. In front of all the people I asked, "What is your requirement?" My son-in-law suddenly said, "Nothing, nothing!" And then I didn't hear any more about a dowry.

Quaker from Aotearoa/New Zealand

I want to share two examples of cooperation in the economic field. Our Quaker office at the United Nations in Geneva has a program that involves the World Trade Organization and collaborates with delegations from those countries without money for resources. The non-governmental organizations and government delegations from many such countries can't afford legal and technical help. If you know of issues within your own countries that are coming before the World Trade Organization, and you would like to collaborate to prevent the power of multi-national organizations to take away rights, for instance to intellectual property, or to enforce economic measures that are not good for your country, then do make contact with the Quaker organization in Geneva. There is a possibility for collaboration between developed and developing countries.

The other example is an ecumenical organization called Oikocredit (www.oikocredit.org.uk). It started in Europe and churches there are able to ethically invest money for churches in developing countries. Your money counts as shares. It brings you dividends which you can then return to the organization. The organization works with partners who practice microcredit and grass-root development in many countries. While it's a church-founded organization, it's open to everybody. The partners that do grassroots development may be religious or non-religious. Our national Quaker body in Aotearoa/New Zealand puts money into the organization every year. I'm proud that some of our money is there, making a difference at the grassroots level. And because Oikocredit is quite large, it can afford the infrastructure to support the grassroots. So, as I see it, we can have a kind of *creative* globalization that works *with* people, instead of corporate globalization that works against most people for the benefit of the few.

Quaker from Australia

I'm aware that we're talking about poverty and that it's a huge problem. But I'm not sure how we can talk about poverty without talking about affluence. It's a problem as well. I'm very aware that I need *your* help, my sisters and brothers in the developing world, about how *I* may repent because I am captured by prosperity. There's a desperate need for me in the first world to practice jubilee, to move away from charity, where I merely feel good about being "nice" to people who are suffering. I need to move to solidarity with people where we're aware of the principalities and powers that keep *me* captive to a dream that is other than God's dream of creation. It's an entrapment that comes at the cost of God's good earth and the poor around the world. Do you have any ideas how you may help people like me to repent?

Ashok Solanky

What as rich people can we do? The first thing is to see to our own basic needs. Whatever is left over should go to help those who really are in need. Make that point clear to those affluent persons who live close to you.

Chapter 13

THEME: POVERTY IN ASIA

Group Discussion Editorial Summary

Editor's note: The following is an editorial summary of a group discussion about poverty in Asia in relation to conflict and violence.

THE PEACE CHURCHES have a tradition of simple living. A simple lifestyle is more than a nonviolent lifestyle—but what does this mean in our own situation? What does it mean in this time and place for each of us here? We come from different countries. We come from different situations. Some of us are urban and some rural. What does it mean to live a simple lifestyle in Asia? What are the obstacles we face in living the simple lifestyle? How does a simple lifestyle relate to overcoming poverty? What do we mean by poverty?

Poverty can be considered from both the vantage point of spiritual poverty of our minds and also economic poverty of our communities. Poverty is not only a problem for individual persons; it is also a structural problem involving economic and political practices. If we understand poverty in economic terms, it refers to persons who do not have access to clean drinking water, medical care, sanitation, education, and who live in depravity. The main causes of poverty in developing world countries are overpopulation and unemployment, which in turn cause shortage of food and lack of basic amenities like sanitation, health facilities, and education.

Such considerations lead to concerns about charity, which is a matter of simply providing food or other provisions. Real help goes beyond charity. Often charity is given when there are natural disasters, such as floods or tsunamis. It is also given as aid for refugees or in the times of immediate need. There are ways in which charity can be given for long-term development to promote education and aware- ness so that people can learn to live independent of such assistance.

Charity is a part of the social structures in India that promote beg- ging. There are communities that have been following the traditional ancestral roles of receiving charity, and they have been excluded from the social support they require to escape poverty. Several non-govern- mental organizations are working on this problem. In some parts of India landlords own major portions of the land, and this has pro- moted violence. These landlords are now subjected to harassment by a communist movement, and this movement is gaining momentum in south India and central India. The farmers are choosing sides, and it is a major concern for the government of India. Sometimes the state gov- ernment polarizes the people, and the farmers are often the victims

Also there are racial, cultural, and religious dimensions to poverty, which can be seen in the differences of class and caste in India. There may be similar injustices in Japanese culture. Women in India are frequently considered to be second-class citizens. Overcom- ing poverty must include women of lower status. Rural women in India often have lower status, but in urban centers their fortune has advanced. So cultural injustice must be overcome to diminish poverty.

From Antonio Gramsci's point of view, poverty is part of the struggle against the hegemony of the ruling classes, the police, and the military. Gramsci disagrees with the Marxist analysis of replacing capitalism with communism. Nevertheless, from his vantage point poverty is the result of a monopoly of economic and political domina- tion. The emerging order is one of chronic capitalism that oppresses many people. The solution is to form a capitalism that can uplift the people.

So what should we do as the Historic Peace Churches? How can we have solidarity with the poor in our pluralistic societies? Is a soli- darity of the poor a possibility? For example, can poor Christians and poor Muslims unite to combat poverty? Does poverty unite the poor, or are the poor divided by political and religious institutions? Is the interest of the wealthy to keep the poor divided by engendering con- flict? Finding a practical response is a primary issue for peace. The best way to combat poverty is not by working within relationships foreign to the poor but by forming real relationships among the poor. Is it possible for different religious groups to work together in to en- gage poverty in Asia?

We need to focus on stories of success in overcoming poverty, including stories about women. One of these success stories is common knowledge in India. Amul is the brand name of the largest distributor of milk and milk products in the world. It is a successful cooperative that was created by women contributing milk in small quantities. The amounts of their contributions could be from five liters to fifty or a hundred liters per day. This cooperative, which started as a small movement, has gained national and international recognition. Today Amul is one of the most popular brands in India, and women continue to play a vital role in supplying milk to this dairy cooperative. Amul chocolate and milk products are very popular in India. Starting out as a small initiative by rural village women, the cooperative has gained worldwide recognition.

Liche is another popular national brand that is run and managed by women. Women make pepper crispies in their homes in the rural villages, and their enterprise has brought about significant economic development for them. Amul and Liche provide two examples to focus our attention upon successful enterprises that could serve as models for others to follow.

Activists in the Philippines are working to reduce poverty by using more and more natural resources. They do not use the petroleum, but instead they use bio-products to produce energy. Removing pollutants reduces poverty. From the perspective of India and the Philippines, education is important in reducing poverty. Most developing world countries face problems of unemployment, so education is crucial. Another important step to reducing poverty is to give marketing support to the farmers. Asian farmers have so many problems because they are dependent on nature, climatic situations, and the fluctuation in the prices of what they produce. The church can lend its influence to support of markets for farmers, including cooperative market enterprises.

In India the caste tradition is no longer practiced in the Christian churches. Asians cannot stop globalization, but they need a capitalism that is shaped by morality. Let Christians work to stop the extensive use of child labor in Asia. Let Christians look back to the life of the early church in the book of Acts and consider how Christians can be a community of love, practicing the economy of love in a global economy.

Part VI
PRINCIPALITIES AND POWERS

Chapter 14

ENGAGING THE POWERS, PRINCIPALITIES, AND EMPIRE—A QUAKER PERSPECTIVE

Dale Hess

INTRODUCTION

The Quaker theologian, Walter Wink, has written a trilogy (which now runs to five parts) that explores the subjects of the domination system and engaging the powers and principalities.[1] By powers and principalities Wink means the spiritual dimensions of the social, political, economic, religious, and cultural structures that affect our lives. These include, for example, institutions, corporations, churches, organizations, ideologies, rituals, philosophies, governments, and economic systems. They have both visible or outer dimensions (e.g. buildings, personnel, equipment) and invisible or inner dimensions (e.g. spirituality, culture, collective personality) associated with them. The domination system forms when a network of powers and principalities becomes integrated around idolatrous values.

Society needs powers and principalities to function. They serve good and valuable purposes (e.g. schools, hospitals, factories). But they can also do great harm and propagate violence, poverty, hatred,

environmental destruction, war, and genocide. Because of this, the re-
bellious powers need to be identified (named and unmasked), transformed, and redeemed to reflect God's love.

We can summarize Wink's ideas in the following way:

The powers and principalities are—
- good
- fallen
- redeemable

We are called to—
- name the powers (prophetic role)
- unmask the powers (prophetic role)
- engage the powers (prophetic and priestly role)
- transform the powers (priestly role)

Quakers from their beginnings have been actively engaged with
the powers and principalities, both in prophetic and in priestly roles,
in an effort to transform them.[2] Quakerism arose in the seventeenth
century, a century later than the Anabaptists, at a time of greater pluralism.[3] There was still polarization between the church and world,
and true believers could look forward to suffering; their faith would
be tested, but not as many Quakers died of their treatment as Anabaptists. The social conversation was therefore less difficult and Quakers
became more outward looking and optimistic about the transformation than the Anabaptists. The Brethren (German Baptist Brethren)
arose in the early eighteenth century from an Anabaptist and Pietist
background and consequently took a position toward the world closer
to the Mennonites and other Anabaptists than to the Quakers.[4]

Quaker engagement with the powers, principalities, and empire
has included the struggle for religious toleration, gender equality,
penal reform, church reform, governmental reform, peace initiatives,
draft resistance, war-tax resistance, anti-slavery work, justice for Indigenous peoples, justice for refugees (e.g. the Acadians), justice for
foreigners, justice for other marginalized peoples, care for the insane,
war relief, education reform, conflict resolution, employment creation
schemes, healthcare, honesty in business, simplicity in lifestyle, and
other areas.

In this chapter I will attempt to link (1) Wink's analysis of engaging the powers, principalities, and empire; (2) theological arguments
advanced by Robert Jewett and John Shelton Lawrence that have been
used to support a culture of empire and those for a culture of earth

community; (3) a brief overview of empire from an Australian point of view; (4) a psychological analysis of the culture of empire and earth community proposed by David Korten and the social cosmology typology suggested by Robert Burrowes; (5) the need for action and the role Quaker Testimonies play in creating a life-affirming future. We are called to respond to the challenges of the powers, principalities, and empire by naming and unmasking the powers, engaging the powers, and transforming the powers, i.e. breaking the silence (prophetic witness), ending the isolation (priestly witness), and changing the story to affirm life (prophetic and priestly witness).

THEOLOGICAL BACKGROUND

Robert Jewett and John Shelton Lawrence describe two theological threads running through the Bible, both relating to the domination system.[5] One they call *Zealous Nationalism*, which says that the only way to redeem your enemies is to kill them. Wink calls this the myth of redemptive violence.[6] This thread is also associated with other myths, such as the concept of *Manifest Destiny*, which was used by the United States to justify waging war on Mexico and on Native Americans for purpose of territorial acquisition; and the *Captain America Complex*, where an everyman figure possessing superpowers uses undemocratic means to lead his country to achieve democratic ends and rid the world of supervillains.[7]

The other biblical thread is *Prophetic Realism*, which says we should relate to others, including our enemies, with love, justice, and respect.[8] This stream is most fully realized in the ministry of Jesus. He overturned the concept of *the chosen people* and welcomed the hated Samaritan; he advocated a nonviolent lifestyle.[9]

The two threads, Zealous Nationalism and Prophetic Realism, are illustrated by the following examples.

ZEALOUS NATIONALISM

- Moses: Yahweh will fight for you. Several generations later in the era of Elijah and Elisha, this becomes total war against Yahweh's presumed enemies at home and abroad.
- King Hezekiah and King Josiah revived zealous nationalism.
- In the Book of Deuteronomy the narrative is that Israel would prevail in battle if it obeyed the law. The prophetic message is blunted in Joshua, Judges, 1 and 2 Samuel, 1 and 2 Kings.

- Ezra and Nehemiah developed a narrow, nationalistic perspective. The Maccabees revolted. Daniel saw the enemy as demonic and ought to be annihilated.
- In the Book of Revelation, Prophetic Realism, including message of Jesus, is submerged within zealous images. God's Word as defined in Isaiah, as a redemptive force replacing warfare, is now transposed to an image of annihilation. The image of Jesus as the Lamb is now transposed to wrath of the Lamb. The saints prevail no matter how destructive the battle.

PROPHETIC REALISM

- Amos and Hosea countered the tradition that defined the nation as Yahweh's agency of wrath against heretics and foreigners.
- Isaiah criticized reliance on foreign alliances and sophisticated arms systems.
- Jeremiah warned of the consequences of following the course of fanatical nationalists. Isaiah voiced the concept of Suffering Servant redemption.
- Jesus rejected bringing in the messianic kingdom through violence.
- The early Quakers reinterpreted Revelation in terms of Prophetic Realism and the War of the Lamb based on nonviolence.

Under Zealous Nationalism, a rigid stereotyping of the saints and enemies develops. The saints are entirely pure and enemies are entirely corrupt, deserving of death. These views culminate in the books of Daniel and Revelation. Early Friends took a different view. They read the book of Revelation to mean engaging in the Lamb's War to transform the whole world by the Spirit, rather than carnal weapons. "The Lamb and his followers . . . wrestle not with flesh and blood which God has made, but with spiritual wickedness exalted in the hearts of men and women, where God alone should be."[10] This process begins with a personal, inner transformation of the individual to combat pride and self-will.[11] "They were changed men [and women] themselves before they went about to change others. Their hearts were ripped open as well as their garments changed, and they knew the power and work of God upon them."[12] Because of Friends' belief in the universality of the Inner Light (see the section on Testimonies below), each person has "that of God" within and therefore each life is precious. Early Friends undertook a nonviolent revolution and expected to see social and political changes. The concept of Zealous Nationalism is used to justify the system of domination and exploitation of today's empire, which is discussed in the next section.

EMPIRE TODAY

I now present a brief overview of four aspects of empire: military, human rights, economic, and environment. Other faith communities have carried out more detailed analyses of empire, including the theological bases for responding to it.[13]

Military

Today's empire is primarily, but not solely, based in Washington, D.C.. To pursue its foreign policy and economic objectives the United States has adopted a military doctrine of "full spectrum dominance" with nuclear weapons as the cornerstone of this doctrine.[14] The aim is for Global Engagement (GE), the combination of global surveillance of the Earth (see anything, anytime), worldwide missile defense, and the potential ability to apply force from space. Australia is deeply involved in this strategy by hosting the Joint Defense Facility at Pine Gap and the Australia-U.S. Joint Communications Facility at Geraldton. Both of these facilities enable the U.S. to fight wars in Asia and the Middle East. The Pine Gap Facility is part of missile defense; a system of offensive war-fighting designed to control and dominate space.[15] The Harold E. Holt Naval Communications Station at Exmouth is part of the U.S. worldwide nuclear submarine force communications network.[16]

in addition to these facilities, Australia supports the U.S. global strategy by sending troops to Iraq and Afghanistan, participating in U.S. war game exercises, e.g. Talisman Sabre and RIMPAC, and gathering joint intelligence. Australia is also involved in the four-power partnership of strategic alliance (between Australia, the United States, Japan, and India) aimed at containing China.

The militarism of the Empire has global reach. The Pentagon maintains a vast network of at least 766 military bases in 140 countries around the world to support its aspirations for hegemony.[17] Over the past three years, Australia's defense spending more than doubled to integrate Australia's defense forces within the U.S. military system and advance interoperability.[18]

Human Rights

The wars in Iraq and Afghanistan, undertaken as part of the "War on Terror," continue to inflict a horrific toll on the populations there. More than 650,000 civilians (over 2.5 percent of the population) are estimated to have died in Iraq to the end of June 2006 because of the war. A more recent survey released in September 2007 puts the number at 1.2 million Iraqis.[19] Human rights are disregarded. Legal safeguards, such as *habeas corpus*, are swept aside by anti-terrorism legislation.[20] In many countries abductions, murders, renditions, torture, and imprisonment without charge have been carried out as part of the war on terror. Airspace and ground facilities of neutral countries, e.g. Ireland, have been co-opted to fight the war in Iraq. Australia has supported the use of the detention camp at the U.S. Naval Base in Guantánamo Bay, Cuba, where hundreds of people have been held without charge with little hope of a fair trial.

The legal framework under which international relations depends has retrogressed in the war on terror. International disarmament treaties and conventions, obtained through years of difficult negotiations, have been abrogated in the pursuit of empire.

Economic

Neoliberal economic theory, known as the "Washington Consensus," underlies empire.[21] Australia supports this. Three international structures, the World Bank (WB), the International Monetary Fund (IMF), and the World Trade Organization (WTO), exert enormous global economic influence. Many developing countries are in debt and poverty due in part to the neoliberal policies of the WB and IMF, notwithstanding their stated intention of relieving poverty. Both the WB and IMF require the country receiving loans to adopt policies to structurally adjust its economy, policies that require reduced spending on health, education, and development, devaluation of the currency, decreased financial regulations to encourage foreign investment, and increased privatization.[22] The WTO draws up the rules for trade and can override environmental regulations, labor standards, and other laws it considers to be barriers to trade. Voting power in the WTO, WB, and IMF depends on the financial contribution and thus favors the rich countries; all three institutions are undemocratic.[23]

The gap between the rich and the poor widens. Access to resources becomes paramount. Oil and natural gas are key resources because they provide the energy to drive the economy and provide the ability to project military power. Hence the Middle East, Iraq, Iran, and Afghanistan become central to hegemonic strategies. But other resources are also important. Australia sells (or is planning to sell) uranium to the nuclear weapons states of China, India, and Russia in an effort to achieve short-term economic gains. Unfair trade agreements (both within the WTO structure and bilateral free trade agreements outside it) and other practices of the WB, IMF, and WTO, open up the resources of developing countries to the rich countries and erode workers' rights.

Corporations and governments of the Empire are immersed in the military-industrial complex, and economies are constructed that depend on the sales of arms.

Environment

Corporations and governments for many years have not adequately cared for the environment. Urban air pollution is currently estimated to lead to about 800,000 deaths a year and climate change to about 150,000 deaths, but as global warming increases the latter number is likely to increase to many millions.[24] The United States and Australia are the only countries that have stated that they do not intend to ratify the Kyoto Protocol to the United Nations Framework Convention on Climate Change.[25]

The World Wildlife Fund produces a report every two years that tracks the populations of 1,313 vertebrate species—fish, amphibians, reptiles, birds, mammals—from all around the world to survey the Earth's biological diversity and the health of ecosystems.[26] In the period 1970 to 2003, the Living Planet Index fell by 29 percent, indicating a dramatic deterioration in natural ecosystems. The largest impact is felt in the Tropics. The decline for tropical terrestrial species is 55 percent, for tropical freshwater species the decline is about 30 percent, and for marine species in the Indian Ocean and the Southeast Asia region the decline is greater than 50 percent.

KORTEN ON UNDERSTANDING
THE PSYCHOLOGY OF EMPIRE

David Korten in his book, *The Great Turning*, provides insights into understanding the psychology of empire based on integrating the research of many prominent specialists in the field of human development.[27] He outlines five levels of consciousness: magical, imperial, socialized, cultural, and spiritual. These levels correspond to human growth and maturation processes in Western society.

The first to third levels of consciousness correspond to the Culture of Empire, where relationships are hierarchical and are based on domination. There is a paradigm shift or pivot point in the development of consciousness which occurs in the third or socialization level. From the upper part of the third level to the fifth level, the consciousness supports a Culture of Earth Community, where relationships are based on partnership rather than domination. The move from the Culture of Empire to one of Earth Community requires expanding one's cultural horizons beyond the local group and accepting the concept of an inclusive, pluralist society. This consciousness sees diversity as a source of enrichment, of new ideas and perspectives, rather than as a threat. The highest level of consciousness is based on an integral worldview and spiritual pluralism.

First Order: Magical Consciousness

The Magical Consciousness category includes *Fantasizers* who live in an Other World and place their faith in magical protectors; they depend on external figures to make things magically right, and a sense of betrayal results when they fail to do so. Members are young children, two to six years of age, and fantasizing adults, e.g. economists who believe that markets will turn greed into public good. For them the lines between fantasy and reality are blurred.

Second Order: Imperial Consciousness

In the Impersial Consciousness stage the members are *Power Seekers* in My World who play up to the powerful; they exploit the oppressed; they believe conformity to expectations of authority figures yields rewards; they justify bad behavior with excuses. The stage begins about age seven, when the child discovers order in the world; the child identifies with superheroes, and his/her perspective is self-referential. It also includes adults, who divide the world into friends and enemies; they define good as serving their interests and evil as conflicting with their interests. Truth is defined as what they want it to be.

Third Order: Socialized Consciousness

Socialized Consciousness entails a group comprising *Good Citizens*, who live in a Small World and play by the rules of their identity group; they expect a fair reward for working hard. They include the swing voters; they have the ability to see self through the eyes of another but are unable to grasp complex systems relationships. This stage begins about age eleven and is a transition stage. Adults in this group internalize the values and social roles of the prevailing culture. This group is pivotal because it can adapt either the dominator culture or the partnership culture.

Fourth Order: Cultural Consciousness

The Cultural Consciousness class includes *Cultural Creatives*, who live in an Inclusive World and see the possibility of creating inclusive, life-affirming societies that work for the benefit of all. This stage is achieved through the capacity to question the dysfunctional cultural premises of empire and to risk rejection from the systems that demand loyalty. If sufficient maturity is reached then cultural truths of other cultures are recognized. Cultural consciousness is rarely achieved before age thirty because corporations and institutions discourage it.

Fifth Order: Spiritual Consciousness

In Spiritual Consciousness, the last category, are the *Spiritual Creatives*, who live in a complex, evolving Integral World, which they engage as evolutionary co-creators. Here members relate to diverse people and situations in search of an ever deeper understanding of life's possibilities. This includes elder statespersons, teachers, and religious sages. The members are grounded in universal principles of justice, love, and compassion. They approach conflict not as a problem to overcome but as an opportunity to learn, and they seek ways for its transformation. They promote restorative justice instead of retributive justice.

Further key considerations of Korten's approach

- It is important to recognize that fear causes a regression to a more primitive state of consciousness.
- Perfect love casts out fear (1 John 4:18).
- As noted by Albert Einstein, "No problem can be solved at the same level of consciousness that created it." (For further details, see Korten's book).[28]

THE BURROWES SOCIAL COSMOLOGY

An alternative typology to Korten's Western dynamic or evolutionary model for understanding the Culture of Empire and the Culture of Earth Community is the static or asymptotic model given by Robert J. Burrowes in his book, *The Strategy of Nonviolent Defense: A Gandhian Approach*.[29] Burrowes defines the social cosmology or culture as comprised of four components: the pattern of matter-energy use, the set of social relations embraced, the prevailing philosophy about the nature of society, and the strategies adopted for dealing with conflict. Among contrasting factors to highlight in relation to the

Culture of Empire and the Culture of Earth Community are these:

THE CULTURE OF EMPIRE

- The pattern of matter-energy use: non-renewable matter-energy use;
- The set of social relations embraced: patriarchal, capitalist, racist, and imperialist social relations;
- The prevailing philosophy about the nature of society: life is seen as competitive and material growth is valued;
- Strategies for dealing with conflict: employ laws, and police and military violence that promote the interests of elites.
- It is shaped by Zealous Nationalism.

THE CULTURE OF EARTH COMMUNITY:

- The pattern of matter-energy use: renewable matter-energy use;
- The set of social relations embraced: non-hierarchical society and highly participatory;
- The prevailing philosophy about the nature of society: all life is considered sacred; there is a spiritual and physical connection to the Earth; diversity is valued;
- Strategies for dealing with conflict: laws are egalitarian and conflict is resolved through cooperation and consensus;[30]
- It is shaped by Prophetic Realism.

We stand at an important juncture in history. Empire and the global domination system have created a number of life-threatening problems. These include—

- Peak oil (the availability of cheap energy and transport is coming to an end because oil reserves are being exhausted);
- Climate change (which will bring droughts, floods, landslides, bushfires and sea-level rises, creating widespread social disruption and food insecurity);
- Wars over resources (which will exacerbate the depletion of oil and other resources);
- Collapse of the U.S. dollar (the United States has a monumental balance of payments problem largely due to its military expenditures which could trigger worldwide economic instability).[31]

These problems are interrelated and their effects could be felt simultaneously.[32]

The need to act is urgent, and the problems we face are extremely difficult. We will need to draw upon all of the spiritual resources available from all traditions. The Asia-Pacific region offers great human and spiritual resources in this regard, encompassing many traditions. The Alternatives to Empire Project and the Our World in Crisis Course are attempting build on these resources.[33]

We need to engage with empire and move toward an Earth Community. This will require prophetic (witnessing) and priestly (reconciling) roles. It will require—
- Breaking the Silence: truth-telling (prophetic role);
- Ending the Isolation: community-building (priestly role);
- Changing the Story: changing the future to affirm life (prophetic and priestly roles).

This is a continuous turning process—a *metanoia* that transforms the powers and principalities and ourselves.

We also need to keep in mind that those in power often use the politics of fear to retain their power. Fear has the effect of making people regress to a lower level of consciousness. Faith communities, however, can offer hope. They can break the silence, end the isolation and build community and change the story. The Quaker testimonies are how Quakers are responding to change the story. These are ways that promote peace (including justice and nonviolence), simplicity, integrity, equality, community, earthcare (including environmental sustainability). The source of our strength, nurture, and guidance is from the Inner Light, the Christ within.

QUAKER TESTIMONIES

Quaker spirituality has developed over more than 350 years, during which time certain beliefs and practices have become part of the way of life for Friends. The "beliefs" described in this paper are not to be understood as dogma but are derived from and are rooted in our common living experience.[34]

Religious testimony: Everyone is endowed with the Light within

As Friends, we believe that we can have immediate and direct access to God through the Inner Light. Early Quakers spoke of this light as the Spirit of Christ. George Fox was fond of saying, "Christ has come to teach his people, himself." This is identified with the *Logos* in the Gospel of John 1:9, which says that "The true light, which enlightens everyone, was coming into the world." (This is sometimes known as "the Quaker verse.") This direct access through the Inner Light enables us to know the Truth; with effort and testing it enables us to discern God's will. The Inner Light helps us recognize evil, and if we are faithful to the Inner Light, it turns us toward good.[35]

As Friends we believe that not only can we discern God's will, but with the help of God we can do God's will. This is a concept of radical obedience to the holy. George Fox has described it as "[to] live in the power of the Lord." Friends try to follow George Fox's admonition to "Let your lives speak."

Quakers believe that all of life is sacramental. Our outward life is an expression of our inner life. Because of this, special outward observances, such as the Lord's Supper (Holy Communion) or baptism, are unnecessary for Friends.[36]

Religious testimony: The community gathering in Meeting for Worship

The Quaker experience combines the individual experience (as described above) and the community experience where individual actions and concerns are shared and tested with the wider body of Friends. We meet for worship in silence, waiting for God to speak to us.[37] Out of the silence, worshippers may receive a message that they are moved to share with the group through vocal ministry. After the message is delivered, the meeting once again is enveloped in silence. Often everyone in the meeting feels a very deep sense of unity without a word being spoken. This is commonly referred to as a "Gathered Meeting for Worship."

In Quaker Meetings for Worship for Business, decisions are taken by discerning "the sense of the meeting" rather than by voting. This is a reflection of the concept of unity and the gathered meeting. The tension between individual and community discernment promotes growth: Friends belong to a faith community and, as such, have responsibility and accountability in their relationships with one another.

Why did the Religious Society of Friends survive when nearly all of the other dissenting groups of seventeenth-century England have disappeared? George Fox preached individual liberty and the ability to experience the Spirit of Christ firsthand. Quaker individualism promoted equality, democracy, republicanism, pluralism, and tolerance.

But individual liberty has its downside. There have been schisms, disputes, splits, disagreements, and power struggles within Friends, tendencies that lead to disintegration. George Fox recognized the importance of "Gospel Order," a new covenantal relationship of the gathered community of Friends with God in which Christ taught and guided the community now. It was Fox's genius that saw the introduction of corporate organizations; the Meeting for Worship for Business, Elders, and Overseers; the Yearly Meeting, etc., to oversee the life of the meeting and to nurture this covenant relationship. These organizations produced guidelines and procedures which, over time, set limits to individual liberty, thereby enabling the corporate wisdom and discernment of Friends to act as a brake on eccentric influences. [38]

Social Testimonies

The religious testimonies are expressed through the social testimonies; the two are part of an organic whole.[39]

Peace

The Peace Testimony is perhaps the best known of the social testimonies.[40] Quakers came into being just after the English Civil War (about 1650). This was a time of social and religious turmoil, a time when government was insecure and plots and uprisings were a constant threat. Religious persecution and intolerance were common. Leading Friends publicly adopted a position of rejecting war and violence. The 1661 Fox-Hubberthorne Declaration to King Charles II is seen as a definitive expression of their nonviolence.[41]

Since there is "that of God in every person," Friends believe it is wrong to use violence and contrary to the gospel. Not only do the victims of violence suffer, but also the perpetrators of violence do spiritual harm to themselves. In the words of George Fox, Friends also work "to take away the occasion for war." Friends believe that evil can be transformed and overcome with love and reconciliation, and we work to establish "the peaceable kingdom." Peace includes inner peace, peace within the family, within the community, within the state, within the nation, within the region, and globally.

Peace is built on justice and mercy. This includes just economic, political, civil, and social relationships—recognizing that our well-being is intimately tied up with the well-being of our neighbors and of the planet. Early Friends protested against unjust laws, such as those restricting people's ability to worship as they pleased, but they also protested against severe punishments, including the death penalty. Friends have been influential in Britain and the United States in reducing the number of crimes to which the death penalty applies. Australian Friends have been taking action to achieve the same result in this region of the world.

Equality

Women have played a major role in the Society of Friends since the beginning.[42] Of the sixty-six who evangelized Britain with the Quaker message (the "Valiant Sixty"), twelve were women. Friends have been among the first to recognize and promote the full participation of women in the home, church, and school and in other social, civil, and political contexts. Early Friends scandalized authorities with their view that all people, including those despised or thought to be inferior or to be enemies by English society (Jews, Arabs, Turks, Africans, Native Americans, heathens, etc.) were gifted with the Inner Light, sufficient for salvation.

This continuing belief that all people are equal under God has been central to our experience. Friends have been leading advocates for the abolition of slavery. They have worked to promote justice and to improve economic and social conditions of the poor and of indigenous people; they pioneered efforts in prison reform, care for the insane, and war relief work.

Because of their views on equality, Friends refused to take off their hats or bow before "social superiors" or persons of authority. In court this practice frequently led to severe prison sentences. Even the few early Quakers who remained in the military forces during the 1650s treated senior officers as equals. Not surprisingly, they were seen as a threat and promptly cashiered. Friends used plain language, i.e. Friends used the familiar terms "thee" and "thou," rather than the then-subservient "you." They opposed using titles when addressing other persons in order not to honor one person above another. Friends' commitment to equality is also seen in their conscientious resistance to hierarchy in Quaker organization and worship. There are no priests: all are called to minister.

Integrity

Early Friends bravely called themselves "The First Publishers of Truth" because they felt they were professing religious truth in the same way as the first Christians. Integrity always has been an essential part of being a Quaker—integrity of the individual and in relation to others and to God.[43] Part of this commitment to integrity is to not lie. This commitment includes a refusal to take oaths because of the biblical command by Jesus not to swear oaths but also because of the implied double standard that one only tells the truth under oath. Friends' refusal to take an oath of allegiance to the king often led to severe prison sentences. Friends' commitment to the truth, sincerity, and honesty has been demonstrated in public life and in business.

Because early Friends were not allowed to enter the professions, many went into business. They gained a reputation for fair dealing and for fixed, fair prices (rather than haggling). Thus many Quakers prospered in business. Friends continue actively to witness to truth and integrity today in a wide range of areas, including humane governance, justice, human security, public administration, science, overseas aid, and ethical investments, among others.

Simplicity

Quakers have adopted a simple style of personal dress, furnishings and possessions, avoiding unnecessary and excessive ornamentation. This also includes plain, direct speech, and avoiding unnecessary, flowery language. This striving for simplicity is reflected in a lifestyle of moderation.[44] It helps us to focus on holy obedience rather than the accumulation of possessions and also to not use resources that others need. A commitment to simplicity is reflected in building sustainable systems, for example in trade and agriculture, in caring for the environment, and promoting the right sharing of resources. This moderation extends to the use of tobacco, alcohol, and drugs. Gambling, with its promise of unearned wealth, is not in accord with the simplicity testimony.

There is a growing discernment within our Society worldwide of testimonies to community and earthcare.

Community

From the beginning, Quakers emphasized the importance of community within the Meeting for mutual support and nurture.[45] Friends' commitment to reconciliation and inclusiveness meant that they have been active in building community in society, including with those marginalized by society. Friends have also been active in building the community of nations, e.g. at the Quaker United Nations Office and with international relief and service programs.

Earthcare

Earthcare, Friends' commitment to the environment and sustainability is related to the other testimonies[46]. Friends have recognized that they are stewards and have a responsibility to preserve God's creation in the natural world because it is the source of the material and spiritual nurture for everyone on the planet. We are connected to each other and all living and non-living things in the environment.[47]

Australian Friends have established a number of programs and institutions to help carry out the Testimonies. An ABC *Compass* television program in 2004, *Quakers: Seeking the Light Within*, featured Friends School in Hobart and Quaker Service in Australia and the Asia-Pacific region. Quakers also have offices at the United Nations in New York and Geneva, an office in Brussels (promoting peace, human rights, and economic justice), an office in the Middle East (promoting peace and reconciliation programs), and an office in Washington, D.C. (witnessing to the US Congress). In Australia the Quaker Peace and Legislation Committee witnesses to the Australian Government.

In *Quakers: Seeking the Light Within*, a Friends' Meeting for Worship was filmed showing the silent meditation and vocal ministry. Several of the social testimonies were discussed: Ro Morrow on simplicity and equality; Mark Deasey on equality; Sarah Davies, Jo Vallentine, and Peter Jones on peace. Each year the Backhouse Lecture, which deals with aspects of Friends' religious and social testimonies, is given at Australia Yearly Meeting.[48] The Swarthmore Lecture performs a similar role in the United Kingdom,[49] as does the Pendle Hill pamphlet series in the United States.[50] These resources are available in Regional Meeting libraries in Australia.

CONCLUDING REMARKS

Friends also have weaknesses and failings and do not always live up to the Testimonies. I think the main reason we find it difficult and struggle in our witness is that we are part of the Empire, often without realizing how much we are integrated into it. This shows the importance of naming and unmasking the powers, and breaking the silence.

The Empire can make us feel powerless. What can I do to change things against such overwhelming forces? Often we think we must achieve immediate results, but we forget that the major impact of the work of Anthony Benezet, John Woolman, Elias Hicks, Sarah and Angelina Grimké, Lucretia Mott, Abby Kelley, and other Quakers on the slavery issue was not felt until decades later. They saw their task as living faithfully and being persistent. We may never know the impact of our witness. Franz Jäggerstätter's pacifist witness against the Nazis cost him his life. His courage was little known until Gordon Zahn wrote *In Solitary Witness* two decades later. Daniel Ellsberg read it and was deeply moved by Jäggerstätter's example, and it led him to publish *The Pentagon Papers*, which changed the culture of support for the war in Vietnam.[51]

Another factor is the loneliness of the witness and the courage required to face the hostility of the Empire. Our failings indicate the need to strengthen our support and affirmation of each other in our witness. The challenges posed by empire are so great that no one person can do everything, yet each of us can do something.

Our struggle to live up to the Testimonies, to change the story of domination, reflects the need for our lives to be deeply rooted in the Spirit. Our efforts often suffer because our prayer life and worship are not deep enough. The Social Testimonies and the Religious Testimonies are entwined. Our individual and corporate witness embodied in the Social Testimonies calls us to extend ourselves fully in the Religious Testimonies, which are the source of our strength. They encourage us to live our lives to the full measure of Light given to us. We are called to discern anew what the Testimonies mean in our present political and socio-economic situation. Our power comes not from domination but by letting our lives speak.

As George Fox wrote, while jailed in Launceston Prison in 1656:

> And this is the word of the Lord God to you all, and a charge to you all in the presence of the living God: Be patterns, be examples in all countries, places, islands, nations, wherever you go, so that your carriage and life may preach among all sorts of people, and to them. Then you will come to walk cheerfully over the world, answering that of God in every one. Thereby you can be a blessing in them and make the witness of God in them bless you. Then you will be a sweet savor and a blessing to the Lord God.[52]

Our task is to carry out the nonviolent Lamb's War, as Sandra Cronk reminds us:

> We are asked to love as God loves, showering sunshine and rain on the good and evil alike. We are not told in the Sermon on the Mount what the outcome of our actions will be. But we may assume that closing off our love to an antagonist carries no possibility of change in our relationship, while continuing to love holds out the possibility of transformation. Indeed, if we raise defensive barriers and become angry, we have already lost the Lamb's War. We have been drawn into the fallen structures of hatred and bitterness. We have lost the war, because we no longer manifest God's abundant and transforming love. If we choose love, the peaceable kingdom has already come to birth in our lives. If we choose hatred or fear, the kingdom is far away.[53]

The primary point I would like to leave with you can be summarized as follows: We need to break the silence (truth-telling), name the powers, unmask the powers (these are prophetic roles); we need to end the isolation (build community—this is a priestly role); we need to change the story, affirm life, resist the powers nonviolently, and transform the powers (these are prophetic and priestly roles). The way that Quakers are approaching these tasks is through our religious worship and Social Testimonies of peace, justice, nonviolence, simplicity, equality, integrity, community, and earthcare. To achieve our goals we need to change the prevailing culture from one of empire to one of Earth Community. This in turn means a spiritual transformation, a metanoia, a turning, both for ourselves and for society.[54]

NOTES

1. Walter Wink, *Naming the Powers: The Language of Power in the New Testament* (Minneapolis, Minn.: Fortress Press, 1984); *Unmasking the Powers: The Invisible Forces that Determine Human Existence* (Minneapolis, Minn.: Fortress Press, 1986); *Engaging the Powers: Discernment and Resistance in a World of Domination* (Minneapolis, Minn.: Fortress Press, 1992); *The Powers that Be: Theology for a New Millennium* (New York, N.Y.: Galilee Doubleday, 1998); *When the Powers Fall: Reconciliation in the Healing of Nations* (Minneapolis, Minn.: Fortress Press, 1998); Ray Gingerich and Ted Grimsrud, eds., *Transforming the Powers: Peace, Justice and the Domination System* (Minneapolis, Minn.: Fortress Press, 2006); William Stringfellow, *An Ethic for Christians and Other Aliens in a Strange Land* (Waco, Tex.: Word Books, 1976); *Conscience and Obedience: The Politics of Romans 13 and Revelation 13 in the Light of the Second Coming* (Waco, Tex.: Word Books, 1977); Willard M. Swartley, *Covenant of Peace: The Missing Peace in New Testament Theology and Ethics* (Grand Rapids, Mich.: William B. Eerdmans Publishing Company, 2006), 222-253.

2. The name *Quaker* was first used by Justice Gervase Bennet of Derby as a term of derision for George Fox and John Fretwell when they were on trial for blasphemy in 1650. *The Religious Society of Friends* is the most widely accepted name today. In this article I shall use the terms *Quakers* and *Friends* interchangeably.

3. John H. Yoder, *Christian Attitudes to War, Peace and Revolution: A Companion to Bainton* (Elkhart, Ind.: Goshen Biblical Seminary, 1983), 205-233.

4. Carl F. Bowman, *Brethren Society: The Cultural Transformation of a "Peculiar People"* (Baltimore, Md.: The Johns Hopkins University Press, 1995), 41-45.

5. Robert Jewett and John Shelton Lawrence, *Captain America and the Crusade against Evil* (Grand Rapids, Mich.: William B. Eerdmans Publishing Company, 2003). Captain America is a comic book character, Steven Rodgers, initially rejected by the Army as medically unfit, but who then was turned into a super-soldier by a scientist working for the military. He now leads the U.S. fight against evil.

6. Wink, *Engaging with the Powers*, 13-31; *The Powers That Be*, 42-62.

7. Jewett and Lawrence, 27-43; 55-78; Michael Northcott, *An Angel Directs the Storm: Apocalyptic Religion and American Empire* (London, U.K.: I. B. Tauris,

2004), 14-43.

8. John Howard Yoder, *The Politics of Jesus,* 2nd. and rev. ed. (Grand Rapids, Mich.: William B. Eerdmans Publishing Company, 1994); Peter Brock, *The Quaker Peace Testimony:1660 to 1914* (York, U.K.: Sessions, 1993); Hugh Barbour, "The 'Lamb's War' and the Origins of the Quaker Peace Testimony," in *The Pacifist Impulse in Historical Perspective,* ed. Harvey L. Dyck (Toronto, Ont.: University of Toronto Press, 1996), 145-158; Donald F. Durnbaugh, "The Brethren and Non-Resistance," in Harvey L. Dyck, 125-144.

9. Jewett and Lawrence, 52.

10. James Nayler, *The Lamb's War against the Man of Sin,* 1658, reprinted by Hugh Barbour and Arthur O. Roberts, *Early Quaker Writings, 1650-1700* (Grand Rapids, Mich.: William B. Eerdmans Publishing Company, 1973), 106. For a discussion of George Fox's view on the Book of Revelation and The Lamb's War, see Douglas Gwyn, *Apocalypse of the Word: The Life and Message of George Fox* (Richmond, Ind.: Friends United Press, 1991), 179-207; T. Canby Jones, *George Fox's Attitude Toward War* (Richmond, Ind.: Friends United Press, 1984).

11. Hugh Barbour, *The Quakers in Puritan England* (Richmond, Ind.: Friends United Press, 1985), 40-41. Hugh Barbour and J. William Frost, *The Quakers* (New York, N.Y.: Greenwood Press, 1988), 33-35.

12. William Penn, *Preface to the Journal of George Fox,* 1694. See Matt. 7:3-5 and: http://www.hallvworthington.com/wjournal/journalintro.html

13. World Alliance of Reformed Churches, *An Ecumenical Faith Stance Against Global Empire,* Manila, the Philippines, July 13-15, 2006, http://warc.jalb.de/warcajsp/side.jspnews_id=809&part_id=0&navi=6; Empire Task Group, 39th. General Assembly of the United Church of Canada, *Living Faithfully in the Midst of Empire,* http://www.united-church.ca/economic/globalization/report and Appendices; Justice, Peace and Creation Team, World Council of Churches, *Alternative Globalisation Addressing Peoples and Earth (AGAPE),* http://www.oikoumene.org/index.php?id=2986; also see David E. Anderson, *God and Empire,* http://www.pbs.org/wnet/religionandethics/week1209/exclusive.html

14. Joseph Gerson, *Empire and the Bomb: How the US Uses Nuclear Weapons to Dominate the World* (London, U.K.: Pluto Press and the American Friends Service Committee, 2007).

15. United States Space Command, *Vision for 2020.* http://www.fas.org/spp/military/docops/usspac/visbook.pdf; Ben Zala, *Heavens on Fire: The Issue of Ballistic Missile Defence for Australia and the World* (Melbourne, Aus.: Medical Association for the Prevention of War, 2004), 28 pp.; for Pine Gap, see http://www.globalcollab.org/Nautilus/australia/australian-security-general/joint-australian-us-intelligence-facilities; Brendan Nicholson, "US gets military base in Western Australia," *The Age,* 15 February 2007. See http://www.theage.com.au/news/national/us-gets-military-base-in-australia/2007/02/14/1171405295243.html

16. Naval Communications Station Harold E Holt (NCS HEH), 21°56'S 114°07'E. http://www.globalsecurity.org/military/facility/exmouth.htm

17. Nick Turse, *Planet Pentagon: How the Pentagon Came to Own the Earth, Seas, and Skies.* http://www.commondreams.org/archive/2007/07/11/

2435/

18. David Fickling, "Australia doubles defence spending in desire to become top military player," http://www.guardian.co.uk/australia/story/0,12070,1141402,00.html

19. Gilbert Burnham, Riyadh Lafta, Shannon Doocy, and Les Roberts, "Mortality after the 2003 invasion of Iraq: a cross-sectional cluster sample survey," *The Lancet,* October 11, 2006. Gilbert Burnham, Shannon Doocy, Elizabeth Dzeng, Riyadh lafta, and Les Roberts, "The Human Cost of the War in Iraq: A Mortality Study, 2002-2006." A supplement to the October 2006 Lancet study. NGO Coordination Committee in Iraq and Oxfam, *Rising to the Humanitarian Challenge in Iraq*, 30 July 2007. http://www.oxfam.org/en/policy/briefingpapers/bp105_humanitarian_challenge_in_iraq_0707

20. "In the five years after September 11, the [Australian] federal Parliament has enacted 37 new [anti-terror] laws, or one new law every seven weeks. They cover everything from banning speech through to new sedition laws to detention without charge or trial to control orders that permit house arrest to closing down courts from public view." George Williams, "Anti-Terror Laws," *Perspective* (ABC Radio National), 28 February 2007. http://www.abc.net.au/rn/perspective/stories/2007/1857402.htm

21. Variants to the neo-liberalism, including the Washington Consensus Plus, Neo-conserative Neo-liberalism, Neo-structuralism, and Global Social Democracy, are discussed by Walden Bello, "The Post-Washington Dissensus," *Foreign Policy in Focus*, see http://www.fpif.org/fpiftxt/4569

22. Susan George, *A Fate Worse Than Debt* (New York: N.Y.: Grove Weidenfeld, 1988) 29; Susan George and Fabrizio Sabelli, *Faith and Credit* (Boulder, Colo.: Westview Press, 1994).

23. Richard Peet, *Unholy Trinity: the IMF, World Bank and WTO* (London, UK: Zed Books, 2003).

24. Brrie Pittock and G. Dale Hess, "Sustainable Atmospheric Management," in *Extending Schumacher's Concept of Total Accounting and Accountability into the 21st. Century,* Cheryl H. Lehman, Series Editor and Kala Saravanamuthu, Special Guest Editor, *Advances in Public Interest Accounting*, vol. 14 (Bingley, U.K.: Emerald Group Publishing Limited , 2009), 193-224.

25. The Rudd Government, elected 24 November 2007, has promised to sign the Kyoto Protocol; however a coalition of Australian conservation organizations rates the new government's overall climate change program only 1.9 out of 5. See http://www.thebigswitch.org.au/index.cfm?page=ourPoliticians.parties

26. Chris Hails, Jonathan Loh, and Steven Goldfinger, eds., *Living Planet Report 2006*, World Wildlife Fund International, Institute of Zoology, and Global Footprint Network, 2006. See http://assets.panda.org/downloads/living_planet_report.pdf

27. David Korten, *The Great Turning: From Empire to Earth Community* (San Francisco, Calif.: Berrett-Koehler Publishers and Kumarian Press, 2006), 41-56. Also see Joanna Macy, *The Shift to a Life-Sustaining Civilization*: http://www.joannamacy.net/html/great.html. In theological terms The Great Turning is called *metanoia*, a transformation of the heart or a spiritual conversion.

28. Korten, *op.cit.*, 41-56.

29. Robert J. Burrowes, *The Strategy of Nonviolent Defense: A Gandhian Approach* (Albany, N.Y.: State University of New York Press, 1996), 1-2.

30. See Riane Eisler, *The Chalice and the Blade: Our History, Our Future* (New York, N.Y.: HarperCollins, 1995); *The Real Wealth of Nations: Creating a Caring Economy* (San Francisco, Cal.: Berrett-Koehler Publishers, 2007); Bruce D. Bonta, *Peaceful Peoples: An Annotated Bibliography* (Metuchen, N.J.: Scarecrow Press, 1993). See, http://www.peacefulsocieties.org/

31. Energy Bulletin, *Peak Oil Primer and Links*. http://www.energybulletin.net/primer.php; Pittock and Hess, *op. cit.*; Michael Klare, *Resource Wars: The New Landscape of Global Conflict* (New York: Holt Paperbacks, 2002), 304 pp.; Chalmers Johnson, "A National Intelligence Estimate on the United States," *Harpers Magazine*. http://www.informationclearinghouse.info/article16260.htm

32. Korten, 57-73.

33. *The Alternatives to Empire* is a project initiated by the International Movement for a Just World (JUST), Pax Christi Australia, and the Commission for Mission of the Uniting Church in Australia, Synod of Victoria and Tasmania, to facilitate a dialogue among faiths to vision an alternative to the hegemonic ways of Empire. See http://alternativestoempire.org/. The *Our World in Crisis? Course* is a 10-week course offered annually to members of the Melbourne community, sponsored by Pax Christi Victoria, the Islamic Council of Victoria, the Commission for Mission of the Uniting Church in Australia Synod of Victoria and Tasmania, Oxfam Australia, World Vision, Australia Volunteers International, Asia Education Foundation, Victorian Local Governance Association, Australian Education Union Victorian Branch, Victorian Council of Social Service, Medical Association for the Prevention of War, Psychologists for the Promotion of World Peace, and the La Trobe University Centre for dialog, to understand better the issues of development, environment, human rights, peace, democracy, our rapidly globalizing world, and Australia's place in it. See http://www.josephcamilleri.com/owic/inddex.htm

34. Howard Brinton, *Friends for 350 Years*, revised by Margaret H. Bacon (Wallingford, Pa.: Pendle Hill , 2002); Wilmer Cooper, *A Living Faith: An Historical and Comparative Study of Quaker Beliefs* (Richmond, Ind.: Friends United Press, 1990); John Punshon, *Testimony and Tradition: Some Aspects of Quaker Spirituality* (London, U.K.: Britain Yearly Meeting, 1990).

35. Insights into the Quaker religious testimonies are collected in the booklet, *Advices and Queries* (see http://quakersfp.live.poptech.coop/qfp/chap1/1.02.html); and the books Britain Yearly Meeting, *Quaker Faith and Practice* (London, U.K.: Britain Yearly Meeting, 1995) (see for example http://quakersfp.live.poptech.coop/qfp/index.html), and Australia Yearly Meeting, *This we can say: Australian Quaker Life,Faith and Thought* (Armadale North, Aus.: Australia Yearly Meeting, 2003) (see http://www.quakers.org.au/pubs.shtml).

36. Many Friends feel that the world religions (including indigenous religions and insights from secular humanists) possess Truth and, like Bahá'ís, see the unity of all religions. However, within Friends there is a diversity of

belief, some members are more Christocentric while others are more Universalist.

37. Buddhists, Yogis, Sufis, Taoists, and some sections of the Roman Catholic community share Friends' religious testimonies in their practice of silent meditation and experience of mysticism. Their practice, though, tends to concentrate on the individual experience, while Friends' mysticism is corporate mysticism grounded in Christian concepts. In some parts of the world, Friends' meetings have adapted a pastoral system and the worship service is planned in advance; however, in Australia meetings are based on unprogrammed, silent worship.

38. Larry Ingle, *First Among Friends: George Fox and the Creation of Quakerism* (Oxford, U.K.: Oxford University Press, 1994).

39. Jonathan Dale, *Faith in Action: Quaker Social Testimony* (London, U.K.: Quaker Books, 2007). The Mennonites and Church of the Brethren share these social testimonies. The Mennonites, Church of the Brethren, and Quakers have been called "the Historic Peace Churches." Other denominations, e.g. Dukhobours, Moravians, Hutterites, Bruderhof (the Society of Brothers), and the Amish, have also carried out a witness to these testimonies. Individuals from other traditions, e.g. Tolstoy (Orthodox), Gandhi (Hindu), Abdul Ghaffar Khan (Muslim), Thich Nhat Hanh (Buddhist), Dorothy Day and Philip and Daniel Berrigan (Roman Catholic), Martin Luther King Jr. (Baptist), have become prominent, especially in the areas of peace and equality. In recent years, many of the mainstream Christian churches have become very active in taking up these testimonies.

40. Gerard Guiton, *The Growth and Development of Quaker Testimony, 1652-1661 and 1960-1994: Conflict, Nonviolence and Conciliation* (Lewiston, N.Y.: Edwin Mellen Press, 2005); Dale Hess, *A Brief Background to the Quaker Peace Testimony* (Melbourne, Aus.: Victoria Regional Meeting, 1992); Rosemary A. Moore, *Light in Their Consciences: Faith, Practices and Personalities in Early British Quakerism, 1646-1666* (University Park, Pa.: Pennsylvania State University Press, 2000); Meredith B. Weddle, *Walking in the Way of Peace: Quaker Pacifism in the Seventeenth Century* (Oxford, U.K.: Oxford University Press); Brock, 1993.

41. Margaret Fell wrote and presented an earlier declaration of the Peace Testimony to Charles II in 1660, signed by George Fox, Richard Hubberthorne, Samuel Fisher, William Caton, and nine other leading Quaker men. Isabel Ross, *Margaret Fell: Mother of Quakerism* (York, U.K.: William Session Book Trust, 1996), 127-28. Edward Burrough addressed Parliament and proclaimed Quaker nonviolence in 1659. Guiton, 2005, 55-56, 85.

42. Phyllis Mack, *Visionary Women: Ecstatic Prophecy in Seventeenth-Century England* (Berkeley, Cal.: University of California, 1994); Christine Trevett, *Women and Quakerism in the Seventeenth Century* (York, U.K.: William Session Book Trust, 1991).

43. Wilmer Cooper, *The Testimony of Integrity* (Wallingford, Pa.: Pendle Hill, 1991).

44. Catherine Whitmire, *Plain Living: A Quaker Path to Simplicity* (Notre Dame, Ind.: Sorin Books, 2001).

45. Lewis Benson, *Catholic Quakerism: A Vision for All Men [and Women]*

(Philadelphia.: Philadelphia Yearly Meeting, 1968).

46. Susannah Brindle, *To Learn a New Song: A Quaker Contribution to Real Reconciliation with the Earth and its Peoples*, James Backhouse Lecture (Armadale North, Aus.: Australia Yearly Meeting, 2000).

47. Australia Yearly Meeting is considering issuing a statement on "Earthcare."

48. See http://www.quakers.org.au/old_pubs_bl.htm

49. See http://en.wikipedia.org/wiki/Swarthmore_Lecture

50. See http://www.pendlehill.org/bookstore/pamphlets.php

51. Thomas E. Drake, *Quakers and Slavery in American* (New Haven, Conn.: Yale University Press, 1950); Jean R. Soderlund, *Quakers and Slavery: A Divided Spirit* (Princeton, N.J.: Princeton University Press, 1985); Gordon Charles Zahn, *In Solitary Witness*, rev. ed. (Springfiled, Ill.: Templegate Publishers, 1986); Neil Scheehan, *Pentagon Papers* (New York, N.Y.: Bantam Books, 1971).

52. George Fox, *The Journal of George Fox*, ed. John L. Nickalls (Philadelphia.: Religious Society of Friends, 1997).

53. Sandra Cronk, *Peace Be with You: A Study of the Spiritual Basis of the Friends Peace Testimony* (Philadelphia: The Tract Association of Friends, 1984).

54. It is a pleasure to acknowledge the generous help and encouragement of Robin Arnold, Bruce Bonta, Joe Camilleri, Kevin Clements, Mark Deasey, Adrian Glamorgan, Ted Grimsrud, Gerry Guiton, Mark Hurst, Doug Hynd, David Johnson, Deb Kent, Nelson Kraybill, Jarrod McKenna, Jason MacLeod, Sieneke Martin, David Purnell, Doug Sewell, Willard Swartley, Mike Thomsen, Jo Vallentine, Walter Wink, and Ben Zala in the preparation of this manuscript.

Chapter 15

CHRISTIAN PEACEMAKER TEAMS IN ISRAEL

Christina Gibb

THE CHRISTIAN PEACEMAKER TEAMS were organized as the result of a speech by Ron Sider at the Mennonite World Conference in 1984. The challenge that he issued was that Christians should be prepared to take the same risks in the cause of nonviolent peacemaking as we take for granted for soldiers who are acting on a different basis. He was thinking in terms of thousands and thousands of Christians forming a nonviolent peace force based in our faith, which would counter the threats of war and the actuality of war throughout the world.

The organization that has developed is still very small. There are about thirty full-time members and about two hundred part-time ones like I am. First of all it started with the Historic Peace Churches, Mennonites, Quakers, and the Church of the Brethren in the United States getting together to work out what would be needed to create a peace force and peace teams working on these principles.

From the early nineties onward, Christian Peacemaker Teams, or as I will refer to it from now on, CPT has put teams into a variety of places of conflict, always—and this is important part to what we do—at the invitation of local people who are suffering in a situation of conflict. The invitation is necessary so there are always local partners also committed to nonviolence, nonviolent resistance, or nonviolent peacemaking of one sort or another.

CPT quite rapidly became much more ecumenical, though there are still, I think, more Mennonites in CPT than any other single denomination. But now it includes Christians of many different traditions: Catholics, especially those from the Catholic Worker part of Catholic church, Anglicans, Episcopalians, Presbyterians, Methodists, Lutherans, and many others, including people who have no specific church affiliation but who still are drawn to Christ and feel able to join in our common worship every day.

CPT has engaged in many places of conflict. Two teams are active within the United States. One team is working to expose the evils of depleted uranium, its use in atomic weapons, and its dangers as radioactive waste. They are also engaged in advocacy and lobbying work in Washington. Another team serves in the southern border of Arizona, where United States is building a wall to keep out illegal migrants from Mexico. More and more these migrants have been forced to cross over in the desert, where hundreds of them have died. The immigration laws are extremely unjust. On the one hand many employers in the United States want the migrant labor, but on the other hand the migrants have no rights at all. They will be sent back to Mexico and severely punished if they do reenter the United States illegally.

Teams have been active in several places in Canada, where the conflicts have been those largely between First Nation people, the indigenous people in Canada, and large multi-national companies exploiting their land. A team has been working in southern Mexico. A South American team has been in Colombia for some time. Another team has been serving in Iraq, where four CPT workers were taken hostage. One of them, Tom Fox, was murdered in 2006, and the other three were safely released.

The CPT team that has been active for the longest time is in Hebron, in the West Bank, the occupied territories of Palestine. I've been part of the team for over four years, volunteering for three months each year. Since I became a member, the team has become more international in that most members are from the United States, though quite a few are from Canada. Some are from Britain, both England and Scotland; and a few are from Europe, one from Italy, one from Germany, one from Sweden. One person is from the Philippines, and so far I am the only member from Asia. I hope Asian participation will be changing soon, in that several people in Australia and New Zealand are interested and have taken first steps toward discerning whether this is the right thing for them to do.

What do we do? CPT usually does five kinds of things wherever it is serving. First of all we are a *presence*, a nonviolent presence in the situation of conflict along side those who are suffering in the conflict. Second we do *accompaniment*. We look out for individual persons or groups of people who ask us to make sure, in so far as we can, that they get safely to their destination, wherever that may be. We *monitor* human rights abuses, taking photographs and writing whatever we see happening that is an abuse of human rights. We also take part in *nonviolent direct action*. In Hebron this means actions normally led by Palestinians. They know what they want to do and the part they would like us, as their international supporters, to take in any action they plan. And fifth, we *raise awareness* about the situation in the place of conflict, so that the stories get told about what is actually happening on the ground to the people who are suffering in the conflict.

Another aspect of CPT is how we live. We live together as a small Christian community wherever the team goes. We try to practice the testimonies that would no doubt be expressed somewhat differently by Mennonites, Quakers, and Brethren, but which in fact we have in common. We live simply. We are not like those international groups in situations of conflict who live according to the standards of the country from which they come, in a sort of enclave separate from the people they are there to serve. Rather we deliberately choose to live among our people and on the same standard as theirs.

Our decision-making among ourselves is much like Quaker decision-making. We listen to one another for what seems to be the right way forward, and we listen for God's will within the particular situation for this group of people at this time. We share equally the various jobs that need doing. We all take turns leading our worship together each morning. We also take turns doing the cooking, washing the dishes, writing up the log each day, and doing the cleaning that needs to be done that day. I should also say that we are people of all ages, from twenties up to up to people in our seventies. I'm not quite the oldest, but nearly so. I think there is one member in her eighties. Living in a community of mixed ages, including both men and women, is very stimulating. We try to be living examples of what we stand for.

Our decision making, as I said, is among us all by consensus, or by the discernment of God's will among us. The same is true for our relationship with the headquarters, which is in Chicago. We don't really speak of a headquarters, but rather of the office in Chicago. One support person in Chicago is particularly responsible for contact with the team in Hebron. However, he and the team in Chicago are not the ones who make the decisions about what we do on the ground. By contrast, other local groups with whom we work quite closely can be told by their headquarters located elsewhere that their situation has become too dangerous and they must withdraw, whereas they may have a very different perception of the situation. Situations often look much more dangerous from a distance than they do when you are actually living there. We make the decisions about the important things like leaving or staying. Of course we consult with our colleagues in Chicago, but we are not overridden by some central policy not connected to what is actually happening.

But let us consider the situation in Hebron, where my CPT team was serving. The situation there is that since 1967 Israel has occupied the whole of the West Bank, and there is no Palestinian state. The Palestinian population includes three and a half million people in the West Bank together with another million and a quarter in the Gaza strip. Israel has occupied the whole area during the years since the occupation started, and increasingly Israel has placed more and more restrictions on the Palestinians. So the occupation heavily impacts the lives all Palestinians. Most Palestinians are Muslims, but some are Christians. Ever since the time of Christ, Christians have been in Palestine. They are now quite a small proportion of the population, but we need to remember that Christians are living there among the much larger Muslim population.

Our team was based in Hebron in the southern part of the West Bank. Hebron is the city of Abraham. If you read Genesis 12–24, you will realize that again and again Abraham came back to Hebron. Also Hebron was the place where Abraham bought the plot of ground to bury his wife Sarah. We are talking about 3,800 years ago, the time of Abraham. The Cave of Machpelah is below the large stone enclosure which was built by Herod 2,000 years ago. So it's been a sacred place for a very long time.

This site is sacred to all three Abrahamic faiths: Jews, Christians, and Muslims. At one time it was a Byzantine church, circa 300 to 600. Following their invasion shortly after the time of Mohammad, the Muslims built a mosque there. The crusaders conquered the area and built a Christian church. Finally, Salaheddin, or Saladin as we more commonly know him, ejected the crusaders and built a magnificent mosque. The site is also very sacred to Jewish people, who look to Abraham as the founding father of their faith. It is the second holiest site in the whole of Israel and Palestine for both Jews and Muslims, the most sacred being Jerusalem. So it is not surprising that when the Israelis conquered the West Bank the first place they wanted to be able to settle with Jewish people was Hebron.

Hebron is a city of 150,000 Palestinian Muslims, and it has no indigenous Christians. The Palestinian Christians are in and around

Bethlehem, Jerusalem, Nazareth, and elsewhere. About 500 fanatical Jewish settlers have pushed their way into Hebron and settled, against all odds, immediately right inside the city. It takes about 2,000 Israeli soldiers to protect them, so you can imagine that this is a place of great tension. Palestinian people have always lived there and consider it their land. During the past 2,000 years Jews have been living in the Holy Land, but not in any large numbers. Many Jewish people returned to Palestine from various parts of Europe following the Holocaust to form the state of Israel, promulgated by UN decree in 1948. Now that they have returned, Israelis claim it as their land on the basis of God's promise to Abraham three thousand eight hundred years ago.

The Jewish people say the covenant was through the descendants of Isaac, Abraham's son. The Muslim tradition is that the covenant came to them through the descendants of Ishmael, also Abraham's son. So the two peoples are very distant cousins. The Muslim people still have the use of the main prayer hall, but about ten years ago the Israeli government and army enforced a division within this mosque, so that half of it is now a synagogue. You can imagine the tension that the whole situation creates. Two peoples, both with ancient links to the land, one with continuous links, the other with a gap of two thousand years. However, since the Holocaust in the Second World War, the Jewish people are in desperate need of their own country, so the conflict continues.

What do these two peoples living together in this one bit of land mean to Hebron? Consider the plight of a Palestinian shopkeeper who makes sieves in the main market place. Over his head above the Palestinian shops is a part of one of the Israeli settlements. The Israelis have extended the property they have built to come out directly above the shops. They throw their rubbish down upon the Palestinian properties below. The Israeli army has put up netting here to catch the rubbish. One finds pieces of concrete, pieces of old furniture, and all sorts of rubbish chucked down from above. At other times when they are not throwing the larger stuff out, they throw out water and sewage. This is an example of the extreme animosity of the settlers toward the local inhabitants.

Consider another example of what the occupation is doing, in this instance, the wall on the West Bank. The Israelis have built a concrete wall nine meters high on Palestinian land that is well within the Green Line, the armistice line established in 1948. The wall snakes its way by a very circuitous route right down the west part of the West Bank. More often than not, Palestinian land is cut off on the Israeli side of the wall and then is taken over by Israeli settlers. Whereas the wall is promoted by Israel as a security and defense measure against terrorists and suicide bombers, it has in fact been a means by which Israelis can settle on Palestinian land. The Israelis call this creating facts on the ground. All through the peace talks during the 1990s and beyond, Israel has continued building settlements and settler-only roads that criss-cross the West Bank, cutting the West Bank into tiny little cantons.

A favorite occupation of Palestinian youth is to throw paint balls at the towers along the wall. Bethlehem has been enclosed on three sides. Think of the plight of the people of Bethlehem, cut off from their lands. Jerusalem is only five miles away, yet they are walled off from their natural markets in Jerusalem. They have no access to Jerusalem without a special permit. CPT has started a campaign called, "Bethlehem behind the wall: No way to the inn." We suggest that people may like to symbolize what is actually happening by building a wall around a Christmas crib, a crèche, or a manger scene. The shepherds and the wise men are on the outside; they can't get there. It is a very simple, powerful symbol of what has happened in Bethlehem.

As well as the wall, a really terrible instrument of Israeli policy is to demolish people's houses. Houses are demolished if close to settlements. They are demolished if close to the main Israeli bypass roads, which link all settlements. They are demolished for so-called administrative reasons. It costs a great deal of money for Palestinians to apply for building permits, and chances are they won't get one. The Israelis are just trying to stop the natural expansion of the population. Palestinians have large families; nine or ten children are quite common. A family with three generations living in one house becomes much too crowded, because the brothers and sisters also have large families. So they build a modest little house, one or two rooms on their own land with their own money, and the Israelis put a demolition order on it straightaway. The house may not be demolished immediately, but the family always has this threat hanging over it. Are the bulldozers coming tonight? Will my house be demolished?

A courageous Israeli peace group, the Israeli Committee Against House Demolitions, works closely with people to rebuild their houses that have been demolished. It is a humanitarian act, but it is also more. They build one house each year with a team of international volunteers as an act of resistance to the situation into which the Palestinians have been put.

The Israeli soldiers are a cross-section of Israeli society, aged eighteen, nineteen, or twenty; quite often one is able to get into conversation with them. Loving our enemies, we try not to demonize anybody and to treat everybody as a fellow human being, despite what we see the soldiers doing.

Frequently they invade Palestinian houses during the nighttime, ransacking the house, probably taking one of the men into detention. On one occasion in Hebron, we managed to follow the soldiers in before they shut the door to our neighbor's house. Once we were in the house, our neighbors would not do what the soldiers told them to do. The soldiers said, "You must tell them to go home." They said, "We cannot; they are our friends and neighbors. Hospitality requires that we never tell people to leave." So we stayed. The soldiers had been planning to spend the night in that house and had taken over one room completely. Since we were clearly also staying, eventually after about two hours, they left.

On another occasion, a large group of soldiers were out at night in the Old City. They were entering every single house and rounding up all the men between about thirty-five and sixty. They put them all in the big space in front of the mosque and behind the police barricades, making them all sit on the ground behind the police barriers. They said they were doing a survey. In what situation do you ever need to round up all the men in the middle of the night, not saying what you are doing with them, and leaving the families traumatized? The women didn't know whether they were going to see their husbands again that night or that year. Nobody knew what was happening, so the whole civilian population were terrorized. In fact the soldiers let them go by about one o'clock in the morning. Once they got all the men out of their houses, they let them back in again. They didn't detain anybody that night.

As we worked with our Palestinian friends and colleagues, I was constantly inspired by the strength of the nonviolent resistance of some of our Palestinian neighbors. They have been persevering day after day, week after week, and year after year. The Palestinian terrorists are often in the news, but one seldom hears about the nonviolent activists and all the ordinary people who are not part of the active peace movement, like that sieve merchant with his little hardware store in the market place. They persevere in refusing to be moved, staying put no matter what, through thick and thin, resisting nonviolently by just being there. This gives you a hint of what CPT is doing, being alongside these Palestinian friends and neighbors and alongside the Israeli activists, as we work together for peace with justice for everybody in this land.

Chapter 16

ETHICS OF NONVIOLENT INTERVENTION AND ACCOMPANIMENT: PERSONAL PRESENCE AMID UNEQUAL POWER

Elizabeth Duke

Just then a lawyer stood up to test Jesus. "Teacher," he said, "what must I do to inherit eternal life?" He said to him, "What is written in the law? What do you read there?" He answered, "You shall love the Lord your God with all your heart, and with all your soul, and with all your strength, and with all your mind; and your neighbor as yourself." And he said to him, "You have given the right answer; do this, and you will live." But wanting to justify himself, he asked Jesus, "And who is my neighbor?"
—Luke 10:25-29

Jesus told the story of the priest and Levite who passed by the wounded man, and the Samaritan who came to his rescue. "Which of these three, do you think, was a neighbor to the man who fell into the hands of the robbers?" He said, "The one who showed him mercy." Jesus said to him, "Go and do likewise."
—Luke 10:36-37

ETHICS IS THE STUDY of what is right and good. This is not the occasion to recapitulate more than 3000 years of discussion on the foundation of ethics. So I take the story of the good Samaritan to illustrate the foundation I shall use as follows: Ethics involves my relation to other people; anyone whom my actions affect is my neighbor; I am called to love my neighbor as myself. How does this relate to nonviolent intervention?

I am talking about personal nonviolent intervention, known as accompaniment or presence—being present in a scene of actual or potential violence in the hope that this presence will prevent or reduce violence and offer protection to those threatened. There are many other forms of nonviolent intervention, such as humanitarian relief, action at the United Nations or other international political bodies, diplomacy, facilitating discussions and understanding between parties in conflict, serving as a broker in negotiations. This chapter considers *personal presence in circumstances of unequal power*, where people—perhaps a civilian population, or a body with a peace witness, or human rights defenders, or other parts of civil society—are subject to violence and oppression by a stronger party. The stronger party may be a state actor or some other group that uses violence to control others. The reason for such presence, witness, or accompaniment is that the presence of outsiders, especially nationals of powerful countries, deters these actors from violence since it will receive unwelcome publicity, because the witnesses are there. This principle involves several ethical dilemmas that I will discuss later.

Most commonly nonviolent intervention of this kind is undertaken by volunteers through organizations that have evolved for this purpose. Some of these are Christian Peacemaker Teams (an initiative of the Historic Peace Churches), the International Fellowship of Reconciliation, Peace Brigades International, Friends Peace Teams, and the Nonviolent Peaceforce. Some of the ethical issues I raise here are questions for such bodies about intervention, while some belong more to individuals who are considering voluntary service. My personal interest in these questions comes from a period I spent considering whether or not I was called to undertake volunteer accompaniment in Colombia. I spent time learning from the Fellowship of Reconciliation and from Peace Brigades International. My discernment eventually brought me to the conclusion that I should take part in a two-week Fellowship of Reconciliation "delegation" in Colombia, then become a supporter of their work from home in Aotearoa/New Zealand. So I speak of nonviolent intervention from the outside, not from personal experience.

Because I come from a "Western" country, I am looking at nonviolent intervention as an outsider going into another country. The truly good and brave people in this context are those who live in countries where there is institutional violence and oppression, people who risk their freedom and their lives every day to support human rights or to build peace. *They* cannot take a plane home if things become dangerous. Yet they act and they speak. I heard a priest in Colombia say, "We could remain silent and have no trouble. But we will *not* remain silent." This paper is dedicated to such people.

PERSONAL ETHICAL QUESTIONS

Anyone considering whether or not to undertake nonviolent intervention has to ask many personal ethical questions. At this stage I want to rule out one line of argument. Faced with questions such as, "Do I have a right to give up other commitments, to involve my family in loneliness, anxiety, and perhaps financial loss, or to risk my life when there are contributions I might make to society?" someone might answer, "Well, nobody asks these questions when people engage in military service. The risks are taken as normal." However, it is very dangerous for those who are committed to nonviolence to copy the arguments of those who use violence as a tool. If our actions are not directed by our own standards of right, we had better give them up. So what are the questions, and how might we answer them?

At the core of personal ethical decisions is the question, "What is it right for me to do? What am I called to do? What is God's will for me in this decision?" There are many external paths to an answer: my own suitability for the service, the potential impact of the action on other people, guidance from biblical and other tradition, consultation of others, models to follow. In the end, taking all these into account, the answer is inward, coming from prayer, reflection, patience, and thought. I have asked the last question first. Here are some of the other considerations.

Do I have the right to undertake the risk of personal harm or death? At this point I wish to honor the memory of Tom Fox, member of a Christian Peacemaker Team in Iraq, a Quaker from Baltimore killed in Baghdad in the service of God's peace. Both humanist and Christian ethics are clear that one should not avoid death at all costs, and there are times when it is right to undertake a risk voluntarily. Models in civil society include landmine disposal, the fire and rescue services, and medical care in epidemics. These are circumstances in which the risk comes with an activity necessary to society. Is it right to enter a situation of risk that could be avoided? Common opinion would see some occasions as morally wrong, e.g. driving dangerously; some as morally neutral, e.g. mountain climbing; and some as morally right, e.g. entering fast-moving water to save someone in trouble.

All who undertake risks need to ask whether they are seeking psychological satisfaction, such as the courting of death by some young drivers, or the thrill of possible martyrdom. The latter danger was recognized early by the church under persecution. The church in Smyrna wrote an account of the martyrdom of Polycarp and other faithful around the year 156, which makes it clear that they would not deny their faith to avoid death.

> The Proconsul continued insisting and saying, "Swear, and I release you; curse Christ." And Polycarp said, "Eighty-six years have I served him, and he has done me no wrong: how then can I blaspheme my King who saved me?"

But the same letter tells of Quintus, who "had forced both himself and certain others to come forward of their own accord" but then in fear swore by the divinity of the emperor and offered incense. "Therefore, brethren," wrote the church of Smyrna, "we do not commend those who surrender themselves, for such is the teaching of the gospel." The reference is probably to Matthew 10:23, "When they persecute you in one town, flee to the next."[1]

This Christian understanding points to an ethical model that one should not *seek out* martyrdom or death in a good cause, but that the danger of death should not deter us from right action.

Dag Hammarskjold, who died in office as Secretary General of the United Nations, spoke of such physical and moral courage.

> How would the moral sense of Reason—and of Society—have evolved without the martyrs to the faith? Indeed, how could this moral sense have escaped withering away, had it not constantly been watered by the feeder streams of power that issues from those who have forgotten themselves in God? The rope over the abyss is held taut by those who, faithful to a faith which is the perpetual ultimate sacrifice, give it anchorage in heaven. Those whose souls are married to God have been declared the salt of the earth. Woe betide them, if the salt should lose its savour.[2]

My neighbors, anyone whom my actions can affect, include my family, friends, and others close to me. Anyone proposing to go into a setting of violence to engage in accompaniment must realize that this will cause anxiety to those who care about them. If others are finan-cially dependent on them, do volunteers have a right to ask them to do without that income for a period? What about children or others who are emotionally dependent?

These ethical questions do not have simple answers. If it is other-wise right to undertake the risk, should it be avoided because it causes others anxiety? We might try a moral balance, weighing anxi-ety against the harm that may be prevented by the nonviolent pres-ence. But how do we balance an almost-certain anxiety against a re-duction in violence that cannot be guaranteed? There is no simple cal-culus for ethical questions. One answer might be that if the action is otherwise right, the moral course is to undertake it, while granting those who are anxious a realistic picture of the level of danger (for ex-ample, that the organization has been sending volunteers to this country for twenty years without any one being harmed). The bal-ance may be different if somebody close to the volunteer might suffer psychological and physical breakdown. All these things must be taken into account.

Financial dependence and the needs of children are very strong ethical obligations. If the volunteer has not discussed with family members whether it is right to go, can the decision be considered eth-ical? One answer might be that perhaps the action is right, but the tim-ing wrong. Is it necessary to spend time building up a financial re-serve, or waiting till children are more mature? Sadly, the need for nonviolent intervention will still be there in two or twenty years' time. Those considering volunteering for nonviolent intervention are probably already involved in various activities of service to their neighborhood, religious community, and society. Spending time away will impose extra burdens on others. Such existing commit-ments cannot be an absolute obligation. In time all of us will need to hand over our responsibilities in life. While it will be right to consult those who could be affected by one's absence, the deciding voice must lie elsewhere.

ORGANIZATIONAL AND PERSONAL QUESTIONS: THE IMPACT OF PRESENCE IN THE PLACE OF WITNESS

Any who propose to go to another country to engage in nonvio-lent intervention might be challenged as to their right to intervene in the politics of another country. It could be argued that outsiders lack cultural and political understanding of the situation and do not have the commitment to that country required of those who live there. This needs to be taken very seriously. If nonviolent intervention of the type I am describing is applied in situations of unequal power, then those intervening are attempting to affect the power balance. By what right do they meddle? The Samaritan could have told himself that what happened on the road between Jerusalem and Jericho was a Jewish internal matter, not concerning him as a transient. However, the very point of accompaniment or presence is that the outsiders are there to bear witness. They can be effective just because they are outsiders. Organizations that send in volunteers undertake careful training to help them understand the cultural and political situation.

The various organizations that engage in accompaniment have differing understandings of how far their roles as protectors extend to witness, such as spreading news of atrocities and calling for international pressure to end them. Sometimes they will pass on information to another body, like Amnesty International, rather than undertaking pressure themselves. One type of international leverage is to use the process of nomination for awards, such as the Nobel Peace prize. The Peace Community of San José de Apartadó in Colombia was nominated in 2007. Whether by presence or by publicity, those who engage in nonviolent intervention are declaring that they understand all to be potentially their neighbors, despite artificial political boundaries. Just because the intervention is not in their own country, it is likely to have more effect.

Is intervention a waste of time, energy, and resources? How can those who intervene show that they will make conditions better in the long run for those whom they accompany, when cruelty, greed, fear, and violence are so prevalent? Human history is not subject to controlled experiment. We cannot re-run it, changing one factor, to see what happens. An accompaniment organization cannot know for sure that it will make a difference. The best determining criterion for the decision is the experience of those who have been accompanied. If they believe that accompaniment has been of value and request more, this is an indication that the work has not been ineffectual.

A more subtle moral question is, "What right do you have to intervene in this situation, when your presence may enrage those in authority or with power, and provoke them to harm either you or others?" If my presence induces someone to commit violence, then perhaps I have the moral responsibility for that violence. This does not seem to me a valid argument. It is too close to blaming the victim of rape for being there. If the commitment is to peacemaking, then the accompanier will respect the human person and child of God in those who threaten violence, and treat them in a way which may make them less violent. One peacemaker in Northern Ireland said, "These violent men will speak to me and trust me to carry messages to the other side, because they know I don't want to kill them."

The Quaker founder of Pennsylvania, William Penn, argued, "We are too ready to retaliate, rather than forgive, or gain by love and information. And yet we could hurt no man that we believe loves us. Let us then try what love will do. For if men did once see we love them, we should soon find they would not harm us. Force may subdue, but love gains."[3] Sadly, Penn was not absolutely right. Humanitarian workers and peacemakers have been attacked in many countries. Peacemakers cannot be sure that those who commit violence will trust their motives. Nevertheless, it is not true that nonviolent intervention is responsible for violence from the aggressor. The violence was there already.

What impact will the presence of accompaniers have on those who receive this service? Is there an argument that, like those who receive material aid, they may become dependent on outside support and fail to develop their own resources? The argument about material aid is very complex, and it is not a true parallel. The regular practice of accompaniment organizations is to intervene only when their presence is requested and when there is a very real danger to a community, a human rights lawyer, a trade union organizer, or others who are seen as a hindrance to those in power. These people have already relied on their own resources to the ultimate, and many have lost friends or family to violence. If the intervention does not take place, the chances are that those who request it will not end up resourceful and independent but dead.

A difficult ethical question is whether those who intervene have the right to endanger people who support them in their work—drivers, interpreters, property owners who rent space to them. These people and their families may be seen as easier targets than the foreigners. One could say that the income from such work is much needed, but do peace workers have a right to bring people into danger because of their poverty? This dilemma cannot be avoided altogether. Organizations working in Latin America insist that their volunteers have fluent Spanish, which eliminates the need for interpreters, but in many countries where work is undertaken the language is not widely studied elsewhere. Though volunteers are sent to immersion courses, they are not likely to be fluent enough to do without interpreters. Drivers and interpreters may be willing to undertake the risk because conditions are already so violent that they do not expect anything worse. Wherever local people are to be involved in providing services, an ethical principle would be that of informed consent. The outside organization must also take great care to protect such people.

Questions of justice and equity arise when an organization decides to undertake intervention and accompaniment. The supply of volunteers is limited. By what right does an organization settle resident volunteers in one village and not another? Why accompany one endangered human rights lawyer out of seven? The Fellowship of Reconciliation has two peace volunteers living fulltime in the main rural village of the Peace Community of San José de Apartadó. The community has a newer settlement, formed after an armed police post was set up in their original township, and the outlying villages uphill. These are visited only occasionally by these and other volunteers. Are some being helped rather than others? This is not an unusual dilemma. Anyone in any country wishing to give effort or money to a good cause has far too many to choose from. For example, if wells are dug in one village through development aid, does this put its inhabitants in a position of economic control over those in neighboring villages?

Some criteria help to determine the choice of accompaniment. Organizations do not decide where to come in; they respond to clear requests from within the country. A village might be helped because it had declared itself a peace zone, but not if the army was attacking it because it had in reality engaged in guerrilla activity. A lawyer threatened for defending human rights could be accompanied but not one whose wealth attracted attacks by gangs. We need to do the good which is presented to us, rather than doing nothing while setting up some kind of competition of danger and inviting applications. It would not be right for the Samaritan to leave the injured man on the Jericho road while he went off to check whether on the Bethlehem road there was someone with more urgent need.

If the presence of outsiders offers protection to those threatened, what happens when the outsiders go? Armed men wearing balaclavas visited one woman living near San José de Apartadó. "Are the gringos still in the village? Tell the people that when they are gone we will come and kill them." One can imagine that hatred might become worse because violence has been thwarted by the presence of the accompaniers. This danger is recognized by organizations, who aim, through successions of volunteers, to remain present as long as they are needed. In time countries undergo political changes that reduce the power of violence. Chile is a current example. We cannot guarantee that accompaniment will continue as long as it is needed. We should still undertake it, provided the organization gives its best efforts to ensuring continuity. "We are not called to be successful but to be faithful." It is something if one generation of children is enabled to grow up in their own homes with living parents rather than becoming orphans or taking refuges in overcrowded cities.

Those who go unarmed are often challenged: "You are stupidly getting into trouble. In the end the armed forces will have to risk their lives to rescue you." This was said when three of the kidnapped Christian Peacemaker Team in Baghdad were discovered and liberated by British troops. One answer could be that it is more right to go into a country to help peace among its people than to kill them, and that peacemakers do not request or expect intervention by the military. This is a special case of a dilemma that faces all who are committed to nonviolence, whether or not they perceive it. Are they taking advantage of the society in which they live, which is protected externally by military forces and internally by police who if necessary will use force?

One answer is that a good government has the right to use force to maintain a peaceful society. Paul argued that "the authority does not bear the sword in vain. It is the servant of God to execute wrath on the wrongdoer" (Rom. 13:4). A number of early Quakers also adopted this position, taking nonviolence to be a personal and religious commitment. Today some argue that, while nation-states should not engage in armed activity, the cause of peace requires that the United Nations have troops to protect those attacked. A more rigorous commitment to peace is based on the perception that violence breeds violence. When the military, however well trained, are in a position of power, abuses will follow. Costa Rica abolished its armed forces in 1948. Improved health and education in that country show that nonviolence is not always a path to martyrdom.

However, Costa Rica is an exception. Most governments have armed forces. How are those committed to nonviolence to live in states which use force, however democratically they are governed? Returning to our subject, how are those engaged in nonviolent intervention to act, in a context where violence rules? The ethical answer might be to recognize that, although we are part of an imperfect world, we are not to be conformed to it but to live in a society governed by force in such a way that we are helping to transform it.

One ethical dilemma is built into the very nature of accompaniment. Why does the presence of foreigners deter some acts of violence? Because they are citizens of countries that have international power, which can make things difficult if any of their nationals are harmed. I have New Zealand and British passports. If I had been arrested in Colombia, the British embassy would have taken notice. Britain is an ally of the U.S., and the Colombian government depends on U.S. military and economic support. Does this mean that nonviolent intervention is rooted in the military and economic power of such countries as the U.S. and its allies? Is nonviolent accompaniment total hypocrisy?

It would be dishonest not to recognize why international volunteers have leverage. One answer might be that accompaniment is a way of beating swords into ploughshares, of converting international power to the side of human rights, not of oppression. This is very dangerous; those who go along with force or injustice, thinking they can modify its effects, usually find themselves compromised and in the service of harm not of good. Perhaps the dilemma is insoluble. Perhaps the ethical solution is to engage in accompaniment, if called to do so, while also working to modify the policies of one's own and other powerful countries. Many of the accompaniment organizations take this position, and call on their supporters to use their rights as citizens to affect their governments.

Very rarely is it simple to choose the right course of action. For individuals considering nonviolent intervention, and for organizations practising it, guiding principles are trust, experience, and discernment, grounded in love of one's neighbor.

NOTES

1. W. H. C. Frend, *A New Eusebius: Documents Illustrating the History of the Church to AD 337* (London, U.K.: SPCK, 1987), 20-24.

2. Dag Hammarskjold, *Markings* (New York: Alfred A. Knopf, 1993), 96

3. William Penn, *Some Fruits of Solitude*, Part I, 544-6

Part VII
OVERCOMING VIOLENCE

Chapter 17

SEEKING CULTURES OF PEACE

Forum of Opinion

MENNONITE FROM AUSTRALIA

I am from the Mennonite Network in Australia and New Zealand. I just want to reflect on our discussions and what they have meant for me. As the discussion has progressed, we've dropped the barriers evident at the beginning between the various groups from around Asia. Those differences seemed to disappear as people had the chance to have a voice. I think it to be a crucial principle that our differences disappear as we have a chance to voice them.

So often we have things inside ourselves about which we feel unhappy, and we are not able to put them to one side until we actually express them, talk about them, and give ourselves a voice. The groups representing different nations were so happy the day after they were able to sing, to talk about their stories and their experiences; whereas before, they all seemed removed and separated. First it was the Mennonites, and then the Quakers, and then the Church of the Brethren. As each group had the chance to express their own story, they felt free. The worship began to grow, to become more wonderful and inclusive. I felt the same way myself. Before speaking, I was looking around and feeling a bit on the outside. When I had the chance to speak, I suddenly felt different. I was one with you.

Maybe a large part of the problem of religious pluralism is that we don't give others the chance to tell their stories; and because so many have no power of a voice, they feel they must explode their stories with a bomb. They want to get attention by blowing up some people, because they feel that otherwise they have no chance to speak. When people are listened to and have a voice, they feel a sense of freedom. I believe this applies to poverty as well, because the poor are dispossessed and have no power, so they feel that they have no voice. We don't always give them a voice by giving them money. When we create the opportunity for the poor to have a voice and be heard, then even in their poverty they have power. Therefore a voice is more powerful than poverty.

The same is true with injustice. When we give people a chance to be able to voice their concerns and to be heard, then they feel that they can perhaps find a way out of the injustice that they are suffering. Our brothers from India feel like a minority group in their own culture. About three percent of the people in India are Christian, and about six percent in the province of Gujarat are Christian. They felt that they had no opportunity to give voice to their own stories. Here they had the opportunity to tell their stories, and I saw the joy on their faces as they did so. I have learned that something so simple and fundamental as giving people the opportunity to speak, to tell their stories, to have that voice is so important. It's been crucial for me personally to observe that in a very fundamental way we can begin making peace by allowing each other to be heard.

MENNONITE SPEAKER FROM INDONESIA

First, how do we overcome the poverty? I know that many people in Indonesia live in poverty, especially in the village area. And I know that many of them go abroad to seek work in other nations and end up as prostitutes. So how do we overcome the poverty? Second, what shall we do together as the Mennonite churches in Asia? I feel that many churches do not care to help other churches, even in the same denomination. Now is the time we can help each other. Third, I suggest that we establish an association in every country. In Indonesia, we have three Mennonite synods. Perhaps we can arrange to confer together because of our government officials sometimes limit our opportunity to raise questions with them. So we as Christians need to do something to support our programs.

MENNONITE FROM KOREA

From these conversations I learned many things. Consideration of peace includes shalom, pluralism, injustice, and poverty. I believe we should develop a network of centers of education for pastors in Asian countries so that we can bring this kind of peace education to the churches. Pastors must learn first, then the people. In Psalm 34:14 through the mouth of King David we have the biblical instruction, "Seek peace and pursue it." But before saying that, he emphatically said, "Depart from evil, and do good." And Paul in Galatians 6:9 instructed us, "Do not grow weary in doing what is right, for we will reap at harvest time, if we do not give up."

MENNONITE-BRETHREN CHURCH MEMBER FROM INDIA

We have gathered here and heard from different churches and different nations pertaining to the themes religious plurality, poverty, and injustice. I have learned that we are all sailing on the same boat. When we hear from Filipinos, Indonesians, Japanese, Koreans, even Indians, we are in the same boat. I used to feel we in India are uniquely living in a pluralistic society. We have continual struggle and tension between these religions. But I find all of us are facing the same situation. When we come together, we share our experiences. This gives us extra strength to cope and bear up when we go back home.

We often feel we are the only minority living in a much larger religious group. In my own country, India, the Christians are a minority, three percent of the people. Among these three percent Christians, Mennonites are a very, very tiny minority. We have larger Catholic, Protestant, and Orthodox Church populations. If you go to many Christian churches and ask about the Mennonites, most don't even know who Mennonites are. But I learned that the situation in which I live is similar to that in other nations of Asia. This gives us a boost, an encouragement to continue our work.

The same is true regarding poverty and injustice. All of us are facing poverty and injustice. The exceptions are the Asian nations that are more affluent: Japan, Korea to a certain extent, and possibly Australia. Most Christians in Asia, including the Mennonites, are under the poverty level. So these conversations give us a stage where we can identify each other, where we can see each other sailing in the same boat. Probably this will help us to pray for each other in a better way. Whenever I remember Indonesia I will remember that some Christians are struggling for justice; some churches are opposing the nuclear atomic power station; I need to support these sisters and brothers with my prayers.

The prime minister and government of India wanted to sign an agreement with the U.S. Atomic Energy Department, but most of the alliance partners opposed it. Now there is tension between the majority ruling party, the minority parties, and the major opposition. Each group has its own pros and cons. They say these are the benefits and costs, advantages and disadvantages. However the common person does not understand. Atomic energy can be used in a positive way, but it is dangerous because the byproducts can be negative.

In our own city we have a small atomic energy plant. It provides electricity to the manufacturers. By mistake, the plant let loose a small amount of waste into a small pond. The next day we saw all the fish in the pond had died. Atomic waste is so dangerous, not only for fish but also for humans. The same accident could happen to people. Unfortunately, that picture is not shown to the people. They show only the advantages of having more electricity. I hope we will clearly point out the pros and cons, so that we can educate our own people. We are a small light, but one day we may be a big light. Any movement in the world starts with one or two people. It grows and becomes a big movement. Maybe God wants the Mennonite people in Indonesia to do that. Let's do that in Jesus' name.

INDONESIAN MENNONITE SPEAKER

These conversations helped me to consider seriously our missions and contacts, poverty, religious pluralism, injustice, ecological crisis, sufferings, racial and gender discrimination. I believe our church's mission contacts can help to bring peace in our land. But many of our churches, especially in Indonesia, are not conscious of these contacts and have not made the issue of peace a main concern or mission. So I propose that we ask the leaders of the churches make a programmatic effort to bring awareness to our local churches and to make the issues of peace an the integral part or even the essence of their church's mission.

SPEAKER FROM THE MENNONITE CHURCH IN INDONESIA

I have learned in these conversations that to create peace in this world, we have to build good relationships. We have to build a strong network between the churches, between the churches in our own countries and those in the world, between the churches in Indonesia,

India, Japan, North America, and Australia. If we build good relationships, we can have the possibility to bring peace, to speak up about the possibility in this life of bringing God's kingdom to this world.

MENNONITE BISHOP FROM THE PHILIPPINES

I just want to say that we have a limited time to work for peace in our land. I ask you to spend two or three minutes every day in prayer. We have same God, and we have two knees to kneel down and pray to God. I do believe our God is an unlimited God. So just take time every day to pray for our networking, for peace in our land. I believe our prayer will change our world to be better.

MENNONITE SPEAKER FROM ASIA

We Mennonites have had conversations with Catholics, Lutherans, and other groups, and these churches have similar religious practices to ours. But I have heard that some of the churches do not believe in baptism. They don't even take even Holy Communion, but they do get married in their church. How far can Mennonites and other Anabaptists take religious pluralism in combining with such groups? Christians are known for their peacemaking and other activities, but if they do not accept Jesus Christ as their personal savior by taking baptism, how they are Christians? Anabaptists stress following Jesus Christ even more other churches. How far is too far in religious pluralism?

MENNONITE SPEAKER FROM ASIA

John Roth, who is a professor of Old Testament at the Goshen College in Indiana, said that when we conform too tightly to our own traditions, we take a dangerous risk. Anabaptism arose in the sixteenth century as a result of Catholics sticking too tightly to their own traditions. We have our own traditions, including baptism, but then we also are in danger of judging other people. During the Reformation time, such judgments led the Catholic people to kill Anabaptists. So we have to be careful to pray about such judgments.

SPEAKER FROM AUSTRALIA

The differences between the Brethren, the Friends, and the Mennonites in our discussions show that we are practicing our own religious pluralism. By peacefully assembling and discussing, we show how we can go back to our own countries and embody religious pluralism. The fact that there are believers here who don't get baptized is insignificant in the whole stream of our being together as the body of Christ. Some people are the hands, some people are the feet, and some people are the mouth. What makes us unique as Christians is that we understand other denominations. People in Australia sometimes say, "Why would I become a Christian when all you do is fight among yourselves?" That is why we are in this gathering. We are demonstrating religious pluralism so that when we go home to our churches and our communities, we can demonstrate the same religious pluralism.

MENNONITE SPEAKER FROM ASIA

In these conversations are three denominations, Friends (Quakers), Church of the Brethren, and Mennonites. By sharing with one another to do good, we are doing the good in common. The Bible says, "Do not be weary in doing what is right" (Gal. 6:9). So in our own life, in our own thinking, we perceive what peace is and what justice is. We perceive how we could seek peace and how we pursue it but always from out own point of view as Friends, Brethren, or Mennonites. Whatever each of us can do toward pursuing or seeking peace, let us do it. If we cannot do it, let us ask the others to help us.

MENNONITE SPEAKER FROM JAPAN

In Japan before World War II, the emperor was treated like Jesus Christ, or like God. People worshiped the emperor. In the old days, Christians were persecuted, and during World War II they were put in jail. After World War II, all of this stopped. Since then we do not have persecution in Japan. A person is free to be religious. In Indonesia and India, Muslims and Christians live together, but in Japan, we have no Islamic people. Indeed, Islamic people can stay in Japan, but very few do. I have learned here at this conference that Japan is changing its attitude toward religion. In recent years Christmas has come to be accepted. Christmas is no longer only for Christians. Everybody goes grocery shopping; sings jingle bells, jingle bells; and feels Christmas happiness. Nowadays Christmas is a Japanese tradition. But here in Indonesia, everything is so different. In our discussions I have learned how to make peace in our church, our country, our community.

MENNONITE BISHOP FROM THE PHILIPPINES

I remember that the speaker from India said to us, "We cannot pursue peace and justice without money." Now I would like to share with you that in the Philippines we have no money. But we can influence our government officials, especially the high school or elementary principals, to do something about peace in our land. We can encourage teachers to let their pupils write something about peace. They could write about how peace can be increased in their respective homes by saying, "Mama, Papa, the peace of the Lord be with you." It will reduce misunderstandings. No money is involved.

SPEAKER FROM INDIA

I am talking with the respect to the context in India where I live. When we speak in India about the society or social life, we hardly feel any difference among the religions, whether Christian, Muslim, Hindu, Buddhist, or even other religions. We mingle, sit together, eat together, talk together, and work together. The encounters don't bring out any differences, which is a good thing, one that should be continued. However, when we start talking about religion, exclusiveness begins. Then one is Christian, another is Muslim, and so on and so on. If we want to promote peace, then I believe we will have to talk less about religion. Every religion has the claim that it is the right one. Christians also have the same claim. So as far as living peacefully, having a harmonious society, I think the binding element is culture. Even here in Java, I find that culture is the link between all the religions. So we should promote a culture in which religion does not separate us.

How we express our faith is a very big issue directing how we encounter one another. I remember the GKMI (Mennonite) president Aristarchus Sukarto telling us that the biblical passage John 14:6, in which Jesus says, "I am the way, the truth, and the life," means that the type of life Jesus lived we should also live. Only then are we following the way of which he spoke. Jesus did not hand us a personal answer, but rather he has shown us the way; he has shown us the light. I believe we should take that way. On this point everybody is agreed: the Muslims agree, the Hindus agree, even other religions agree. Living that kind of life will bring peace to the world.

MENNONITE SPEAKER FROM AUSTRALIA

I believe Jesus came not to start a new religion but to show us a way of life and to bring us life. I think only when we are able to share that love and that way of life that we can build bridges of peace. Unfortunately, religion is about trying to put things in a box to protect them, when our lives should be open, inclusive, accepting and inviting. What I want to take back to the Anabaptist Association in Australia and New Zealand is the importance of partnership, because we can grow only when we get alongside other people. I believe it is very good for all of us to think of other churches as partners. We are working in different ways, but we can share and support one another. Giving and receiving goes both ways.

I am involved in a project in Manly, Australia, which has a partnership with Manado in Indonesia. It is a two-way partnership, because those of us who live in Manly have learned so much from the people in Manado. We have had people going to and returning from Manado, and their lives have been changed because of what they have learned from the people there. Partnership is always equal, not one above the other, but it is also about respecting our differences. Being equal means both giving and receiving. I am from the Anabaptist Association, which is a network, not a church. It includes people from all over Australia and New Zealand. I want to be able to say to them that it's important for us to partner not only with Anabaptists in Australia and New Zealand but also with people outside in Indonesia, India, Philippines, and Japan. I want to make them aware that there are some very wonderful and exciting things happening.

MENNONITE SPEAKER FROM INDIA

We are trying to make openness compatible with being Christian. We are compromising the exclusiveness, but it's all right. Sometimes in India we have a problem with the Pentecostal groups. We are peace-loving Mennonites, and most of our chapters are more than 100 years old. Pentecostals are more recent and are growing rapidly. They feature healing, and everyone gets sick so understands the appeal of healing. In their preaching and teaching they call for healing through prayer and services of healing. They bring everyone together, Christian and non-Christians, thank them, take pictures outside and get money somehow. But that makes us part of the picture too. Sometimes we Christians make problems for the other Christians, and that is wrong.

We have a hospitality program in our church, and we have a training course for general nursing and for nursing aids. We were taking only Christian girls, but then a few years ago we started to take non-Christian girls when they apply. One non-Christian girl came and we told her, "You have to live in the hostel. You have to come to chapel and church." She agreed. After three years training, she told her non-Christian friends, "They are not asking me to become a Christian, but I am following Christianity." She was a regular attendant at church and became a member of the choir. She didn't receive baptism, but she learned something that was beneficial for her. So this girl's story shows how we preach. Preaching is to include others in our way of living, to teach by example. If we love the others, they will love us.

I worked in a government job where I was the only Christian. Al my coworkers were Hindu, but I had a good relationship with them. I went to their places, they came to my place. They came for Christmas, and I went to their festivals. We ate together. Between us was a relationship from the heart which is love, the love of Christ, which we have learned. So we can be in mission not only by preaching or telling but also by showing through our relationship who we are, how we love, and how we forgive. This is the practical preaching we need.

BRETHREN SPEAKER FROM INDIA

In overcoming poverty we should start from our local church. Changing the unjust economic system in our country will be very difficult, and changing the economic injustices in all the world will be even more difficult. Therefore I think it best for us to start in our locality. The church must be pay attention to our own church property to bring peace in our land. We can also start with our own church to be in a good relationship with other groups and other religions. The local church can't be exclusive. We must open our relationships with other groups and other religions. I think we should start with our local church, and then we can can work to develop good relationships with all churches in all the world.

MENNONITE SPEAKER FROM JAPAN

I appreciate what my brother said about some of the causes of poverty in India. Instead of growing cotton that can be exported for maximum profit, perhaps they should grow food that can be eaten in India. So I looked back at my own country's history. In the early twentieth century the world economy collapsed and Japan suffered in a major way. To overcome poverty Japan turned to the resources of overseas lands. So it is crucial that we are talking about how to overcome poverty in a just way, and not any means whatever.

Nearly seventy years ago Japan attacked Pearl Harbor. Some decades before, a major earthquake hit Japan and many people died. The biggest financial contributor at that time was the United States. Later a museum display featured an old poster of the Red Cross saying, "Americans, stand up and help the Japanese people who are suffering. If you don't act now, many people will die from hunger." So they stood up to overcome poverty and suffering. Some decades later the same country attacked Japan, but it is because Japan attacked Pearl Harbor first.

Our problem is not just to overcome poverty but also to create a framework by which we can work at overcoming poverty in a just way. Especially we should first try to find a way to work within our own resources. You already know how Japan tried to colonize Korea, entered into China, and even reached as far as Indonesia. Before we expect others to help by sending their resources, we should find a way to use our own. We may be able to do something for ourselves first. But if the problem is beyond us, then we may turn to others for help. As Christians we should work together, volunteer, and help each other. By so doing, we can show the rest of society what it means to work to overcome poverty in a just way.

SPEAKER FROM INDIA

What have we learned from these discussions? The first thing I have learned is that many people all around the world are struggling to build peace among their neighbors and between the nations. Second, it is crucial to build a global network with each other. So I will bring this issue to our church and then try to develop some network, some new relationship. The third thing is probably small, but crucial. To work toward making peace, the starting point is relationship. Develop a good relationship with each other, between individuals, within churches, and within countries, and these relationships can flourish into more peaceful communities.

MENNONITE SPEAKER FROM INDIA

The question before us is what can we implement from what we are learning in our discussions together. In India we Mennonites already have a national association, the Mennonite Christian Fellowship of India, for which I work as director. We have several types of programs, including a program of peace and justice. In parts of India, we are facing Maoist communist violence. This type of violence is very intense in some regions, so we are planning a peace promotion program in those regions. For next year we have already planned to bring together a peace promotion team from among the religions in those communities. We will train the pastors who will work with the community. The pastors will choose persons whom we will also train.

From our discussions I am thinking we will develop another program. We have been discussing global warming and atomic energy with the threat of radioactive waste and nuclear proliferation. So I think we will share those ideas with the larger pool of community people. Already we are taking a different approach to global warming. Because trees attract rain and many parts of India face a drought situation, we are conducting a program of planting trees to prevent drought. Trees also convert carbon dioxide to oxygen, and carbon dioxide is a cause of global warming. So the tree planting will also contribute to the reduction of global warming. We will be taking our Mennonite program of concern about global warming program to the churches and the common people of India.

We will also promote opposition to nuclear power, even though we may be going against our government. The government has taken up the development of nuclear power, and is collaborating with the United States to produce it. Some political parties, including the Communist Party, are opposing nuclear power; so if we promote this program, we may be branded as communists. In any case, it is a good thing that, through the church's platform with the community, we can make the people aware of the danger of nuclear power.

MENNONITE SPEAKER FROM INDIA

I would like to tell you, as the previous speaker has mentioned, that in India we have a Mennonite Christian Fellowship. Under this umbrella, we give vocational training to students with no money. We can also provide relief assistance to the poor through this organization. A few years ago the Mennonite church in India wanted to help a local congregation with about twenty-five Christians families. The majority of people in that community are non-Christian, and they are quite poor. They don't have any means of subsistence other than one crop. The same is true of everyone in that general area. Though they have some land they cannot make it productive, because it is not fertile land. Working together, the Mennonite Central Committee and Mennonite church developed a relief program for the area. Each family, whether Christian or non-Christian exchanged its one acre of unproductive land for one acre of productive land.

Everyone had to work together. All had to work for their own field and also help the others. They were getting food for their work. That work helped each and all, and it was a witness. Each family received one acre of productive land, and it was their land. We provided help with irrigating their fields, and we demonstrated modern methods of raising rice with better yields. This is one way we can help to do justice while relieving poverty.

MENNONITE SPEAKER FROM JAPAN

Sometimes we contrast mission in opposition to relief. Mission proclaims the gospel, plants churches, and is evangelical. Relief provides vocational schools, agricultural assistance, and help for the poor. How are we to balance programs of mission, church planting, evangelism, and relief? The Mennonites are putting them into one category, one kind of program. They keep them together as a whole to make peace, to save people, to help, to support, to restore.

MENNONITE SPEAKER FROM JAPAN

I gave you the historical illustration of what happened in the past, over half a century ago. Now I give you a modern illustration, and I would like to know what you think about this issue. The point I am making is that overcoming poverty does not necessarily lead to peace. The United States fed Japan and we attacked them. Later the United States fed us after World War II, but that did not lead to a witness for Christ, for there are not many Christians in Japan. Now consider the North Korea issue. In the past the general thinking was that if we gave North Korea material assistance, like rice or other aid, they would be good-hearted, and we could go a step further toward the normalization of relationships.

It didn't work that way. The nuclear and abduction issues came up, and things are messy now. So the government is saying, or at least some groups of people are saying, we should not send any food or other assistance to North Korea until they return the people whom they have abducted from Japan.

Regarding the issue of overcoming poverty, more recently Japan has neither continued to give aid to North Korea nor to help the victims of the flood or disaster. If we did, do you think such aid would at least bring about a softening of the hostility? History has not proven that to be the case. As I asked before, how do we overcome poverty in a just way, relating it to the Christian witness, so that it is not just feeding the hungry? I don't know a practical way in the case of our relationship with North Korea.

SPEAKER FROM AUSTRALIA

I understand a bit about what you are describing, and it seems to me that the conflict goes back for many, many centuries. I think you can see a similar pattern of distrust happening in many other countries where conflict has become a part of the history and culture between races or between nations. How to address such conflict in an effective way is very, very difficult, and is not quickly solved. It takes time, just as it has taken hundreds of years to create this culture of distrust or mistrust. Overcoming it may take some time. I always think that building peace takes a long time, but bringing peace to an end can take a very short time. You can work for peace for many, many years and sometimes it only takes one word for that peace to be lost.

I see that happen in marriage. I have two friends, very good friends, who are currently going through divorce in Sidney. They spent many years building their relationship, but it took only one event to end it. Now they are going through tremendous pain, and I am trying to be a peacemaker between the two. Sometimes when you are the peacemaker, you end up becoming caught in the middle. One will say, "Ah, but you are more of a friend to the other one," and the other will say, "Why are you trying to be a friend to the other one?" So one is caught in the middle. Peace work is challenging, and it is no wonder that Jesus was crucified.

I don't really know the cultural differences between Japan and North Korea, but it might be helpful to look for creative, practical ways of doing something together. Is it possible to invite a small group from North Korea to come to spend time in Japan? That may not be possible yet, but it's a project to work on. We have come from different places to be here, to eat together, to sing together, to laugh together. We haven't quite wept together as you said, but there might come a time when we weep together. Being together in these ways, we find the walls of separation have fallen down. So the Japanese might go to North Korea and live there for awhile to allow this type of integration to happen, even if very slowly. Whether it will work or not, I do not know. Yet it could be an inspiration of something to dream about and to pray about, and the Spirit of God might allow one or two doors to open. Who knows many doors may open beyond that.

MENNONITE SPEAKER FROM JAPAN

A group of us from Tokyo, including several persons from the West, visited the Korean Anabaptist Center in South Korea as part of an exchange program recently. The Korean Anabaptist Center works with North Korean defectors. We were able to spend time and share a meal with a young man who left North Korea, and we talked about many things. In terms of Japan and North Korea getting to know each other better, the two countries are still in a process of normalization, so we can't travel and visit each other freely. I am really grateful for the work of the Korean Anabaptist Center and also Grayson Peace Church, who are playing the role of mediator and helping Japan really to understand what is going on with the North Koreans. We are all human, and when we are face to face, communicating with each other, sharing meals together, and eating the same food, we all understand that we are not totally different people. We want the staff of the Korean Anabaptist Center to know how grateful we Japanese Mennonites are for what they are doing.

MENNONITE SPEAKER FROM JAPAN

My brother, all Japanese people and soldiers did what was wrong. My wife said to me just recently that she forgives me, and I very much appreciate it. I said to her, "Thank you very much for your forgiveness." Our relationship is sometimes very good, sometimes very difficult. Sometimes in a long history, some things are forgotten and some are not, but it is good to talk about it openly. In that kind of conflicted history I am very thankful to Jesus Christ. He's the only one who can provide the way for people to make up with each other. He's the only one who can mediate the differences between countries, not only between Korea and Japan, but also other countries that have fought against one another.

I want to thank the Mennonites and others who visited those taken to Korea after the Korean Civil War. They also provided vocational training for orphans and they started a program for reconciliation between Japan and Korea. In the 1960s they held conferences for reconciliation between Japan and Korea. Somehow those conferences were discontinued. More recently the Mennonites are again working to bring people together. Church members in Japan come to visit Korea and they have a good relationship together. They sit and talk together openly from their hearts. Also brothers and sisters from Korea visit Japan and they have a good relationship together. These exchanges are an effort at community building, a kind of a peacemaking with and for each other, and they are a very good starting point. Thank you for your hard work in exchange programs with our country so that we can learn to know one another. .

SPEAKER FROM INDONESIA

Economic injustice against the poor is to be found in Indonesia. No medicine is available for the poor people even though they are dying. Even Christian hospitals have no medicine for the poor. No education is available for the poor, even when the poor are more capable than the rich.

MENNONITE FROM INDIA

I should communicate the vision of this conference with others, not only with the people of my church, but with my neighbors and my community. I have to build relationships. I have to look for other persons of peace and make relationships with them. Also I need to pray and to enlist others to pray for the peace movement.

SPEAKER FROM INDIA

I am involved with a radio ministry full time. We send out seven broadcasts in eight different languages of India, Nepal, and Bhutan. One of the programs is called Giver of Peace in my native language, and the program is truly a giver of peace. When we share the gospel message, we receive letters from the listeners, who write to us that the word of God has touched their hearts and they have received peace in their lives. Many broken families have been united, and people have come to know the Lord. I thank God for the possibility to share the gospel through the radio.

SPEAKER FROM JAPAN

Australia has appointed Kevin Rudd to be prime minister. For eleven years John Howard was prime minister. Why the change? What difference does this make for policies about global warming, climate change, segregation of aboriginal people, discrimination, or the war on terror?

SPEAKER FROM AUSTRALIA

The change of political parties in Australia probably has more to do with internal issues than external issues. Primarily, a lot of people thought it was time for a change. However the big issue was an industrial work relations campaign. I suppose issues that were globally based, like Australia being involved in Afghanistan and in Iraq, might have pushed some people toward a change. However, I think primarily it had to do with internal issues. People were scared that they would lose their jobs in a new industrial relations climate.

One way that we can to bring peace in that area is to give the new government a chance. Give them a chance to do what it is they want to do, and then work with the local communities to come up with a solution. Australia seems to be in a position where internally it's fairly stable. We don't have a lot of the religious issues that are found in other countries, although there are some. We're free to worship in whatever way we want. We are also free not to worship, and most people don't.

SPEAKER FROM AUSTRALIA

Many churches in Australia are fairly conservative. A wide branch of the church was very supportive of going to war in Iraq, Iran, and Afghanistan, and of the war on terror, especially since the September 11, 2001, attack on the Twin Towers in the United States and the October 2002 bombings in Bali, Indonesia.

One thing we try to do as a peace church is to share the message of peace among the other churches, pointing to the Bible where Jesus says if someone slaps you on the cheek, turn your other cheek also (Matt. 5:39). That takes a lot of communication. It is something we've been going over in our church, and talking about with other churches in our area to bring them closer to our view. It has caused friction between the pastors and heated discussion among leaders of those churches.

However, the longer the war goes on, the more people get tired of it. So from a peace church perspective, we probably should start healing some of the internal rift between the people and the government. Even though we have a new government, it is still the government that sent our soldiers in to fight in the war. Healing the rift is lot easier said than done.

SPEAKER FROM AUSTRALIA

We used to complain about South Africa's apartheid policies, but some of the Australian polices were much worse. Under our last government there was no formal apology to our indigenous people. My family is English, and I should probably stand and apologize to all of you, because when the British went to Australia, we dominated and oppressed the indigenous people. Since then, our Australian governments have carried on the same policy of not treating our indigenous people as human beings.

The big issue is that many of our aboriginal people are Christian because they have lived in mission institutions and have had Christianity forced upon them. They have lost many their tribal ways, and as a result they have lost much of their identity. My church along with a group of other people is active in Youth with a Mission. We are trying to help the tribal people to reconcile their culture with Christianity. It takes a great deal of effort. In Australia much of what we have to do is to roll up our sleeves and work side by side. Creating relationship is the only way you get anything done in Australia. That is how it all starts. It can take twenty-two, twenty-three, or twenty-four years before you can even talk to aboriginal people about Jesus after you've met them. Purely and simply, they want to be able to know who you are and where you come from before they trust you.

MENNONITE SPEAKER FROM JAPAN

Indonesia has 200 million people, hundreds of islands, and many cultures. It is a country with Islamic people, many cultures, and many races. So, how do you live with plurality?

MENNONITE SPEAKER FROM INDONESIA

I try to view religious plurality in the perspective of the church. The church should be a peacemaking community. It should be a community that shares the gospel of peace with the world by promoting peace and justice in its own context. The goal is to empower civil society as a whole to deal properly with injustice, extreme poverty, suffering, racial and gender discrimination.

As a part of civil society, the church has to relate to other parts of the society. In its context, the presence of other religions and beliefs has to be appreciated properly and positively. Religious plurality can be viewed as the richness of spiritual traditions governing life. In other words, religious plurality is a chance for the church to share its good news in a way that brings improvement, even transformation, to the society at large. In the context of Southern Asia, the church plays a transformative role together with people of other religions and beliefs. In joining hands with people of all religions and beliefs, the church is addressing the problems of justice, extreme poverty, suffering, and ecological problems.

So I feel positive about religious plurality, because it offers us a richness of spiritual traditions affirming life. What the church has to do is open itself to make way for dialogue and cooperation with other people of various religions and beliefs.

MENNONITE SPEAKER FROM JAPAN

How about Philippines? You are a nation with many Christians, predominantly Roman Catholic, but also including Islamic people. Of course you have conflicts in your country, not only political, but also economic. What are the special issues to address in your country?

MENNNONITE BISHOP FROM THE PHILIPPINES

In the Philippines we are concerned about the political assassination of our leading citizens. At least nine hundred activists and journalists have been killed since 2001. Recently the UN issued a statement that the armed forces of the Philippines are implicated in the political killings. We in the Philippines are joining together with other churches to encourage our government officials to convince our president to put a stop to these political killings. The harassment and killing have also been directed at evangelical pastors. In the hinterland of northern Luzon, two pastors from churches that include indigenous people were assassinated, and again the culprits are believed to be the government's soldiers.

Mindanao is our greatest problem. The Bangsamoro separatist Islamic group does a great deal of damage in southern Mindanao. They introduced terrorism and disrupted peace and order. Many suicide bombings have have occurred in Manila and southern Mindinao. I have joined a new group called the Christian Bishops and Ministerial Association of the Philippines, and I am now one of the directors. With our different church conferences joining together, we hope to influence our governors, our senators, our congressmen, and especially the president to put an end to the murder and corruption. During my college days the number one example of corruption was China. Now the Philippines is considered as number one in corruption. So we really have to curb corruption. We need your prayers and your help, along with the prayers and help of all our people and bishops. I thank the Lord that I have been given the opportunity to be with you. At least I have learned something about how to work at peace and reconciliation.

One of the practical things we plan to do to promote peace is to invite all elementary teachers and principals throughout the country to become involved. We plan to urge them to ask their pupils to write essays about bringing peace to the conflicts Filipinos are experiencing: peace in our land, peace in our home, peace in our community, peace in our country. Then the powers of disruption will decline. We will try to encourage children to say, "Mama, Papa, let the peace of God be with you." I know this can make a great impact on the parents. It is the best we can do because we have no money. At least we are trying to strengthen our people. Regarding corruption, I recommend that all pastors meet with the police in Bible studies. It is something I've been doing.

Regarding poverty in the Philippines, eleven million persons live in households in which the per capita income is less than one U.S. dollar per day. The exchange rate for U.S. dollars in the Philippines is 42 pesos. Imagine a family of three, a family of five, or a family of six with a per capita income of only 42 pesos a day—one dollar a day per person for a family. Ninety percent of the members of the Integrated Mennonite Church in the Philippines, 3,500 persons, belong to households whose family per capita income is less than one U.S. dollar per day. My wife has been leading my home church in a livelihood project, and I believe this is one way to overcome poverty.

Before I go back to my country, I want to say the most important thing, my dear colleagues in Christ, is to pray. To pray, to pray, to pray! That's what we need today. To pray. Let your knees be calloused. Pray!

MENNONITE SPEAKER FROM KOREA

In our country the Mennonite church and the Anabaptist Korean Center try to build a network with other denominations to provide alternative service for the people who have conscientious objection to military service. Since military service is mandated, we are trying to find an alternative to such service. There is much violence around us, so we are also trying to develop a peace education center. We are working on a program of mediation between offenders and their victims. We encourage people who are in prison to meet together with their victims, and we try to encourage some kind of reconciliation. We are also trying to develop a peace academy or peace institute for East Asia, including Japan, Taiwan, China, and Hong Kong. We want to communicate more with other countries.

MENNONTE SPEAKER FROM JAPAN

In Japan we have a constitution in which Article 9 promotes peacemaking. Many people give verbal support to Article 9, but in fact only a small minority party in the Diet (the legislature) strongly support this peacemaking article. As a Mennonite, as a member of a nonviolent church, I've been thinking and praying for that one small party of the Diet to give strong public support to Article 9.

SPEAKER FROM INDONESIA

Pluralism has both a positive and a negative impact in Indonesia. I believe we must have a new concept of mission in the Indonesia context in order that the negative impact of pluralism can be overcome. How do we define the Christian mission? On one hand we should be proclaiming the gospel, and on the other hand we should be showing the love of Christ. In the Indonesia context I believe the best mission approach is to show the love of Christ. Openly proclaiming the gospel in our region is very dangerous—very, very dangerous! In my opinion, to overcome the negative impact of pluralism in Indonesia, we need to encourage a new concept of mission: to show the love of Christ.

MENNONITE SPEAKER FROM INDIA

Let me share something about the initiatives in the church in India. We may consider them in two areas: one within the church, and the other outside of the church. Consider first what we are doing within the church. I come from the Mennonite Brethren who are in south India. We also double as a center for peace studies. Our intention is that through this center we want to educate our own people by giving them the skills of mediation and peacebuilding. In line with this we have introduced courses into our Bible college, so that our students, the future leaders of the church, will have peacemaking tools with which to work. We also conduct training programs at the national and local levels. We want to help the churches to take peace initiatives within their congregations and their communities.

Now consider what we are doing outside of our churches. Bishop Ambrocio of the Philippines was saying we should take Bible classes to the police. In our society that may not be possible because we are such a small minority, but I want to share this. A few years ago our government realized that the police are not very effective with the stick and gun. I don't know about other countries, but in my country, if you are in the hands of policemen, you will be nicely beaten. The first job they do is beating. They know how to beat and how to extract confessions from a person who is apprehended. So people try to escape from the police. They hide somewhere and they use whatever means they have to avoid arrest. The government has come to understand this.

We have an institution called the Henry Martyn Institution in Hyderabad, which is very close to a police training center. This center trains bureaucrats in the police department and other high officials from all over India. These officials learned of peace initiatives in the Mennonite church, and they approached the Mennonite Central Committee (MCC) staff in Calcutta to come and give training to young probationary police officers. Our Indian MCC staff who are in charge of the peace program went there and trained these would-be police and high officials. This was one initiative we have taken outside of the church.

A second initiative is in south India where I come from. There you often have community tension. So, some of our Christians, Hindus, and Muslims got together, and with the help of the government, we formed peace committees. Wherever trouble erupts, we go there and talk to the people of the community. Of course we often get threats. The Muslims threaten us, the Hindus threaten us, and always the Christians are in between. It is a privilege of Christians, and a fact well known in India, that Christians are peace-loving people. They never retaliate; they never fight. This is a testimony to the church in India, and we take this testimony wherever we go. Even when there are quarrels in small villages, our committees go there. They take the initiative to talk with the local leaders to address the problems and reduce the tension in those communities.

Let me say that the Mennonite church in India is a very, very small minority. India has about one billion people, and only 2.5 million are Christians. Among the Christians, you have Catholics, Protestants, and Orthodox. Mennonites, Church of the Brethren, Friends, and other peace-loving churches are very minute. Yet God is using us in a small way in certain parts of India to help, or provide, or take initiatives in building peace and harmony.

Chapter 18

THE ROLE OF THE CHURCHES IN OVERCOMING VIOLENCE

The Peace Churches

MENNONITE CHURCHES

The Mennonites gathered here are from a wide cross section of the Mennonite church. It has been enlightening for me to see the way the Mennonite church in Indonesia, India, Japan, Korea, the Philippines, and even Australia all have the same core values, even though we have different issues challenging us and different ways that we work at them. Here are some of the practical things we discussed.

In these discussions we learned about justice, religious pluralism, and poverty. Atsuhiro Katano stated that injustice is universal. Injustice is found in every single country in the world, no matter how big or how small it. For me, one of the main injustices is that the westernized societies don't want to share their technologies and better ways of doing things with the developing countries.

Regarding climate change, the developing countries want to emulate what the developed countries have done, because it has worked. They don't want to look at their own things in their own way. The developed countries have technologies that they can share with their brothers and sisters in the developing countries so that developing countries don't have to go on continually polluting and damaging the environment. After all, we do have only this one world.

We need to build a global network of relationships, and we need to look at local issues in a global context. Some governments are under the influence of the United States to build nuclear power plants in their own countries. They think they can produce lots of extra power, without the negative damage of atomic waste. The Western societies have not informed the developing countries that there is no such thing as clean nuclear power

We are reminded in Psalms 34:14, "seek peace and pursue it," and in Galatians 6:9, "Do not be weary in doing what is right." We as Christians and as Mennonites need to be seen doing good, not just saying we are doing good. To create peace in our world we need to build a strong relationship between the churches in our countries and those in other countries—but not only with the churches outside our countries. We Christians need to create relationships with Muslims, Hindus, and Buddhists. We also need to create relationships with those people who don't believe there is a god. Without that cooperation and that relationship building, we are not going to have peace.

Living together peacefully is not just to live together peacefully as human beings, but we also need to live together peacefully with all of God's creation. The lion and the lamb will lie down together (Isa. 11:6, and 65:25). We are not really sure as to how we were going to go about doing that, but relationship will cause that to happen. With FPLAG we saw how the church in Indonesia started talking to a radical Muslim group, and after five years a friendship is growing. It has broken down the barriers. It is hard to hate your friend. It is hard to hate someone you have lived with, you have slept with, you have worked with, you've cried with, and you've laughed with because you share the same struggles. When you are standing face to face, it's hard to not see persons for who they are and what they are as human beings.

One reason Mother Teresa won the Nobel Peace Prize was that she was willing to go out and do the hard work in her community, the hard work of creating peace, of being a peacemaker. We need to be able to do that as well in all societies. We need to be about the work of making peace before the conflict starts. Jesus didn't come to start a new religion but to show a way of life, a way of looking after the world and the people who are in it. The Historic Peace Churches should be an example of this way of life throughout our communities.

We considered some of the issues in India, especially the nuclear power plants India is in process of building. With less than three percent of the population, Christians in India cannot address the issues of nuclear power by themselves. Nor can the Mennonites, Quakers, and Brethren, with less than one percent of the population, raise this issue by themselves. We need to work together with other groups. We need to start a network with other groups and with other people who are like-minded. We need to show those who favor war that making peace is a lot better for them. To build peace takes a long time, but to destroy it takes a very short time. For two countries to have a peaceful relationship with one other often takes decades, and then a single word can destroy that peace. We need to work continually at keeping peace when we have it, because something can always go wrong, something can always be said to cause peace to break down.

Injustice cannot be erased with money. Countries have sometimes tried to pay money to compensate for past injustices. That really doesn't heal an injustice. It just gives money to the persons who were the victims of the injustice. The only way that we can heal an injustice is to change what happened to cause that injustice in the first place.

We recognize that we can't work at peacemaking alone; we have to do it together. Even though we may begin in small ways, only by working together can we actually bring about social change. Sometimes social change cannot be envisioned from where we are. Sometimes it can be seen only when we look back. Many wonderful changes have taken place, changes that we only later begin to appreciate. The environmental movement has brought about massive social change. If you compare where we stand today with where we were we stood twenty years ago, I think you will agree that our communities have a new awareness about the importance of caring for the environment. Twenty years ago there was little awareness of the issues, except for a small minority. We acknowledge that we as individuals, as groups, as communities, and as nations need to begin to implement plans. Therefore we have identified what we want to focus on in the various nations that are represented by Mennonites in this discussion: India, Australia, Indonesia, the Philippines, South Korea, and Japan.

In India we feel the need to link with other people that were also on the road in terms of being people of peace. They have an opportunity to broadcast through radio in seven different languages the outcomes from our discussions, so that the news can actually go throughout India and Nepal. And they can teach people skills in terms of peace studies; people want to live peacefully, but they don't necessarily have the skills. So in India we feel the necessity to communicate and teach those fundamental principles and ways of implementing peace.

The new government in Australia offers an opportunity to bring a new direction. As an Australian, I believe we now have a new opportunity to work in areas that have been closed for almost a decade. Our objective in Australia is to network more with other peace groups so as to influence the new government, particularly in the area of reconciliation with aboriginal people and with minority groups and refugees. I think we may to be able to generate a greater sense of oneness as a community, something that has suffered from the divisiveness of the past decade.

For Indonesian Mennonites, the three phrases that came up were dialogue, cooperate, and develop. We want to dialogue, particularly with Muslims. We want to cooperate with other Christians from outside our particular tradition, to win them over to the way of peace. We want to develop new concepts of missions that include peace as fundamental to the way forward.

In the Philippines we have major issues with the current government. In particular, we are concerned about corruption and assassination at the political level. We have an opportunity to work not in isolation but with other Christians to lobby the government to set aside the corruption and to avoid using methods of violence to achieve political objectives. We see the need to educate the youth, particularly in the schools, so as to create a vision of a culture of peace in the new growing generation. We must also pray in all humility before our God to acknowledge that we cannot do this alone, but it will be done only in and through God's grace.

In South Korea, our intention is to promote peace service as an alternative to military service. Compulsory conscription is still required in South Korea, and providing opportunities for community service as a viable alternative to military service is something the churches can pursue. Anabaptists and the Peace Center in South Korea can help local churches to gain skills and information these churches need for a peace movement. The peace churches can also become involved in mediation programs within the prisons to bring perpetrators and victims together to seek reconciliation. We would like to form a peace academy in the part of Asia that includes China, Taiwan, both North and South Korea, and Japan. We acknowledged the enormous difficulties of such an endeavor because of the generations of mistrust in their cultures, but we also acknowledged the possibilities that can come from getting people to relate together and to hear one another's stories. To start a peace academy, very exciting!

Those in Japan believe they have a unique opportunity because of the constitution that was adopted after World War II. Article Nine asserts that promoting peace is fundamental to the new constitution. This opens the possibility of enabling groups to work for peace in their own way and in their own setting. While Article Nine is written in words, it is not fully implemented in action. So many good things could happen.

CHURCH OF THE BRETHREN

Our major concern is poverty, injustice, and religious pluralism in the context of Asia. We are also concerned about global issues, particularly global warming, nuclear power, environmental hazards, and ecological threats. However, as Paulus Widjaja has pointed out, we need to be concerned about global issues in the context of Asia. For many Asians, survival and sustaining their families is their most pressing issue. Families living below the poverty line are continually suffering injustice and often are on the receiving end of local tensions. They are not in a position to think about global warming, nuclear proliferation, climate change, and ecological issues. This doesn't mean that such issues do not bother us. Our focus in the Brethren group has been on what we can do at the grassroots level to find solutions about poverty, injustice, and religious pluralism. Only when we have a healthy society, a society that can sustain itself, then and then only will there be permanent peace. This leads us to consider the following issues.

Our first issue is injustice. As has been often mentioned, injustice is universal. It exists in the workplace, the families, the church, everywhere. Women are on the receiving end of injustice, and children are at risk of injustice. One finds oneself subject to injustice on so many occasions. So what can we do about it? We need to speak about it. We need to raise the level of awareness about it. What in the church can we do? We can be a part of implementing this awareness by setting up a committee that will look into these issues and bring about new understanding to people within the church.

We suggest that when there are tensions within the community, we try to discuss these issues with the various political groups, religious parties, and other groups that are in conflict. We should try to engage these people in together in dialogue , and try to develop community agreements so we can live together peacefully. As we saw from the work of the Interracial and Ethnic Peace Forum (FPLAG), deep divisions made reconciliation very hard work. Setting up committees to respond only during isolated events of conflict will not work. We should make the work or reconciliation a continuing process. Only a continuing process will help us reach for a united and a peaceful and harmonious society.

In India we face such situations of conflict on many occasions. We know many stories about serious provocations. During such provocation, we should try to restrain ourselves and rather to incite the antagonists. One approach is to look for ways and means to bring our issue to the attention of the governments. Peaceful rallies and protest marches are one of these ways. Even at the local level, this can be effective. Peaceful rallies sometimes pay good dividends, and the government relents. We should work with different nongovernmental agencies (NGOs), including Christian NGOs that have influence within government. We should identify the organizations that are effective and associate ourselves with them. We can increase our influence by networking with government officials, working with religious leaders, and engaging political parties. We are not thinking primarily of the national scene. These efforts need to be done within our local communities. We are looking for healthy communities, which in turn will have a wider and wider influence.

Injustice also occurs because we are unaware about law, ignorant of the law. Each and every country promises some fundamental rights to its citizens. India is a democratic secular country. We are a country that promotes harmony and peaceful coexistence with each and every one. Even so, people are subject to exploitation and other kinds of injustices. Why? Even in this modern age, the simple reason is lack of awareness of the law. If one is aware of the law, if we are aware of our rights, then it will be difficult for people to exploit us. So we need to bring awareness, first within our churches, and through our churches to the wider communities. We need to make use of the tools and the rights that are provided by the government. As institutions, as churches, we need to make people aware of their rights, and this can be done by forming small groups.

Regarding religious pluralism, we face an internal conflict as Christians. We face an internal conflict within ourselves because we are living in a pluralistic society. We live with Hindus, Muslims, Sikhs, Buddhists, and with a host of other castes and creeds. At the same time we have to be true to our convictions, our belief in Lord Jesus Christ and the Ten Commandments. It's a tough job because there are so many issues that concern us. When we attend a ceremony, offerings are placed before the idol gods, and then these offerings are given to us. The question in our minds is whether we can accept and eat these offerings, or whether we should we refuse them? Refusal could be offensive to the Hindus and could result in hurting their feelings. But if we take and eat the offerings out of respect for their feelings, we are hurting God. Thereby we are moving away from our convictions and our belief in Christ. It's a real day-to-day issue for us because we live with Hindus, who have ceremonies, pujas, and religious activities on many occasions.

So what are we to do? We are agreed that we need to be faithful to our convictions. We need to tell our Hindu friends, or even our Muslim friends, that yes we are Christian, and for this reason we can't accept these offerings. At the same time we speak very respectfully. Some of us have said that if you speak respectfully, they understand your convictions. But this requires courage, because it could happen in your workplace where your manager could be a Hindu, and he could be presenting you offerings that have been placed before the Hindu gods. Because he is your boss, you will be in a tight spot if you refuse him. This actually happened in our church when our pastor refused his boss, whereas other Christians accepted the offering because they were afraid of offending their boss. People from Western countries may not able to understand this dilemma because such a situation may not have arisen. However, increasingly many Western communities have a Muslim mosque or a Hindu temple and therefore may have experienced such a situation.

This example of the conflict between Hindu customs and Christian convictions is one that we feel deeply. Christian people are alienating themselves from mainstream Hindu society because their Christian convictions stand in the way of developing more integrated relationships with their Hindu neighbors. We need to relate to the large Hindu majorities in our communities, but we also need to stick to our convictions and our belief in Christ. To work toward integration we need to create an understanding of this issue not only for ourselves, but also for all of our church members, because we all face the same situation. Only integration will bring about harmony, so we need integration within our societies with those people who come from different faiths and different backgrounds, especially in a multifaceted and very diverse culture like India.

We have decided first to try to educate our church members, to bring awareness of this message to them, because that is where we must start. Start from where you are, and then go further. Sunday school is another platform where we think that we can teach children, because they are fundamental to the future. They will be the next generation. So Sunday school could be one forum where we could bring them this awareness. Then there are many Christians, including Mennonites, who also have educational institutions. We Brethren have a few. Educational institutions could be used as a forum because there are so many people in our institutions. We find Hindus and Muslims and other students coming to be educated in our schools. We can use these educational institutions as a forum for peacebuilding. We should hold workshops in the schools and then work with other schools in tandem to integrate such workshops. This would be a real step toward a more integrated society, and this would insure peace in the future.

Regarding religious pluralism, we discussed suggestions about how we could visit hospital patients to show our Christian concern for people who are in need, not of money, but of human help. In the stressfulness of life we often don't find people ready to help each other. We could form a team to help patients, to sit with patients for a few hours. Maybe we could help them in their work, or maybe we could help them bring their belongings, or maybe we could bring in food they would like. So we believe that there are ways to get involved with the society and at the same time spread the word of the gospel while integrating more with those in other religious.

Finally we are concerned about the issue of poverty, a major challenge in developing countries. It is not just the problem of people who live below the line of poverty. It's poverty for educated youth who face unemployment. It's poverty for youth who are addicted. It's poverty for persons who have jobs but who are underpaid. We need to work to lift these people. We believe that we will find some of these people, some youth who need training, right within our own churches.

We do not intend to put up institutions for these youth, because that is an expensive proposition. What we are considering as a church is to identify such youth, determine what they like to do, and find a way to help them. Many government programs in India are beyond the awareness of people, even though the government wants to help them. Here is the same thing again, lack of awareness. We can identify the NGOs who have association with the government. In India the government has programs to help, but we need to identify these programs, inform our people, and help the people to take advantage of these programs. When we talk about India or any developing country, awareness is a big issue. Lack of awareness causes severe problems. We as a church should form teams to work on bringing awareness.

We want to have regular assessments of the work we do. We also want to coordinate with Mennonites, Quakers, and other churches in India, as well as work with churches in other countries. We intend to exchange stories among our own churches, which will provide motivation and inspiration to sustain our efforts. The difficult and the most important part is persistence. We may have with ambitious ideas, but after a few days they may all be forgotten. Continuous work is essential. We need to work hard to monitor what we decide because mere words will not solve problems. In the end we need to urge the administrative bodies of our churches to fund and encourage these programs and to set up a mechanism to operate them. The bottom line of our considerations is to work on the grassroots level, first within our churches and communities, and then within the larger society.

THE RELIGIOUS SOCIETY OF FRIENDS

Where there is injustice, there can be no peace. Injustice is a cancer that infects the whole world. It is manifested in the wrong use of power, especially military power; in poverty, debt, corruption. and the theft of resources; and in the walls of caste, class, color, religion, status, and gender, which we build to divide ourselves. Inequalities are deeply rooted in all our societies and in all our lives. We can be educated in such a way that we lose our emotional and spiritual vision. We learn not to see the poverty and injustice around us and of which we are part. In our relationships with one another there are inequalities in our practices, in who is present, who speaks, and who has influence.

Knowing our own involvement, we have to seek to remove the sword from our own hands, to probe injustices in ways that are just and do not perpetuate wrongs. We are inspired by the example of Jesus, who, living in an unjust, oppressed, and occupied country, found creative ways to bring the kingdom as good news into the lives of the poor with healing, nourishment and love. We have to engage in the politics of the eternal. We start with prayer and changed hearts. We continue with actions borne of love, love of the neighbor, and love for the oppressed.

We come from very different cultures and situations. Each of our groups and each of us as individuals have to start where we are. Some of us are Christians in a culture in which we are a minority among those of another faith. Others of us are in a majority Christian culture and need to welcome religious minorities. How are we good hosts and good neighbors? We can form relationships, listen carefully to each other, recognize and support the good work which members of other faiths do, and above all develop respect for each other's dignity.

We need to have patience and continue to respect each other's dignity. We must know each other and not think in stereotypes, and we must be aware of how our views may be formed by the agenda of the news media. If we tell our stories and hear each other's stories, perhaps together we can help transform the world's story. Our peace testimony is enriched by the recognition that it includes the struggle against disease and poverty as well as against war. We recognize also the urgency of climate change, which is already affecting Asia and the Pacific and will soon submerge all other struggles. The ways of peace and justice are the only ways to make a difference that can avoid war. People of all faiths must work together to meet the challenges that face all.

What we can do as peacemakers includes communication and building networks, projects, and actions. Communication with Quakers and with others is crucial. We want to build networks with our own people in every way that we can, but we also want to network with other churches, with other faiths, and with those who have no religious affiliation at all. Then too there are projects and actions. We have some projects already ongoing, such as the Vine and Fig Tree project. We think it's important to inform and educate young people so we can engage them with the issues. We can help each other with projects that train people and help them to train others, so the ways of nonviolence get passed on from one group of people to another.

We can also encourage our Meetings to look at the use of money and investments. Those of us who have money should be sure our money is working for our principles and not against them. Every church needs to be accountable for the use of its money. And of course, finally, as was said earlier, we need to pray and to pray for the Holy Spirit to guide us in the way forward, to help us see what other possibilities might open up as we continue to carry all these issues in our hearts.

MENNONITE RESPONDENT

When I was asked to give my reflection about our discussions, I started to think of the different things we have discussed: religious pluralism, poverty, and injustice. And I noticed that we as participants are an example of both the major and the minor things we have discussed together. Some of us are from countries that have committed major injustices against other countries. Some have come from extreme affluence and some from extreme poverty. And although we come from the same tradition of the Historic Peace Churches, we all have our own ways of expressing our faith and worshiping the Lord, our God. This shows that even within the peace church tradition, we still need to practice religious pluralism. We need to be aware that we do not have the only correct way.

We have lived together, eaten together, prayed together, laughed together, and I am sure that we have also cried together as we have listened to the stories that have been recounted in this book. We have shared from our own experiences what we as a community of Christ are going through in some very crucial issues. And as Christians from Historic Peace Church traditions, we have been considering what is fundamental in our work with Christ. While we have not always agreed, we have always been open to listen to others. We have shown that through creating relationships we can truly bring peace to our lands.

We have recounted where we see injustices in our communities and the ways that we have been able to address them. We have discussed how religious pluralism can be good and also bad, and how through relationships with other religions, we can overcome the differences between us. And finally we have considered poverty and raised more questions than we have answered, but at least we have made a start at getting an answer to those questions. However, I feel the most important thing in our discussions is the realization that the Western world does not hold all the answers. We need to look to our brothers and sisters in Asia and Africa to begin to learn the answers. God has shown me that not to be a part of the cause, I need to be a person who is working on a solution.

CHURCH OF THE BRETHREN RESPONDENT

Jesus said, "Let those who have ears, hear." We heard personal and collective stories of struggle and some examples that give cause for hope. These included courageous actions for peace that have yielded results between Muslims and Christians on this island, perhaps one of the more difficult settings in the world. We came expecting to hear about Muslim/Christian tensions, but some of us were surprised to hear that on this island, the Catholic and Christian churches are separate religions and there is Catholic/Christian conflict. We know that the government's role is relevant in peacebuilding. Sometimes the government is not working well, but it can often be pressed to function fairly. At other times the ineffectiveness and inefficiency of governments stand in the way of justice.

Let me recall a few phrases from our discussion: "universality of suffering," "peacebuilding requires building relationships," "restorative justice can break the cycle of violence," "Christianity in the East is often seen as a foreign religion associated with the worst aspects of the West," "peace and justice require mercy," "powers and principalities can be confronted and transformed." Our discussions struggled to define justice and injustice to see more clearly the meaning of religious pluralism for particular contexts. We celebrate the many church and government efforts to address poverty as a means to reduce injustices that can otherwise erode peace.

We heard how the poor suffer violence and injustice, and how some churches are providing charity. We heard of efforts by the churches to change the circumstances that add to the suffering of the poor. One story left a lasting impression on me. It is the painful story of the young girl in India who offered water to her teacher, and how in the face of the teacher's rejection of her and the injustice she felt as a result, her life has been damaged. I was prompted to contrast that story with other stories where the church provides water, bringing life and wholeness to those communities and bringing peace to their local areas.

We have come to recognize differences between various corners of the Pacific region. Our Quaker friends came from Australia and New Zealand, societies with education and highly developed nations with a global view. Their activism in this context is a witness and a challenge to others in the region. Churches from India and Indonesia feel more restricted in their freedom to speak out to their neighbors and their government. There is real personal and corporate risk in speaking out in these places. As a result a more relational and less confrontational model is used. This model seems to be focused on relationship building and small steps forward.

In closing, my impression is that these discussions will have significant impact on the life witness of the peace churches in Asia. I know they have made a deep impression on the peace churches in India. We hope that the peace churches in Asia will feel uplifted and empowered, as we provided new relationships and fostered energy together around ideas for peacemaking in this region, and we hope that this empowers the peace witness of all churches in Asia and around the world.

RELIGIOUS SOCIETY OF FRIENDS RESPONDENT

John Woolman, 1721-1772, American Quaker has written the following:

There is a principle that is pure, placed in the human mind which in different ages and places has had different names. It is, however, pure and proceeds from God. It is deep and inward, confined to no forms of religion nor excluded from anywhere the heart stands in perfect sincerity. In whomsoever, this takes root and grows, in whatever nation, they are brothers and sisters.[1]

There are many Asians, and all cry out for peace, justice, and mercy. All crave liberation from the many types of violence that holds this continent in its grip: violence, nuclear arms race, terrorism, globalization, political and religious oppression, and absolutist religious and political beliefs. There is deepening poverty, degradation of women, exploitation of children and theft of land and resources. And all this in addition to bloody warfare and the ominous presence of climate change which promises the most terrifying of consequences, both economical and social. These blasphemies are in opposition to the spirit in Christ Jesus and to the kingdom that he proclaimed. It is understandable that we slide into despair and into helplessness at the enormity of our task.

But while there is an ocean of darkness, we believe wholeheartedly that there is also an ocean of light and love. And such light there is! We have heard with humility those who are engaged in life-giving and sometimes-dangerous witness, a witness that is both reconciling and healing. By sincerely welcoming and initiating this witness, we enact our discipleship, our priesthood, and we anoint others. We also know that we are not alone in our struggle; we hope, therefore, that we may join with non-Christians who also love humankind and our planet home.

Our earnest and urgent desire is that this love reach beyond these islands to the whole world. Since God is one that reaches out, we pray that participants at these consultations carry the message of prophetic hope and reconciliation directly to their homes, churches, and meetings, so that from it may grow a fuller witness. Some resulting actions will be necessarily political. We need courage; we are called to remain steadfast in the faith. And with George Fox, British Quaker from the seventeenth century, we can rejoice in saying: "Where peace and mercy do meet, what joy there is!"

NOTE

1. Amelia Mott, *The Essays of John Woolman* (London, 1922), 180.

APPENDIX I

A Message from the Third International Historic Peace Churches Consultation

SURAKARTA (SOLO CITY), JAVA, INDONESIA. 1ST-8TH DECEMBER, 2007

1. To all our sisters and brother in the Historic Peace Churches and in the wider ecumenical fellowship of Christians, we send you loving greetings and the peace of the living Christ Spirit.

2. We, members of the Church of the Brethren, Mennonites/Brethren in Christ and the Religious Society of Friends (Quakers), have come together in central Java to continue the process of consultations initiated at Bienenberg (Switzerland, 2001) and then in Limuru/Nairobi (Kenya, 2004). Two representatives from the Anabaptist Association of Australia and New Zealand assisted us in our deliberations.

3. The above consultations fell under the auspices of the World Council of churches' Decade to Overcome Violence (DOV) program which was inaugurated in 2001. This, the third in the series of four, brought together eighty two men and women from Aotearoa/New Zealand, Australia, India, Indonesia, Japan, Korea, Philippines, the United Kingdom and the United States to share our current theologies of peace and justice and their practical outcomes. Participants brought with them a variety of expertise—pedagogical; dispute resolution, management and transformation; development aid; and peace and social justice activism.

We are grateful for the insights from our first two consultations which may be accessed from the publications that resulted from them—*Seeking*

Cultures of Peace and *Seeking Peace in Africa*.[1]

We are grateful to our caring Indonesian hosts and to their local churches. Their organization and welcome were exemplary and deeply appreciated.

4. Our theme, "Peace in our Land," sought to explore issues of religious pluralism, poverty and injustice in the most highly diverse and dispersed region on our dangerously threatened planet. Formal presentations included theological papers, stories from individuals and/or from churches, groups and Meetings as well as formal worship. Our time together in worship was rich and uplifting. We discovered just how the Historic Peace Churches in this region are a melting pot for western and Asian thought and its ensuing orthopraxis.

The Asian Historic Peace Churches have long committed themselves to the cause of justice, peace and mercy, to the building of the kingdom on earth as this reflects the glory of God's loving intention for us.

5. It is clear to us that the Rule of Love or 'Kingdom' that Jesus set up is antithetical to war and to the manner in which nations and groups prepare for it. We understand war as the greatest of human scandals, the greatest of human sins, a full frontal blasphemy of the precious gift of life.

As we listened to the stories we shared from our experiences in working toward reconciliation and healing, we came to know other forms of warfare. There is the inner war, which we recognized through our common worship, the necessity of looking closely at ourselves, the need for *metanoia*. In the words of St. Francis of Assisi: "If you desire peace with your lips, make sure it is written first on your heart." Do we hear this? Do we truly love our enemies? Do we pray for those who persecute us (Matt. 5:43-44)? How well do we live the Sermon on the Mount? Indeed, how well do we enact the fifth chapter of Matthew? Have we forgotten that Jesus meant it to be taken seriously? Each one of us must ask ourselves these questions, continually guarding against defiling the kingdom that is within and among us (Luke 17:21). There is the war within our homes and neighborhoods. There is the war that separates us from those who are members of different denominations or religious traditions; the Peaceable Kingdom is inclusive of all who come to God, for the Christ cannot be divided (1 Cor. 1:13).

The outer wars that traumatize our region include a regional conventional arms race, nuclear proliferation and terrorism. But they also include the ravages of globalization, which results in deepening poverty, the degradation of women and the exploitation of children on a massive scale. HIV/Aids, political and religious oppression, and bloody warfare continue to mock our simple desire for human flourishing.

These are not mere words to us; we in Asia live through these realities each and every day. In our listening and sharing, our tears unveiled our unity and compassion; our joy affirmed the fruits of the kingdom, the omnipresence and omnipotence of Love, its Life and Power (Gal. 5:22).

6. And hovering above us and more fundamental than all the ills that beset our region is climate change. It is not a theory but a specter that promises ecological and social collapse on a scale unimagined in human history. Our anxiety and sense of urgency determined a plea to world leaders whose meeting on the Indonesia island of Bali coincided with ours.

Our devotion to the peace that Jesus taught and practiced leads us to urge nations to organize for peace and to remove the causes of war as enthusiastically as they currently prepare for war.

7. We speak our truth with love when we say to those in authority that the amount of money spent on armaments and arms transfers, which reaches record levels as each year passes, is nothing short of disgusting. Better indeed to divert the expenditure for the well-being of humanity—to reducing the cruel effects of climate change, to ridding our planet of the nuclear industry and the weapons that inevitably are linked to it, to developing peace-keeping capacities, to building genuine restorative justice systems away from existing punitive institutions, to improving the health of all the children of God, to reducing and eventually eradicating illiteracy—in short, food for the hungry, clothes for the naked and drink for the thirsty.

Our principle is, and our practices have always been, to seek peace and to pursue it, and to follow after the love of God. Wars and other injustices arise out of our turning from this love (James 4:1-3). Sin is separation from God. The greater this separation the harder our hearts become and the lesser will our compassion be. Thus diminished we will never fully enjoy what the Scottish poet Edwin Muir described as the "green springing corner of young Eden." We know in our hearts that this Eden can be restored in not only in our hearts but outwardly among the peoples of the world. We will never surrender this vision and submit to "a yoke of slavery" (Gal. 5:1).

8. We look forward to our final consultation in the Americas in 2010 after which we hope that a 2011 convocation in a place yet to be chosen will present insights from the peace churches from all over the world to the World Council of Churches. The great work of peace, justice and mercy—the work of the kingdom—will continue.

NOTE

1. Fernando Enns, Scott Holland, Ann K. Riggs, *Seeking Cultures of Peace: A Peace Church Conversation* (Telford, Pa.: Cascadia Publishing House, 2004; copublished with Geneva: World Council of Churches Publications; and

Scottdale, Pa.: Herald Press, 2004); Donald E. Miller, Scott Holland, Lon Fendall, and Dean Johnson, eds. *Seeking Peace in Africa: Stories from African Peacemakers* (Telford, Pa.: Cascadia Publishing House; copublished with Geneva: World Council of Churches Publications; and Scottdale, Pa.: Herald Press, 2007).

STATEMENT TO THE BALI CONFERENCE ON CLIMATE CHANGE

To the Leaders of the Nations Gathered at the Meeting of the United Nations Intergovernmental Agency on Climate Change Meeting in Bali, Indonesia

From Members of the Historic Peace Churches (Church of the Brethren, Mennonites, and Quakers) meeting in a Conference in Solo, Indonesia

Our churches have long been concerned with peace and justice for all the people of the world. This year is the sixtieth anniversary of the award of the Nobel Peace Prize to the Quakers. The greatest threat now to world peace comes from climate change and global warming. These expected changes and the consequent struggle for land, water, and resources threaten wars and many deaths. At the United Nations Intergovernmental Agency on Climate Change meeting in Bali, the people of the world have entrusted you with a great responsibility and a great opportunity. Your decisions will cause the people of the world to look back to this time with blessings or with curses. We appeal to you to act with vision, boldness, and courage to give people new hope. The need for action is urgent. The action taken must make a significant difference. We pray that God will help you together to find ways forward which are wise, just and peaceful.

PEACE IN OUR LAND: THE ASIAN CONTEXT OF INJUSTICE, RELIGIOUS PLURALISM, AND POVERTY

Making peace theology relevant to the challenges of conflicts in Asia

**Proceedings of the International Conference
of the Historic Peace Churches in Asia
Lor-In Hotel and Conference Center
Solo, Indonesia
December 2-7, 2007**

SUNDAY, DECEMBER 2
Welcome and Theme Statement: Paulus Widjaja
Opening worship
Speaker: Mesach Krisetya
The Historic Peace Churches: Donald Miller
Welcome by the mayor of Solo, Indonesia

MONDAY, DECEMBER 3
Keynote Address
The Decade to Overcome Violence: Hansulrich Gerber
Theme of the day: Injustice
Between Retribution and Restoration: Atsuhiro Katano
Addressing Injustice: Jarrod McKenna, Jo Vallentine

Small group discussions about injustice
Plenary discussion of injustice led by Elizabeth Duke
Worship led by the Friends

TUESDAY, DECEMBER 4

Theme of the day: Religious Pluralism
Religious Pluralism as a worldview: Aristarchus Sukarto
Relating to Radicalism: Paulus Hartano
Visit to the Kraton Palace
Javanese Views on Harmony and Stages of Life
Worship led by the Mennonites

WEDNESDAY, DECEMBER 5

Theme of the day: Poverty
Stories of Christians and conflict in India
Poverty in India: Ashok Solanky
Small group discussions of poverty in Asia
Christian Peacemakers Team in Israel: Christina Gibb
Principalities and Empire, A Quaker Perspective: Dale Hess
Worship led by the Brethren

THURSDAY, DECEMBER 6

Excursion to the Borobadur Buddhist temple
Attendance at the Ramayana ballet performed at the Prambanan Hindu temple, a traditional dramatic ballet about the conflict between the Hindu deities Ram and Rahwana.

FRIDAY, DECEMBER 7

Conclusions from the conference
Employment Discrimination
Regional and denominational groups
Action group I: What did you learn at this conference?
Action group 2: What can you take home from this conference?
Action group 3: What action plans do you have?
Plenary Session
Approval of a letter to the churches
Approval of a statement to the Bali environmental conference
Closing worship
Songs by Wisma Kasih Voice—a choir of children from Ambon, East Indonesia, all of whom were orphaned by riots

APPENDIX IV

CONFERENCE PARTICIPANTS

Church of the Brethren

Cornelius Solomon	India
Arnold David Macwan	India
Dhirubhai Vasanjibhai Gamit	India
Jayantilal Kalidas Bhagat	India
Gabriel Martin Jerome	India
Musshabber Ismail Merchant	India
Sanjitkumar Pratapsingh Raj	India
Deepakkumar Ishwarlal Rajwadi	India
Kantilal Ratanlal Rajwadi	India
Darryl Sankey	India
Shaileshkumar Samuelbhai Patel	India
Amos Jayant Solanky	India
Ashokkumar Maganlal Solanky	India
Vivek Ashokkumar Solanky	India
Dhansukh Somchand Christian	India
Amitkumar Sudhirbhai Thakore	India
Rameshkumar Williambhai Makwan	India
Scott Holland	USA
Merv Keeney	USA
Donald Miller	USA
Stanley Noffsinger	USA
David Sollenberger	USA

Religious Society of Friends (Quakers)

Elizabeth Duke	Aotearoa/NZ
Christina Gibb	Aotearoa/NZ
John Graham	Aotearoa/NZ

Gerard Guiton	Australia
Dale Hess	Australia
Sieneke Martin	Australia
Jarrod McKenna	Australia
Jo Vallentine	Australia
Janet Scott	Britain
Jairaj Brown	India
Norris Hamilton	India
Devdas Shrisunder	India
Wiwid	Indonesia
Betty Pulido	Philippines
Jaime P. Tabingo	Philippines
Lydia Tabingo	Philippines

Mennonites

David Rouse	Australia
Doug Sewell	Australia
Menno Joel	India
Pradmoud Kumar	India
Roul Manjula	India
Shant Masih	India
Emmanuel Minj	India
Cynthia Peacock	India
Samuel Anton	Indonesia
Ronny Chandra	Indonesia
Timotius Adi Dharma	Indonesia
Eunike Florentina	Indonesia
Paul Gunawan	Indonesia
Paulus Hartono	Indonesia
Stefanus Ch. Haryono	Indonesia
Suis Iranto	Indonesia
Matius Larson Krisetya	Indonesia
Daniel K. Listijabudi	Indonesia
Inneke Lita	Indonesia
Daniel Nugroho	Indonesia
Rudyanto	Indonesia
Saptojoadi	Indonesia
Nindyo Sasongko	Indonesia
Agus Setianto	Indonesia
Nahum Sudarsono	Indonesia
Aristarchus Sukarto	Indonesia
Agus Supratikno	Indonesia

Eko Susanto	Indonesia
Theofilus Tumidjan	Indonesia
Zefanya Adi Waluyo	Indonesia
Janti Diredja Widjaja	Indonesia`
Paulus Sugeng Widjaja	Indonesia
Iwan Firman Widyanto	Indonesia
Kazuhiro Enomoto	Japan
Nobuo Hirokawa	Japan
Yoshirhira Inamine	Japan
Atsuhiro Katano	Japan
Guishik Nam	Korea
Ambrocio Porcincula	Philippines
Amy Erickson	USA
Dan Jantzi	USA
Jeanne Jantzi	USA
Heraldo Siahaan	USA
Hansulrich Gerber	WCC

Local Organizing Committee

Lilik Agus Setiyanto	Indonesia
Agoes Setiawan	Indonesia
Dyah Sri Utami	Indonesia
Antonius Suparno	Indonesia
Yuli Sri Murwati	Indonesia
Endang Ayu Purwaningtyas	Indonesia
Ruth Dwi Yuliawati	Indonesia
Tanti Ayoe Kusuma	Indonesia

THE INDEX

J

K

L

THE CONTRIBUTORS

Elizabeth Duke grew up in England, where she studied Greek and Latin classics and became involved with the Religious Society of Friends, Quakers. In 1976 she moved to New Zealand and taught Classics in the University of Otago while studying theology and Maori (indigenous) language and culture. Elizabeth has served Quakers locally and nationally, and spent seven and a half years with Friends World Committee for Consultation, the Quaker international networking body. After retiring she revisited Colombia with a delegation from the Fellowship of Reconciliation, which supports endangered peace and human rights activists. From a first marriage Elizabeth has two daughters and two grandsons. In 2009 she and her partner entered into a spiritual and civil union under the care of their Quaker Meeting.

Hansulrich Gerber, a Mennonite pastor from Switzerland, was the World Council of Churches (WCC) Coordinator for the Decade to Overcome Violence (DOV) from 2002 to 2009. His office was responsible for facilitating the DOV through its web site, the annual focus, and general networking of churches and movements world-wide. Originally a farmer, then trained as teacher and catechist, Hansuli studied theology in Elkhart, Indiana, United States, and became a pastor. He then worked several years for Mennonite World Conference, first as Executive Secretary of the International Mennonite Peace Committee and then as Secretary for Program. Before joining the WCC, Gerber served ten years as Europe Director for Mennonite Central Committee (MCC). Since 2010 Gerber is Director of the Swiss Forum for Peace Education.

Christina Gibb is Clerk, Dunedin Monthly Meeting, Religious Society of Friends (Quakers), Aotearoa/New Zealand. She has volunteered in Hebron with Christian Peacemakers Teams for several three-month periods of service.

289

Gerard Guiton, a Quaker for twenty-five years, is currently based in Melbourne, Australia. The father of two adult children and a life-long activist for peace and nonviolence, he is a former teacher and development aid worker (Oxfam Australia and World Vision Australia). Currently in formation as a spiritual director, Gerard also leads workshops in Quaker theology and history and lectures in the same internationally. In this capacity he has contributed many articles and papers to Quaker journals in particular. He holds degrees from Manchester and Sheffield universities (UK). His doctorate from Monash University (Melbourne) examined the historical and spiritual underpinnings of contemporary Quaker approaches to military conflict in developing economies with a special focus on apartheid South Africa. It was published as *The Growth and Development of Quaker Testimony* (Mellen, 2005). His current book project, now completed, is a systematic theology entitled *The Way of Revolution: the Early Quakers, the Kingdom of God and the Future of Quakerism*. Guiton served as vice-chair of the Steering Committee which oversaw planning for the 2007 International Historic Peace Conference in Solo City, Java, Indonesia.

Paulus Hartono is director of Mennonite Diaconial Services, an agency of the Muria Christian Church (Mennonite) in Java, Indonesia's most populous island. He is also a member of Forum for Peace Across Religions and Groups, a Mennonite Central Committee partner organization in Solo City, Indonesia. With Hartono's leadership, Mennonite Diaconial Services organized Mennonite and Muslim volunteers to distribute aid, clean up rubble and construct temporary shelters in Pundong in the aftermath of the earthquake on May 27, 2006. That earthquake claimed more than 6,000 lives and destroyed thousands of homes in Java. Sixty-two volunteers from an Islamic malitia group joined with some 260 Mennonite volunteers to help thousands of people and prepare sites to rebuild 100 homes. The joint effort began with a friendship between Hartono and the Muslim militia's commander.

Dale Hess was born in the United States and moved to Australia in 1970. He is a member Victoria Regional Meeting of the Religious Society of Friends (Quakers) in Melbourne and has been active with both Regional Meeting and Yearly Meeting Peace and Social Justice Committees. In addition to his ties with Quakers, previously he was a member of the Lombard House Church (with Brethren members) and the Princeton House Church (with Brethren and Mennonite members). He is a member of the Anabaptist Association of Australia and New Zealand.

Atsuhiro Katano graduated from International Christian University (Tokyo), Chuo University (Tokyo), and Associated Mennonite Biblical Seminary (Elkhart, Indiana, U.S.). He teaches peace studies, international relations, legal studies, and American studies at several universities in Sapporo, Hokkaido. He is a member of Sapporo Bethel Mennonite Church and actively involved in wrinting and teaching ministry on Christian faith and peace issues. He has contributed chapters to *Peace Movements and Pacifism after September 11* (2008) and *Routledge Handbook of Religion and Politics* (2009). He is a steering committee member of Northeast Asia Regional Peacebuilding Institute to provide trainings on conflict transformation, restorative justice, and peace education.

Jarrod McKenna is from Perth, Australia. He is associated with the Religious Society of Friends as well as the Anabaptist Association of Australia and New Zealand. He has organized a group for youth entitled Empowering Peacemakers in Your Community. He has chosen voluntary poverty by living in the Peace Tree Community in Perth.

Donald Eugene Miller is a minister of the Church of the Brethren and Emeritus Professor of Christian Education and Ethics at Bethany Theological Seminary in Richmond, Indiana, where he taught for twenty-five years. From 1986-89 he was General Secretary of the General Board of the Church of the Brethren and a member of the Heads of Communion of the National Council of Churches of Christ in the U.S. He was also a member of the Central Committee of the World Council of Churches 1919-98. He has a Ph.D. in History and Philosophy of Religion from Harvard University, an M.A. from the University of Chicago, and an M. Div. from Bethany Theological Seminary.

Saptojoadi is a pastor of the Evangelical Church of Java (Gereja Injili di Tanah Jawa, *GITJ*), the predominately Javanese Mennonite conference of the north central part of the island of Java in Indonesia.

Ashok Solanky is a pastor from the Church of the Brethren in Gujarat, India. Rev. Ashok Solanky has humble beginnings; he lost his father at the tender age of ten. The youngest of six siblings, he was raised by mother Rahel a devout Christian, who instilled Christian values and the teachings of Christ in her children. Ashok had the call to serve God since his childhood but due to family compulsions he could not attend seminary. Ashok was consecrated as a pastor in 1995; he serves as pastor of the Valsad Congregation of the Church of the Brethren in India. He contributes to the church in various capacities by being on different committees of the Church in India. He has served as Chairman of the Church of the Brethren in India 2009-2010.

Ashok's unfulfilled dream of studying in a seminary has been fulfilled by his son Vivek, who is a student at the Bethany Seminary, U.S.

Aristarchus Sukarto is a Mennonite pastor and synod moderator of the Mennonite churches in Indonesia. He is president of Jakarta Christian University owned by the Presbyterian Church, and he was formerly president of the Christian University of Jakarta, which is owned by twelve churches including the Mennonites. After obtaining a degree in law, he studied Old Testament under the Anglicans and Presbyterians in Indonesia. Then he completed a Ph.D. from the Lutheran Theological Seminary in Chicago with some of his work done at Catholic Theological Union. He is Javanese by birth and his wife is Chinese by birth. He was Muslim until age twenty-one, when he converted to Christianity.

Josephine Vallentine is a peace activist and a former Australian senator representing Western Australia (WA). She was first elected as a member of the Nuclear Disarmament Party, then as an Independent, and later as a Greens WA candidate. She was one of the founders of the Alternatives to Violence Project in Western Australia. She has actively promoted environmental concerns as well as nonviolence. The newspaper Western Australian named her as one of the state's one hundred most influential people ever. She is one of a number of women who have been nominated for the Nobel Peace Prize.

Paulus S. Widjaja is a member of the faculty of theology and Director of the Center for the Study and Promotion of Peace at Duta Wacana Christian University in Jogjakarta, Central Java. He completed an M.A. in Peace Studies from Associated Mennonite Biblical Seminary, Elkhart, Indiana, U.S. His Ph.D. is in theological ethics from Fuller Theological Seminary, School of Theology, Pasadena, California, U.S. He serves as Secretary of the Mennonite World Conference Peace Commission. He was the chair of the planning committee for the Solo conference and presided over the conference.

CPSIA information can be obtained at www.ICGtesting.com
226679LV00004B/1/P